QUESTIONING
GEOPOLITICS

QUESTIONING GEOPOLITICS

Political Projects in a Changing World-System

Edited by
Georgi M. Derluguian and Scott L. Greer

Westport, Connecticut
London

The Library of Congress has cataloged the hardcover edition as follows:

Questioning geopolitics : political projects in a changing world-system / edited by
Georgi M. Derluguian and Scott L. Greer.
    p.   cm.—(Contributions in economics and economic history, ISSN 0084–9235 ; no. 216)
    Includes bibliographical references and index.
    ISBN 0–313–31082–3 (alk. paper)
    1. Globalization.   2. International relations.   I. Derluguian, Georgi M.   II. Greer, Scott L.
III. Series.
JZ1308.D55   2000
327.1'01—dc21   99–049047

British Library Cataloguing in Publication Data is available.

A hardcover edition of *Questioning Geopolitics* is available from Greenwood Press, an
imprint of Greenwood Publishing Group, Inc. (Contributions in Economics and
Economic History, Number 216; ISBN 0–313–31082–3).

Library of Congress Catalog Card Number: 99–049047
ISBN: 0–275–96656–9

First published in 2000

Praeger Publishers, 88 Post Road West, Westport, CT 06881
An imprint of Greenwood Publishing Group, Inc.
www.praeger.com

Printed in the United States of America

The paper used in this book complies with the
Permanent Paper Standard issued by the National
Information Standards Organization (Z39.48–1984).

10 9 8 7 6 5 4 3 2 1

Copyright Acknowledgment

The Northwestern University Research Grants Committee has provided partial support for the
publication of this book. We gratefully acknowledge this assistance.

Contents

Acknowledgments

The editors would like to thank the Northwestern University Center for International and Comparative Studies, and Northwestern University Departments of Sociology and Political Science for their support. The Northwestern University Research Grants Committee has provided partial support for the publication of this book. We gratefully acknowledge this assistance. Isabella Alcañiz provided invaluable editing assistance. Frances Lowe, Judy Gibson, and Judy Kasen lent their administrative expertise, Cynthia Harris was our most trusted editorial ally, and Immanuel Wallerstein proved an amazingly swift reader.

We owe special thanks to the participants in the XXIInd Annual Conference on the Political Economy of the World-System (PEWS), especially those who traveled from as far away as the eastern Mediterranean.

QUESTIONING
GEOPOLITICS

1

Introduction: Repetition, Variation, and Transmutation as Scenarios for the Twenty-first Century

Georgi M. Derluguian and Walter L. Goldfrank

The twenty-first century opens with uncertainties. On the one hand, the world scene continues to look familiar except for the surprising gap in the sites that were the Soviet bloc and the Communist alternative. On the other hand, the breakdown of the Soviet pole, which was long anticipated by the world-systems and geopolitical theories (see Collins, 1978 and 1995), removed the major organizing tension and a large amount of attached meaning from the world as we knew it. The United States remained by far the most powerful state in almost every respect, but it was challenged domestically and internationally to reconfirm its hegemonic status. The main set of the post-1945 interstate institutions such as the UN, the EU, IMF, or NATO were called to the formal word of their charters after decades of relatively quiet subordinate existence. The contradictory notions of "competitiveness" and managing chaos became the order of the day in the centers of world power. Meantime, a larger part of the world population found itself trapped in areas of chronic turmoil and seemingly hopeless marginalization within the world economy. New economic centers arose in East Asia to be hailed as the newest model and the prospective core of the world-economy before they suddenly stumbled in a crisis whose causes were as contested as much else in the contemporary world. All this was occurring amid the major technological and organizational restructuring of the world's production base that led to a substantial increase in the mobility of capital, information, and people across state jurisdictions.

The sum of these transformations came to be called globalization. Nobody earnestly doubts that a major transformation is under way, but there is little agreement on the extent of change, its key areas and prime movers, or the eventual outcomes.We may, however, find at least some agreement in considering globalization an historical instance of regime change. The major theme of globalization debates is indeed the reconstitution of the norms, practices, and institutions (i.e., the regime) that structure the intersecting fields of world power relations, the world-economy, and geoculture. People create and impose the norms and institutions in order to make their actions predictable and therefore to minimize uncertainty. Regimes are inherently conflictual processes because of the differences in the perceived interests and positions of various groups within the world-system. The historical proportion of conflict and cohesion differs significantly over time, forming a cycle that, regarding the world configurations of power, we call hegemonic.

Conflicts and pressures increase during the more chaotic phases of regime transition before a dominant pattern can emerge and become accepted by the majority of actors who would consider the new order to be in their common interest. This always involves some coercion and disempowering directed against those groups that benefit less from the new regime. Yet bare coercion cannot work over longer periods of time without some consent of those who are coerced, and a wider consensus of those middle groups who willingly participate in the order. Machiavelli realized this clearly. Antonio Gramsci's term hegemony embraced precisely such a combination of coercion, consent, and consensus that he considered crucial for the exercise of social power (Gramsci, 1971: 57–58 and 80). These conditions cannot be met without the dominant state or social group within the system being able to support its coercive powers with a sense of moral and intellectual leadership plus the judicial control and the ability to redirect the flows of the means of payment (see especially Arrighi, 1994; Gill, 1990; Keohane, 1984).

It is a difficult combination to achieve and maintain. It always requires a fundamental restructuring of the historical system that evolves continuously and therefore does not allow simple reproduction of past hegemonic regimes. In our view hegemonic order existed in the modern world-system only periodically when the leading state (the United States after 1945, Britain after 1815, and Holland in 1648) acquired the undisputed capability to advance its vision of world governance and present itself as the model for emulation. In each epoch there existed alternative hegemonic projects as well: Spanish counterreformation imperialism against the Dutch, French absolutism against the British, German state corporatism and Soviet socialism against the United States. The defeats of alternative projects (which, notably, always threatened to subsume the capitalist world-economy and the interstate system of sovereign jurisdictions into a directly administered world-empire) were major formative steps in the constitution of new hegemonic order. The key question therefore is whether the current globalization represents the most recent defining moment in the creation of new world hegemony and structuring another era of expansion of the capitalist world-economy.

This volume brings together a very diverse group of authors who explore the ideological, political, and organizational aspects of globalization. Although some of us do not explicitly pursue the concept of hegemonic transitions, we agreed that this angle helps to focus our explorations and avoid the methodological pitfall that Arthur Stinchcombe once wryly called "softheadedness on the future" (Stinchcombe, 1982). The current moment differs from the past instances of hegemonic transitions in the substantially higher degree of rationalization attained within the modern world-system. The evolving social scholarship is itself a historical result and an integral part of systemic rationalization. The future is unpredictable in principle because the social universe is an open complex system. Inevitably there will be the factors that we presently fail to recognize. Almost certainly there operate the countertendencies that substantially meliorate and may eventually cancel the trends that a current public fad proclaims the Hope (the Fear) of our times. The future itself is affected by our collective wills, conflicts, and decisions. Notwithstanding these humbling warnings, it is the responsibility of social scientists to make meaningful statements regarding the arguments that are being advanced in public debates and outline the historical options we are facing.

We use globalization as a common reference point. We doubt that it is an analytically useful term. It is rather the framework and the central marker of the debate about the present state of the world and its future trajectory. This word emerged in the last decade out of the intellectual confusion that was set by the demise of the two powerful and powerfully organizing oppositions—capitalism versus socialism; modernization (whether capitalist or state socialist) versus underdevelopment. Globalization itself is the direct successor of modernization in its bold promise—indeed the demand to spread the Western institutions of market economy and liberal democracy over the rest of the world. In the end (for this will presumably be the end) the world should become a unified and uniform field of isomorphic democratic institutions that would mediate lasting peace among states as well as social groups, and of self-leveling markets that would ensure steady economic growth.

From this angle globalization is evidently a programmatic statement rather than a spontaneous process driven presumably by natural technological progress. It is also a heavily Western-centric program with strong disciplining mechanisms—there are no reasonable alternatives left to making oneself (be it states, social groups, or individuals) competitive and compatible with the proposed global world. The prevalent program of globalization means a return to the original vision of Woodrow Wilson. Wilsonianism was rejected in a post-1918 world torn apart by the economic chaos, the conservatism of European imperial powers, the pressures of socialist movements, and the reactionary challenges of fascist states. It was no more practical in the stable geopolitical and ideological bipolarity of the Cold War. Is the Wilsonian vision about to experience a belated triumph almost a century later and, if so, what could be the actual configuration of such a regime? Will it be an unchallenged *Pax Americana* made possible by the set of alliances and international institutions forged during the Cold War, in the earlier phase of the U. S. hegemony? It is certainly the intent of the U. S. ruling elite and, more widely, the dominant assumption based on the direct extrapolation of the political, economic, and ideological situation of the 1990s.

The prospect of neo-Wilsonian revival, however plausible it may look at the moment, is problematic for the very same reasons—it is so far an unproven political intent, an ideological assumption, and a simple analytical extrapolation of the fleeting situation following the Soviet defeat in the Cold War. One of the lessons of the Soviet demise warns us against simple extrapolations and taking ideological intentions for granted. Some time around 1975 Brezhnev's USSR looked very formidable to its friends and foes alike; it was scoring symbolic victories in the wake of the U. S. defeat in Indochina; it benefited from the detente in Europe; revolutions in Portugal and its fomer colonies; it looked appealing against the disarray and poverty of China in the twilight of Maoism; and let us not forget that the Soviet populations seemed very content with their stable lives and growing prosperity. It is not to say that the renewed American hegemony along Wilsonian lines of a unipolar and politically isomorphous world is totally impossible. Nevertheless, it is presently no more than an assumed possibility and a political project.

The arguments for globalization commonly stress two major processes: democratization and the rapidly increasing unity of the world, tied together by the transborder flows of information, goods, capital, and people. We agree that democratization and unification of the world are real and important trends. Yet we also believe that both processes are no less a challenge to the liberal world order than its foundations. In a world imagined as a global village (rather, given the rates of urbanization, a sprawling global town) worldwide democracy cannot be separated from worldwide equality. Historically, the biggest challenge to liberal ideology was being taken at its word by the impatient masses. (The same was even more true of Communist ideology and, incidentally, became a major factor in the demise of socialist states.) The future of neo-Wilsonianism hinges on its ability to ensure at least a plausible appearance of sustained and sustainable economic growth in the areas whose populations expect that the demise of old developmentalist dictatorships (of a socialist or the Third World nationalist kind) would be followed by renewed prosperity, personal safety, and popular access to the benefits of globalization.

The major doubt is whether there are resources sufficient to cover with investments what now amounts to the entire globe, including places like India, the former Soviet bloc, or Latin America. A closely related doubt concerns the new and yet to be specified institutions that would substitute for the largely extinct traditional mechanisms of community control and welfare. At the beginning of the twenty-first century, a majority of the planet's population are no longer peasants but dwellers of peripheral slums, depressed Rust Belts (the biggest found in the former Soviet bloc), and those pockets of marginalization within the core that Americans call inner cities. The disorganized street crime, addictions, and social decay could no longer be contained by the weakening states of these areas. In most places the immediate outcome of the demise of state-bound developmentalism was the cannibalistic privatization of state assets by corrupt bureaucratic elites and agile intermediaries who, wisely enough, turned their loot into the mobile form of money capital rather than risk fixed investment. This went hand in hand with the privatizations of state coercive apparatuses that competed with the purely criminal violent entrepreneurs, domestically and increasingly at the world level. This was no less true of post-apartheid South Africa than post-communist Russia or Mexico and Turkey. What can contain this disorder? Can we expect the re-empowering and re-ordering of the previous states, or their substitution with something else?

At a sober look the emerging global town looks more like Victorian London or Manchester rather than anything techno-futuristic. In many respects the global social picture of today resembles the situation created by the earlier industrialization in the European core states. Back then the problem could be alleviated by colonial expansion and emigration overseas, but the principal solution found at the time was domestic, thoroughly liberal, and essentially three-fold. It included the extension of suffrage to the propertyless classes; the incorporation of the immediate socialist demands into the state welfare reforms; and the taming and recasting of subversive nationalism into state patriotism (Wallerstein, 1996a). This produced the miracle of the pre-1914 liberal state and belle epoque, although the same enormous strengthening of the state's reach and capacity along with patriotic ideology have also made possible the horrors of twentieth-century warfare. Is the core's liberal achievement of the nineteenth century re-producible on a world scale? In 1917 Woodrow Wilson believed so. Today the outcome still looks very uncertain.

What if neo-Wilsonianism fails again? Presently there is no coherent alternative from the Left comparable to the old socialist project. Resembling the European situation before 1848, most antisystemic protests today are channeled into diffuse and largely irrational forms, including various forms of crime, assaults on the immediate conditions of life, and what has come to be generically called the fundamentalist revival, the ethnic conflict, and race problem. Such erratic pressures are disruptive, but they are not conducive to any positive systemic transformation. There is, of course, the lively universe of new social movements (many of which indeed revive the old causes of European movements from before the 1848 institutionalization of the "Old" Left, possibly with the environmentalists inheriting the scope and élan of abolitionists, and the NGOs becoming the newest missionaries to peripheries). The strength of new social movements is their plasticity, focus on specific issues, professionalization of their staff, and the ability to work with the private and governmental funding agencies. The same is no less the limit on the overall coherence and political strength of the movement sector that often finds itself a dependent force bound to national states and evidently outpaced by globalization. Soberly, the global civil society is today a fuzzy program bordering on utopian vision that is unlikely to coalesce into a practical alternative without a dramatic leap like the movement watersheds of 1848 or 1968 (Steinmetz, 1994, Tarrow, 1994; Tilly, 1995).

There remains the conservative alternative of renewed multisided Cold War famously espoused by Samuel Huntington (1996a). His argument was subjected to devastating intellectual and moral critiques that, however, could not invalidate the political project. Huntington envisioned a world order of multiple exclusions organized around a few rival blocs whose rationale and internal cohesion are expressed in the ideological terms of civilizations. Unlike Huntington or, conversely, the extreme cultural constructivists, we think that civilizations are neither primordial bedrocks of history nor pure products of collective imagination. Civilizations are information networks and comprehensive sets of social practices that primarily evolved around the dominant religions in past world-systems and functioned as their ideological "cement" (Chase-Dunn and Hall, 1997).

Today there is only one civilization, if one wishes to use the term, the civilization of capitalist modernity. Civilizations in plural are particularist claims to the past made for themselves and assigned to others by the continuously reconstituted status groups within the modern world-system in their positioning within the political and economic hierarchy. In this sense Huntington's conservative project is neither unprecedented nor unimaginable. Racism formulated in civilizational terms was the inevitable reverse side of the nineteenth-century liberal belief in universal laws and values necessary to excuse the enduring inequalities of a modern world-system. Civilizational racism was openly central to the ideology of industrial imperialism generated during the British hegemonic cycle and, after 1945 more implicitly, remained the underpinning of the American and Soviet views of modernization and non-European backwardness.

The "clash of civilizations" is an organizing framework for consolidating the world power within a few internally disciplined civilizational blocs. It is also an invitation to eternal geopolitical struggle, for civilizational distinctions are presumably eternal and irreconcilable—which directly leads to a rather dreadful proposition whether another bout of world wars is possible. This question is the center of ongoing debate closely related to the main theme of this volume.

For well over twenty years now, world-systems scholars have been studying hegemonic cycles as one feature of the reproduction and evolution of the capitalist totality. Various economic and political processes have been suggested as causally relevant in accounting for one or more of these cycles, such as technological and organizational imitation of the dominant power by potential contenders, institutional rigidity or obsolescence of the hegemon, foreign investment by the hegemon to the detriment of its own productive base, imperial overstretch, and the rising costs of policing the interstate system. But however crucial these processes have been, an additional process stands out both as an empirical regularity and as a causal necessity: world war.

World war, and by that we mean war involving all the major core powers, has been understood as a crucial mechanism for the transition from one hegemon to another. In the seventeenth century, the Thirty Years' War paved the way from Hapsburg to Dutch hegemony; at the turn of the nineteenth century, the Napoleonic Wars sealed Britain's triumph; and in the twentieth century, what we narcissistically call World Wars I and II were the crucibles in which the United States forged its dominance.

The conception of hegemonic cycles entailing the thirty-year "world wars" was first enunciated in the spring of 1975 when Immanuel Wallerstein presented an embryonic version at a Harvard colloquium. He later published a more refined account (Wallerstein, 1983). In fact, at the same moment that the 1970s global economic recession was leading to a revival of interest in long economic cycles (long waves, Kondratiev cycles), the relative international decline of the United States after Vietnam generated increasing interest in hegemonic or "political" cycles. (For a good summary see Goldstein, 1988). During the 1980s the decline thesis became the focus of considerable controversy well beyond the world-systems community of scholars. This controversy was sparked especially by the publication of Paul Kennedy's bestseller *The Rise and Fall of the Great Powers* (Kennedy, 1987).

In the 1990s, the collapse of the USSR has calmed some of the fears of imminent nuclear war, at least of the all-out variety. Meanwhile, renewed economic vigor in the United States, combined with stagnation in Japan, economic dynamism in China, and the Asian crash of 1998 have cast doubt on the idea previously advanced by many analysts that Japan was on the verge of replacing the United States as the global hegemon. Yet for all the mixed signals of the 1990s, the relation between hegemonic transition and world war has continued to receive attention. One need not be a pessimist to assert that it is perhaps the single most important issue in the study of hegemonic cycles. Indeed, if world war is a necessary mechanism of hegemonic transition, as it appears to have been in the past, then given the present destructive capacity of the most sophisticated weapons, we must hope there will be no more such transitions. However, some of the other processes associated with hegemonic decline and transition do appear to be continuing (Goldfrank, 1999).

In current world-systems writing about the ongoing hegemonic transition, we can discern three scenarios. For shorthand purposes, we may call them repetition, variation, and transmutation. In the repetitionist view, articulated most recently by Christopher Chase-Dunn and Bruce Podobnik (1995), hegemonic dominance gives way first to shared governance by a consortium of leading core powers, then to increasingly conflictful rivalry, and then necessarily to a world war (or "core war") from which a new hegemonic power emerges.

The primary expositor of the variationist view has been Giovanni Arrighi (1994). According to him, each previous hegemonic cycle has entailed a major evolutionary transformation in the organizational scale of the world-system. The current one is likely to decouple economic from geopolitical power, reprising the sixteenth-century hegemonic combination of Genoese bankers and Hapsburg armies with Japanese bankers and the U. S. military ruling the world. Arrighi is moot on the necessity or likelihood of war, although he suggests that power no longer grows from the barrel of a gun.

In the transmutationist hypothesis, finally, the future takes two forms: the first irenic, the second catastrophic. On the one hand, we have the prediction offered by those who interpret contemporary globalization as immanent transcendence of the interstate system by a global class-based hegemony. William Robinson's *Promoting Polyarchy* (1996) is an exemplar, and it too is moot on the question of future wars (see also Stephen Gill and David Law, 1988 and 1989). On the other hand, we have catastrophe, as depicted literally in Warren Wagar's *Short History of the Future* (1989) and metaphorically in Wallerstein's recent invocation of chaos theory to describe the present as a crisis of the system and not merely a regime crisis in the system (Wallerstein, 1996a).

In a 1995 article bluntly called "The Next World War," Chase-Dunn and Podobnik estimate the probability of a major world war as 50–50, and they suggest that the greatest danger will exist in the decade of the 2020s (Chase-Dunn and Podobnik, 1995). Although they focus more on the factors likely to produce or inhibit such a war than on the issue of transition per se, they do evaluate the prospects of the states they see as the three main contenders for twenty-first century hegemony: the United States, Germany, and Japan. Each is associated with a regional trade bloc—NAFTA, the EU, and ASEAN. Each has strengths and weaknesses, and none has overwhelming advantages. The authors imply that the three have somewhat complementary techno-economic specializations, but they do not develop this theme, which has interesting implications for the hypothesis of global condominium. They discount the likelihood of a pan-Asian, Sino-Japanese alliance coming to dominate the globe, which is the implicit view of Andre Gunder Frank's *ReORIENT* (1998), possibly without the Japanese component. At the end, they are moot on the question of who or what is likely to emerge as the dominant power of the next century.

To arrive at their 50–50 prediction of world war, Chase-Dunn and Podobnik evaluate four factors that increase the danger and four factors that inhibit it. The former include heightened economic competition toward the end of a Kondratieff upswing or during a downswing; the "hegemonic sequence" itself; population pressure on scarce global resources; and increased core-periphery and intra-core-country inequality. Their arguments are straightforward, if perhaps overly vague and general. For both Kondratieff and hegemonic cycles, they simply point out that particular cyclical moments are when previous modern world wars have occurred. For population pressure, one can reduce their reasoning to a specification of intensified economic competition. But one could readily counter that thirty years hence is too soon for population/resource imbalances to have major effects on core rivalries, especially since as the authors themselves note, large-scale population growth is likely only in the periphery. For inequality, finally, they speculate that polarization will heighten tensions globally and both within and among core states, thus possibly leading to a far-right or far-left regime in the United States during a period of instability and thence to war. The most recent trend in U. S. income distribution, however, suggests that, at least for this country, we have begun a pendular shift away from the polarization that marked the 1980s and the early 1990s, quite apart from whether or not such polarization is conducive to extremist government.

On the inhibiting side, the authors cite the destructiveness of nuclear weapons, disarmament, international economic integration, and international political norms. As many have proposed, thermonuclear weapons inhibit aggression for fear of mutually assured destruction. But as they counterargue, new weapons technologies could unbalance the situation, encouraging aggression. Disarmament helps inhibit world war by decreasing the likelihood of accident. International economic and political integration are more promising inhibitors. Yet some such integration—for example, regional bloc formation and military alliances—may actually increase the risks of war. They imply that integration that tightens the interdependencies among core states, their corporations, their NGOs, and their citizens reduces the risks of global war. In addition, they give some credence to Bruce Russett's (1993) demonstration that democracies rarely war with each other, though qualifying it with the observation that some democracies may revert to authoritarianism during periods of crisis or tension.

Where Chase-Dunn and Podobnik see repetition, Arrighi sees variation. In *The Long Twentieth Century*, he attempts to understand the present and medium-term future by spending two-thirds of his book revisiting the past. He begins with Venice and the array of Italian city-states of the thirteenth and fourteenth centuries. He emphasizes the dyarchic sixteenth-century European hegemony of Genoese finance capital and Hapsburg/Iberian military power. Only then does he trace the successive ascents of the Dutch, the English, and the Americans. Each hegemonic era, or "systemic cycle of accumulation," is notable not merely for the repetition of structural domination by a single power, but for its unique reorganization of both the leading business enterprises and the regulation of international economic life. Arrighi thus builds variation into his model of hegemonic transition. But it is not just any variation. Rather, it is an evolution of the system in that each new hegemon expands the scale and the scope of capitalism. On the other hand, Arrighi is curiously reticent about the role or necessity of the Thirty Years' War, the Napoleonic Wars, or World Wars I and II. Of these, the Napoleonic receive the most consideration, but more for their economic effects in Britain. Core wars for Arrighi mark the climaxes of hegemonic transitions, but they are not theorized one way or another.

In projecting the future, Arrighi focuses on the recent Japanese ascent based on conglomerates at the top and on vast subcontracting networks extending across East and Southeast Asia. Since Japan is at once too small and too weak militarily to be a candidate for hegemony, Arrighi proposes that the twenty-first century may see a return to the Genoese/Hapsburg variant of dual hegemony, through a marriage of Japanese capital and U. S. military might. This proposition is not dissimilar to and may even be considered as a specification of Wallerstein's (1996a) prediction that the current tripolar core will collapse into a bipolar alignment, with a United States/Japan/China alliance on one side, and an enlarged Europe/Russia on the other. On the last page of his book, Arrighi mentions the possibility of a catastrophic war, but otherwise war plays no role in his scheme for the current transition.

The third recently proposed scenario, what we are calling here the transmutation of global hegemony, appears in irenic form in William Robinson's *Promoting Polyarchy* (1996). No less influenced by Gramsci than Arrighi was, but via Stephen Gill, Robinson uses a fairly conventional Marxist model of the capitalist past. Spellbound by the globalization craze, Robinson sees the present as germinating a qualitatively different future. For Arrighi, world hegemony means one (or perhaps two) state's force-backed, system-transforming, institution-building leadership that evokes consent and willing participation by other core elites. Robinson has a different take. In his view, the repetitive pattern of hegemonic states is finished, with or without variants. Rather, in the era of globalization, world hegemony is becoming the class project of a transnational bourgeoisie (cf. Lesley Sklair)—"The baton will be passed in the twenty-first century to a transnational configuration" (p. 365).

One central necessity of this thesis is that the U. S. government, in its military projection, comes to act as the executive committee more of the global than of the national bourgeoisie. But no evidence for this proposition—which may well be true—is offered in Robinson's pages. He dismisses the tripolar idea (United States/EU/Japan) because of extensive interpenetration at the top; rather he sees the entire competitive nation-state system eroding. World-level multilateral institutions like the IMF, the GATT, the WTO, and the UN are leeching sovereignty from states. Robinson's is really a Marxist cultural-lag hypothesis, based on the idea that the political superstructure is catching up (or at least will catch up) with the economic base. He says (pp. 373–74), "The emergent internationalized state plays a dual role: reproduction of the relations of transnational class domination and reproduction of the asymmetries in the world system." But this is what core capitalist states have always done, even if the world bourgeoisie has not previously been so integrated via transnational corporations.

In the bulk of his book, Robinson argues that the shift in much of the Third World from authoritarian regimes to electoral polyarchy (or low-intensity democracy) is to be explained by the shifting role of the U. S. state from dominating the old nation-state system to acting as agent of the emerging transnational capitalist elite. But he does not prove that this U. S. shift from defending "our" sons-of-bitches to promoting polyarchy was caused by an emergent qualitative transformation in the nature of the world-system, even if such a shift is in fact occurring. Let's compare the present to the turn of the last century, to the hegemonic transition between Britain and the United States. That was a period like ours during which financialization also occurred on a massive scale. In that era there was a major shift toward parliamentarism in many peripheral and semiperipheral countries under the influence of the British model. But most of these parliamentary regimes that flourished in the pre-World-War

I boom were not to last through the difficulties of stagnation and depression in the 1920s and 1930s. Waves of democratization are not a new phenomenon in world-system history.

About the catastrophic version of transmutationism, we have little to add. (See Goldfrank, 1987 and 1996.) It is possible that civilization as we know it may disappear suddenly via nuclear holocaust or gradually via ecological breakdown. The former could happen any time, but our own guess gives it a probability of at most 15 percent, and, if so, during the most acutely conflictful moment of hegemonic transition, should the current one revert to a fiercely nationalistic form. The latter, global ecological breakdown, is a very long-run prospect at most, well beyond the ongoing hegemonic transition, and projecting it probably underestimates human ingenuity.

It is more difficult to say exactly why we distrust metaphorical catastrophism. Perhaps it is a failure of imagination or skepticism borne by personal life experience. More likely, it is the course of the twentieth century with its wild fluctuations between the enormous optimism and universal fears that the world was about to end that teaches us caution and stoic sobriety. The system's demise appears more like a receding horizon than an oncoming asteroid. In our view, there is time for some cyclical repetition and more evolutionary variation before the world-system reaches the human and natural limits that presage transmutation. Arrighi's particular version may well be mistaken, but for the next thirty to fifty years, some variant of the hegemonic cycle seems considerably more likely than either simple repetition or total transmutation. We also like to hope that Arrighi is right that power no longer grows from the barrel of a gun, and that Randall Collins is wrong arguing (including in this volume) that the applicability of geopolitical theory is not affected by the evolution of world-system and the technological advances in weapons and transportation.

We do not claim that our thinking about the current globalization is unbiased or free of uncertainty. In fact, from the outset the explicit awareness of political bias in social science has been the methodological premise of world-systems analysis. Uncertainty about the future is also the fundamental condition of purposive human action. Our collective ability to reshape the social institutions is generally higher during the periods of transition that should be regarded as windows of opportunity. In making this volume we sought to be open-minded and transcend the political and academic kinds of parochialism. In its first twenty-five years the world-systems analysis concentrated on the structures of world-economy; that invited the accusations of disregarding the fields of geopolitics and geoculture. It still remains the major goal to theorize the world as historically evolving totality. The school of world-systems analysis was one among several to move in this direction. It is probably even more difficult to operationalize such a perspective in the specific research programs that go beyond the institutionally encrusted dichotomies of "macro-micro," "qualitative-quantitative," "hard science and humanities," idiographic versus nomothetic, or the triad of "economy-politics-culture" that we inherited from the nineteenth century, (Ragin, 1994; Tilly, 1984; Wallerstein, 1991).

This volume was admittedly designed to present the studies in the currently changing geopolitics of world-system. The austere comparative exposition of the geopolitical and the world-system theory by Randall Collins and David Waller outlines the substantial overlap and the divergent methodological focuses of the two interrelated perspectives and proposes some specific tests regarding the geopolitical realignment after the Cold War. In the course of preparing this volume we realized, however, the impossibility of separating the geopolitics from the geocultural debates about globalization. Even a chapter seemingly as technical as that of Brian Uzzi, Marc Ventresca, and Michael Sacks, which purportedly applies the network analysis toward the hierarchical ranking of states in the world-economy, could not escape the controversy of whether the wealth of one's nation is due to its intrinsic virtue (what at the individual level is called "human capital") or is rather the dominant forms of world culture that obscures with the primordially civilizational formulations the path-dependent and institutionally embedded positions of states within the unequal distribution of economic rewards. The intentionally provocative chapter by Daniel Chirot, who considers himself a world-systems scholar in his own right, presents in a very blunt form what is at the present moment the dominant political project of globalization and the mainstream critique of world-systems analysis in its Wallersteinian formulation. The responses to Chirot's chapter come from the authors (Gill; Cumings; Dirlik; Greer, Ragin, and Beck) who are not disciples of Immanuel Wallerstein, yet whose analyses of the transformations in world power and geoculture seem perfectly germane to the main thrust of the world-systems interpretation of globalization.

Furthermore, regionalization and the creation of transborder networks (that would often look familiar to the historians of pre-capitalist epochs) forcefully emerge as a major theme of globalization. The contributions of Loriaux, Alcañiz, Greer, and Chen demostrate in detail that the emergence of regional blocs is indeed a strong probability that grows not from the alleged civilizational affinities but rather from the emancipation of economic and human geography after nearly two centuries of the attempts by national states to make their jurisdictions the natural containers of every social activity. Derluguian's analysis of Soviet demise suggests that the same processes are occurring in the site of the former Soviet bloc. He combines the geopolitical and geocultural arguments to prove the old claim of world-systems analysis that the USSR was a semiperipheral part and participant in the capitalist world-economy doomed to eventually give up its untenable claims to be a military superpower and a separate world system of socialism. We could not agree in our predictions regarding the future trajectories of Russia and Eastern Europe or China and East Asia. Most of us, however, agree that these two regions present the most acute challenges and uncertainties for the globalization as the project of yet to be defined global governance.

I

RESTRUCTURING WORLD POWER

2

Globalizing Capital and Political Agency in the Twenty-first Century

Stephen Gill

The central argument of this chapter is that key world-order problems today concern the deepening and the extension of the power of capital—a process configured by neo-liberal globalization—and their solution involves new forms of democratic political agency. This is because the extension of the power of capital is a hierarchical and contradictory process that is creative and, increasingly, socially and ecologically destructive, and it generates resistance, opposition, and countermovements.[1]

My argument rests in the proposition that world order is a process that involves structural transformation. Its principal forms of agency are linked to the ideas, institutions, and material capacities of local, national, and transnational political and class formations—what we call here class formations and "social forces." Social forces are bound up with and operate through and across national boundaries and state sovereignties. This means that analyses based on a simplified "states and markets" ontology (e.g., realism, liberal institutionalism, and some world-systems theory and some types of Marxism) fail to capture the social depth and reach of the changes involved. By contrast, what I call the global political economy involves not only international forces (i.e., interacting across national boundaries) but also transnational and global social forces. The global political economy is a complex historical formation that is in movement and flux, an entity that is greater than the sum of its parts (Gill and Law, 1988).

The epistemological dimension of my argument is that we need new forms of knowledge to both better understand world order and to change its direction in a more equitable, democratic, just, and sustainable direction. What is needed for development of the fields of international relations and international political economy are forms of analysis able to explain the constitution, dynamics, and contradictions of the global political economy. This means the ability to relate structure and agency in explanations of contemporary globalization. Such a theory should be able to help us to understand the nature of our historical alternatives—that is, to make our social choices within what Braudel called "the limits of the possible." At the same time we need to realize that these limits, or structures, are made and transformed by collective human agency. And indeed politics is not simply about questions of political economy since it also involves questions of justice and legitimacy, all of which combine in collective action. Thus social and political action requires theory and praxis.

And in contrast to polemics that claim that liberalism provides the only viable approach to human development I will argue the contrary. Indeed, neo-liberal economic globalization has generated global crisis—crisis that goes well beyond currency fluctuations and instabilities associated with the global financial casino. More profoundly, it is a crisis of civilization, society, and economy, involving ecological changes and violence and an increase in human insecurity. Questions are now being raised that link the crisis to the myopic trajectory of our present, hypermaterialistic system of political economy. People are in search of alternatives. Some are on the right (e.g., authoritarian, fascist, nationalist and fundamentalist forces). Some are on the left (justice movements, feminists, oppressed minorities, etc.). The latter, along with new forms of collective action, are discussed in the conclusion.

CAPITALISM AS A CIVILIZATION?

Recently, the question of civilization has come to the fore in the study of international relations. Yet the notion of civilization is by no means self-evident. Braudel (1980) notes that the context for all civilizations today is "revolutions which define the present age" (the industrial, scientific, biological, and demographic revolutions framed by the expansion of capital). Nevertheless, he notes that this does not negate "the permanence of unity and diversity in the world":

We would have to be blind not to feel the weight of this massive transformation which is taking place everywhere, but it is not a transformation which is taking place everywhere, and where it is taking place, it is in forms and with a human dimension and resonance which are rarely ever the same. (Braudel, 1980: 213)

This Braudellian perspective on civilizations is consistent with the more complex ontology hinted at previously—that is, it takes account of unity and diversity across time and space. This means our object of analysis is historicized—it exists in a particular historical time and geographical and social space. As such it has no transhistorical essence, but involves particular forms of existence and consciousness, with their associated hopes and fears, constraints and opportunities, and understandings and perceptions of time and space. This has implications for the study of international political economy (indeed I prefer to use the term "global political economy") and world order. Civilizations—as an aspect of world order—can be likened to an amalgam that is the product of varied historical influences and social flows. Like a great river, a civilization is at once a source and a destination for social, political, economic, and cultural flows. A river flows into and from the seas and oceans, and it carries and modifies their waves, currents, life forms, and sedimentation. Civilizations likewise inflect and reflect the movement of social forces.

When civilization is viewed in this dialectical way as a set of social forces in movement and development, we immediately go beyond theories that create a Manichean universe, of black and white, good and evil, based on fixed unchanging essences. This intellectual and ideological process is akin to one of inclusion/exclusion—that is, it reflects the narrowing of Cartesian rationalism. This type of thinking mystifies and occludes the reciprocal and dialectical relations of social forces that have linked and transformed civilizations over time. Even worse, today it involves a new demonology: fundamentalists categorize civilizations as singular essences, characterized as good and bad, right and wrong. For example, Samuel Huntington and Francis Fukuyama (and in this collection Daniel Chirot) explicitly or implicitly advocate a form of liberal triumphalism, which involves a form of "othering" of people who form part of non-Western or nonliberal civilizations. This practice goes back to the Orientalism of the early Crusades. The assumption of Orientalism is that of the superiority of the "West." This assumption linked to a teleology of progress that goes back to aspects of the Enlightenment, and more recently to the so-called civilizing mission of the "West" in the era of nineteenth century imperialism. This particular idea of the "West" reifies the complexities and diversities of the historical formations of diverse civilizations.

In what follows, I offer an alternative conceptualization that focuses on the revolutionary rise and expansion of capital that lies at the heart of the problems of world order today. By capital, I mean a form of power and a social relation— for example, that between the owners of capital (especially holders of financial capital) and the mass of the society that has little or no capital (most workers and peasants but also small businesses). Indeed, what has occurred over the past 200 years, in an uneven process, is the globalization of capitalism as the dominant form of organization of the political economy and the coordination of social life. Within the context of the *globalization of capitalism*, the speed of change has accelerated in the twentieth century, especially since World War II. Capitalism has become more universal, more productive, and more destructive. Indeed one key civilizational question we need to pose is whether capital has become a force on the planet that is more destructive than creative. A review of the scope, speed, and depth of these changes should make us sanguine about any ideology that suggests that history has ended. If history teaches us anything, it is that it never ends, since it is made by human beings and not by abstract metaphysical forces that are beyond human agency or control—points that will be partly concretized in the rest of this chapter.

Thus a key perspective for understanding economic globalization today is historical and civilizational. From this viewpoint we can see that it is not simply that the world is becoming more integrated economically, involving what David Harvey (1989) has called "time-space compression," but more fundamentally that it is becoming more capitalist. Indeed some of the language in Marx and Engels's *Communist Manifesto*, written in 1848, pointed to the way in which capital was integrating the world and breaking down national barriers, ancient customs, and creating new forms of society:

Constant revolutionalizing of production, uninterrupted disturbance of all social conditions, everlasting uncertainty and agitation distinguish the bourgeois epoch from all earlier ones. All fixed, fast-frozen relations, with their train of ancient and venerable prejudices and opinions are swept away, all new formed ones become antiquated before they can ossify. All that is solid melts into air, all that is holy is profaned, and man is at last compelled to face with sober senses, his real conditions of life and his relations with his kind.

Marx and Engels go on to observe:

All old-established national industries have been destroyed or are daily being destroyed. They are dislodged by new industries, whose introduction becomes a life and death question for all civilized nations . . . industries . . . whose products are consumed . . . in every quarter of the globe. In place of the old wants . . . we find new wants, requiring for their satisfaction the products of distant lands and climes. In place of the old local and national solutions and self-sufficiency, we have intercourse in every direction, universal interdependence of nations. And as in material, so also in intellectual production . . . [capitalism] compels all nations, on pain of extinction, to adopt the bourgeois mode of production; it compels them to introduce what it calls civilization into their midst, i.e., to become more bourgeois themselves. In one word, it creates a world after its own image.

So what are the other main aspects of such globalization today? There are several dimensions of globalization that can be mentioned. They relate to politics, economy, society, ideology, and culture and civilization. First, globalization is not based on free competition as is idealized in neo-classical theory, but on *oligopolistic neo-liberalism* (the world economy is dominated by large transnational corporations). This process is associated with another of Marx's predictions—the tendency toward the concentration of the control over capital into fewer enterprises on a world scale. Giant corporations and institutional investors control the lion's share of world output, trade, and investment flows, and they strongly influence the governments of the world. So the *ideology* of globalization is largely consistent with the worldview and political priorities of big capital as well as the outlook and material interests of affluent minorities in the OECD and in the urban elites and new middle classes in the Third World. Indeed these people often press for government policies that involve protection for the strong and a socialization of their risks, and market discipline for the weak. On the other hand, globalization has gone with growing social inequality and polarization, and the disintegration of earlier patterns of community and association both within and across nations.

Second, in terms of questions of *culture and civilization*, globalization is associated with what Marx called the making of the world in the image of the bourgeoisie. This is not to say that local cultures are completely homogenized by these processes—the process is both more complex and subtle than that. Nevertheless, image makers, spin-doctors, and advertisers of the corporate world are seeking to promote "market civilization," a civilization in which social institutions, including churches, schools, universities, and those in recreation (e.g., amateur sports) are redefined in ways that validate market values and market criteria of success (Gill, 1995).

In sum, as in the nineteenth century, globalization in the 1990s is part of a broader process of restructuring of the state and civil society, and of the political economy and culture. As the events in East Asia, Russia, and Latin America in the late 1990s have illustrated, the process of globalization has been very uneven and unstable. This instability seems to have increased over the past twenty years. At the same time, entire countries (and much of the African continent) and sections of the population are completely marginalized from the process of globalization. Indeed, those who benefit economically from globalization only involve 10 to 15 percent of the world's population.

As previously noted, a third specific aspect of structural transformation is associated with *political and legal changes* that help to *constitute* the emerging global political economy. Of course, Marx stressed the revolutionary implications of capital as a system of surplus accumulation that would serve to constitute (in the sense of create) a particular social formation. However, his political analysis of the *state and juridical system* and what today we would call the global governance of capital on a world scale (e.g., its regimes, rules, regulations, procedures, standards, organizations) was underdeveloped. What Marx hinted at but failed to fully explore were the complex and differentiated ways that the separation of the political and the economic is institutionalized in different forms of state. The generic context is that capitalist states separate the "economic" and the "political" in order to set limits to democratic control over dominant or powerful economic agents so as to support and insulate bourgeois rule, particularly its prerogatives in production and in the capital markets.

Today, this operates both within and across state forms—for example, through international organizations such as the IMF and World Bank, or intergovernmental forums such as the G7 or G8. This creates a capacity to govern the global political economy—although this capacity may, under certain conditions, be rendered largely ineffective by the contradictions of capitalist development (e.g., financial panics, manias, and crashes). Nevertheless, "new constitutionalism" seeks to institutionalize the power of capital (notably giant corporations and institutional investors) within and across state–civil society complexes and regional formations. In much of what follows, this will be our focus: political form of the separation of the economic and political associated with the governance practices of neo-liberal globalization. It involves legal and constitutional changes intended to underpin globalization and to lock in neo-liberalism as the political economy framework that defines future development (Gill, 1995). New constitutionalism is a systematic and conscious project to anchor geoeconomics and geopolitical changes under the dominance of corporate capital and large investors as we enter the new millennium. Thus the shifting geopolitics of the "world system" involves a dialectic between the power of capital and political and social forms (social institutions, customs, etc.) that constitute the basis of global society.

THE POLITICS OF GLOBALIZATION: CONSTITUTIONALIZING THE POLITICAL ECONOMY

Let us initially deal with three "texts" from 1997 that speak to some of the issues I want to raise.

First, in 1997, the *New York Times* reported that the Director-General of the World Trade Organization, Renato Ruggiero, claimed that he and his colleagues in the Bretton Woods institutions were "writing the constitution of a single global economy."[2] Second, at a conference in the UK in October 1997, Columbia University social theorist Saskia Sassen reported on a shift in emphasis among the "elites of transnational corporate capital." Sassen based her assessment on her attendance at the World Economic Forum in Davos during the 1990s. She noted that Davos participants (about 3,000, mainly political leaders and heads of corporations) had previously stressed "market, market, market." Now what was emerging was a significant concern with a "global economic governance" project, a conscious emphasis on the need to more actively mold the nature of the state to provide a more stable political environment for capital. Third, the World Bank's *World Development Report: The State in a Changing World* marks a bold attempt to outline an elaborate blueprint for desirable changes in governance from the viewpoint of economic liberalism. These three "texts" thus indicate that what is occurring is a process of thinking through the nature of political restructuring—or what we might call the reconstitution of state and political forms associated with global economic governance.

The question is why is this project being developed and for whom? What each of the texts speaks to is what I call the "new constitutionism." As I hope to show, this concept helps us to understand emerging political links between the concentration and centralization of capital in the hands of giant transnational corporations and institutional investors. It also shows the links between these social forces and the politico-legal restructuring of state forms. It is reflected in the policies of the international financial institutions and more broadly the G7 governments in attempts to shape the nature of transformation in much of the Third World and the former East Bloc. In this sense, it forms a central dimension of the shifting geopolitics—and patterns of regionalization and state formation as we enter the new millennium.

The new governance discourse is justified by liberal arguments that the international financial institutions and multilateral mechanisms are providing international public goods—such as stronger protection for property rights, which are vital for freedom, peace, and prosperity. Indeed, Joseph Nye, dean of Harvard's Kennedy School of Government, made this argument.[3] Nye is a senior American strategic thinker, a former senior official in the State Department and CIA, an executive member of the Trilateral Commission, and President Clinton's informal envoy to China in the late 1990s. In his *Financial Times* article Nye sought to emphasize that in a global economy, protection of private property rights becomes *more* important, and he stressed that it should be understood as a "a public good" that "depends upon effective government."[4]

Nye's central purpose, however, was to draw attention to a potential legitimation crisis for capitalist state–civil society complexes. Outlining political trends in the OECD, Nye showed that since 1965, there has been a dramatic decline in public trust in not only government, but also major institutions in the civil societies (e.g., in "major companies, universities, medicine and journalism") in a majority of OECD countries. Nye noted that when this was discussed at Davos in 1998, "Representatives from other countries cited similar trends." Nye warned that dissatisfaction might "undermine the public's willingness to provide such crucial resources as tax dollars" and could "erode support for democracy as a form of governance" (sic).

What is significant about Nye's argument is its propagandistic nature—he highlights what he wants to show, but makes no mention of other obvious social trends that might help to explain the decline in credibility of dominant institutions. For example, the media *mirasmus* (a term of Vaclav Havel's) in the United States presents news as disaster, invention, or entertainment. Public discourse is hardly advanced by a media obsessed with scandal and celebrity (e.g., the Bill Clinton–Monica Lewinsky saga).

Other issues Nye might have mentioned as possible explanations for legitimation problems of dominant institutions could have referred to developments in the global political economy. For example, over the last thirty years, as the global political economy became both more capitalist and more integrated, inequality between and within nations has widened (e.g., in the United States), and with this has gone substantial social disintegration. Some of the global statistics are quite striking. For example, the ratio of income of the top 20 percent income earners in the world to the poorest 20 percent has been widening consistently—it was 30:1 in 1960; 61:1 in 1991 and it rose to 78:1 in 1994. The share of the richest 20 percent in global income rose from 70 percent to 85 percent in 1960 to 1991. In this context, there is a new category of plutocrats:

in 1996 there were 358 billionaires who had combined assets that exceeded the total annual income of 45 percent of the world's population—that is, of 2.3 billion people. Of these, 1.2 billion are without access to safe drinking water and 842 million adults are illiterate (a majority of whom are women). There are 158 million malnourished children under five, 1.3 billion living below the income poverty line (statistics from UNDP, 1997). One statistic that is relevant for geopolitical consideration is how the gap between per capita income in the richest and poorest countries is widening all the time: it was 3:1 in 1820; 9:1 in 1913, and rose to 16:1 in 1992 (Moody, 1997: 54). Inequality within as well as across capitalist societies has increased dramatically over the past thirty years, and this inequality intensified after the debt crisis of the 1980s.[5]

THE POWER OF CAPITAL AND NEW CONSTITUTIONALISM

Within this context, global trade and investment are dominated by about 500 mega-sized firms and their subsidiaries. Various estimates suggest that between 40 and 70 percent of all global trade and investment is controlled by these firms. Yet the International Labor Organization estimated that in 1996 one billion were unemployed or underemployed: the unemployment crisis began in the early 1980s with the Third World debt crisis and neo-liberal restructuring (Moody, 1997: 41). Indeed, in 1998 the International Labor Organization predicted that this number would increase rapidly in 1999 because of the global recession.[6]

So evidence points to growing inequalities of power and resources, and dominance of the global political economy by giant corporations and large institutional investors. One key to the success of these firms is the way they have managed to consistently outperform their rivals (and thus "beat the average rate of return"). Jonathan Nitzan (1998) calls this process "differential accumulation." His analysis shows how the income drawn from capital has consistently demonstrated an upward trend since World War II. This finding is in sharp contrast to the arguments of many on the left who point to an accumulation crisis or a crisis of profitability for corporate capital (Nitzan, 1998: 208–9, especially Figures 4a and 4b). The ability to control and to accumulate power is based on legal protection given to private property in capitalist societies. Put differently, the power of capital cannot exist without the application of political authority, legitimation, and a system of coercion and organized violence on the part of the state (Gill and Law, 1989).[7] State power underpins a clear pattern of increasing concentration of capital and power focused in the G7 and OECD.

The accumulation of power has both "vertical" and "horizontal" dimensions. The vertical dimension involves the deepening of control within industrial sectors. The horizontal dimension involves widening market access through entry into new territories, the creation of new products through financial innovation, and so on. With regard to vertical expansion, this process has been linked to the merger and acquisitions (M&A) mania that has gone with downsizing (mass layoffs of workers) that has swept the globe. For example, in the United States in 1997 there was a total of $1.6 trillion of M&A, itself a record. By the end of June 1998 the half-year had totaled $1.3 trillion in M&A. M&A activity rarely produces increases in either productivity or services for customers. Vertical expansion is motivated primarily by the motive of control (i.e., of property rights over future profits and income streams).

The macro-structure of power and control that frames the processes of competition and differential accumulation has been in place—although not without its crises and contradictions—now for roughly a century. Thus most economic activity in production, trade, and investment is focused within the macro-regions of the dominant triad of the global political economy (North America, Western Europe, and East Asia). About three-quarters of all trade and investment flows are between the regions of the triad. This is where the most powerful transnational corporations are headquartered. And since now half of the world's 100 largest economies are transnational corporations (measured in annual sales), not nation states (measured in GDP), we can see how economic power is concentrated in the global political economy (for details see Moody, 1997). This power is armored by the coercive capabilities of the NATO countries, led by the United States, with Japan dependent on the United States for its security in the Asia-Pacific region.

It is in this context that we need to analyze one of the most remarkable but least theorized aspects of the 1990s. Not only the former East Bloc and the Third World, but also the OECD nations have engaged in substantial political and constitutional restructuring, especially with respect to questions of economic governance. This process is what I call the "new constitutionalism" of disciplinary neo-liberalism: it has involved initiatives to politically "lock in" neo-liberal reforms to secure investor freedoms and private property rights for large transnational enterprises. Why has this change taken place and what are its wider political implications?

I argue that this is explained primarily by two sets of structural factors. These are the growth in the power and mobility of large corporate capital and institutional investors on the one hand and increased inter-state economic competition on the other (with the dominance of the United States in geopolitics crucial to both trends). However, structure also means agency: the changes are the conscious product of organized social forces pressing for greater economic opportunities. Elements of the G7 governments and the international financial institutions such as the World Bank and the IMF are central in articulating and implementing the strategic aspects of this process.

So why, in this context, do governments adopt liberal policies? One reason is an intensification of inter-state competition, a competition that involves both economics and strategy. That is, governments (and regional political associations such as the European Union) struggle to represent the "national" or "community" interest, however defined, insofar as this is reflected in the struggle to survive in a more integrated, triad-dominated global political economy in which competitive pressures have increased immensely. And during the 1980s and

1990s, many governments have been persuaded that failure to liberalize their economies, and especially their capital markets, risks losing business and investment to other jurisdictions. Competition involves economic regulation (not deregulation—even a laissez-faire system is a form of regulation), tax incentives, and lowering tax rates to induce investment.[9]

A second reason—which is in effect a restatement of the first—is the increase in the power and mobility of large holders of capital, and the subordination of state policies to their interests. Thus the new era of neo-liberal globalization has gone with a shift in priorities of government—often from a social definition toward a financial one. This requires a strong state apparatus to make sure social order is maintained. For example, governments develop a larger apparatus of surveillance: to put the so-called anti-systemic groups under surveillance as well as to monitor economic activity. The latter is needed to provide credible estimates of economic trends, to demonstrate its potential to investors. Recently the G7 and IMF have pressed nations to maximize their "transparency" to domestic and foreign investors—a further way to increase the structural power of capital by making it, in theory at least, more precise in its application in particular investment locations.

A counterpart to these trends is de-socialization of social reproduction, so that a more market-driven and privatized system emerges: for example, rolling back the welfare state, and its replacement by the "workfare state," with cutbacks in public education, public health care, state pensions, and so on. Both are justified by rhetoric that redefines the citizen as a consumer or as an investor in the marketplace, rather than as a participant in the public sphere. In addition, this rhetoric prioritizes, almost as a categorical imperative, the need to reduce the deficit or the national debt, or both. In this sense, the state is activist in attracting business and creating a more favorable investment climate, whereas it is retreating from other postwar obligations, justified because of fiscal crisis (Gill and Law, 1989).[10]

A third reason is the re-assertion of the centrality and primacy of the United States in the global political economy, a development that can be traced back to the early 1980s (Gill, 1990). The American government has been strongly associated with the promotion of global liberalization and a particular form of limited democratization as a means to strengthen American leadership in global politics (Robinson, 1996). Geoeconomics and what the Clinton administration calls "democratic enlargement" have been central to U.S. geopolitical strategy for almost two decades. Thus we can see attempts to introduce aspects of the American constitutional model. It can be seen in the former East Bloc nations. This process of course originated in the post-World War II settlements in Germany and Japan under the Marshall Plan Administration: political as well as economic reconstruction was central to the constitution of American hegemony within the core capitalist states during the Cold War.

BRINGING CLASS ANALYSIS BACK IN: THE SOCIAL ANATOMY OF TRANSNATIONALIZATION

Nevertheless, it is also crucial to develop a class analysis of these changes and to link the notion of class to both the pattern of social relations and to particular forms of political agency at the international or global level. In this sense the primary agency behind this form of restructuring is not the U.S. government or "American" capital as such, although each plays a fundamentally important role. Rather, I call this agency, following Gramsci, a transnational historical bloc, which connects leading elements of sets of social forces in both state and civil society. This includes leading elements of capital, incorporated labor, and those drawn from important institutions in civil society and culture, such as the political parties, media, churches, education, and so on. A historical bloc seeks to produce a fusion of social, political, and cultural power that aspires to hegemony.[11] In an era of globalization it seems plausible to apply the concept of a historical bloc to transnational class formations. So whereas the identity of most types of labor and many political forces is often national or parochial in orientation, and where the mobility of labor is low, agents of transnational capital are cosmopolitan in outlook, and extremely mobile between jurisdictions and fields of activity. Moreover, these agents are very active in transnational networks of power that sustain their dominance over the world economy, a world economy organized in ways that maximize the structural power of internationally mobile capital (Gill and Law, 1989).

Put differently, a transnational historical bloc is a constellation of public and private power that operates both within and across the territorial boundaries and civil and political societies of nation-states. It is thus a broad set of social forces and a specific transnational class formation. It has political and ideological dimensions. Its political goal is to sustain its dominance in world politics, which in turn depends on maintaining the political and economic conditions for differential accumulation to be possible. This bloc is associated with parts of the state apparatuses of the G7 countries, the IMF, the World Bank and the Bank for International Settlements, and with private agents drawn from the ranks of the largest corporations and institutional investors, and with intellectuals from elite universities and think tanks.[12]

This bloc we can call, for short, the "G7 nexus." It of course involves competition and rivalry within its ranks. It nevertheless contains common interests in certain types of structural and constitutional change in the global political economy. However, although this historical bloc is seeking to institutionalize its dominance through international agreements and treaties, its more fundamental focus of political action is *within* state–civil society complexes, especially of the largest economies of the world. And some of the political activity of the G7 nexus is designed to insulate or protect economic policy from wider democratic forces, as well as from the influence of state capitalist or nationalist political forces.[13]

The goal is to secure private property rights and investor freedoms on a world scale by institutionalizing a more politically hospitable investment climate for the accumulation of capital. Although the policy mix that accompanies this can vary, since the 1980s the latter has been linked to macroeconomic orthodoxy based on market-monetarist principles (low inflation and fiscal austerity). It is also associated with specific initiatives to politically "lock in" neo-liberal reforms and rules-based systems with respect to trade and investment, often using multilateral mechanisms, such as in the World Trade Organization and more recently in the OECD's controversial Multilateral Agreement on Investment.

One general conclusion to draw from this part of the chapter is that we are witnessing an expansion of state activity to provide greater legal and other protections for business, and political effort to stabilize the investment climate worldwide. Many governments have sought to expand the scope of free enterprise as the primary motor force of accumulation, and at the same time, to roll back other aspects of the state's responsibilities by de-socializing risk provision (e.g., dismantling the welfare state or replacing it with the workfare state). In this way there is a change in the institutional balance between state and civil society (e.g., through privatization in pensions, health, education) while at the same time an attempt is made to co-opt potentially democratizing forces into the neo-liberal project. This perhaps explains why both Joseph Nye and the World Bank are so concerned with the problem of legitimation of neo-liberal globalization. Indeed, the World Bank's 1997 report includes a systematic blueprint for the co-optation of forces of civil society into the least central and strategic areas of policy determination. As a tactic to legitimate the attenuation of democracy in economic policy, the Bank encourages "participation" in safely channeled areas, such as in education (e.g., as school trustees), in health, in the social sector, and in the environment (e.g., grazing lands, wildlife, forests, and water sources). The Bank stresses above all the need to keep central control over macroeconomics and strategy. And the Bank also emphasizes strengthening "the rule of law" in the Third World to protect "both persons and property" (World Bank, 1997: 119).

Indeed, suppressing, attenuating, and/or co-opting popular-democratic social forces are central to sustaining the dominance of the prevailing transnational historic bloc. This is because, especially in the context of instabilities and crises of the global political economy, a countermovement, if it attained political coherence, might lead toward authoritative re-regulation, and perhaps a more pervasive popular democratization of control over the political economy. This involves perceptions and social institutions. As central material concessions to the working class associated with the construction of the postwar order erode (e.g., the welfare state), new ideas and institutions are required to legitimate the re-privatization of risk and to sustain minimum consent necessary for social order. The question is, can this strategy succeed?

CONCLUSION: CRISIS, POLITICAL AGENCY, AND CRITICAL PERSPECTIVES

In this new strategic context, a central problem of political theory is how to imagine and to theorize new forms of collective political identity and agency that might lead to the creation of new, ethical, and democratic state forms in a globalizing context. And, in this regard, this chapter has doubtless asked more questions than it is able to answer.

As noted, globalization is not new, although it poses questions that combine the old and the new in unprecedented ways, and these problems require a historical perspective and an understanding of society as something more than the sum total of the interactions of self-regarding rational actors. Atomistic views of the world can be contrasted with those founded on a more organic view of social relations as greater than the sum of the parts, as a set of processes, rather than an aggregate of individualistic interaction. Indeed, as I noted earlier, the contradictions and problems of globalization cannot be fully understood by using the orthodox frameworks of understanding—particularly those associated with neo-realism and neo-liberal institutionalism—that have come to prevail in American studies of international relations. Indeed, these knowledge frameworks often mystify the processes of globalization and directly or indirectly tend to reinforce the status quo—in a very unequal world order that does not provide social justice for the majority of the people on the planet.

Thus what is needed from a critical perspective is a more innovative and historical theoretical framework for understanding and explaining the social and political dynamics of the global political economy. This framework needs to analyze and account for the existing structure of power and authority, as well as its contradictions and weaknesses, in a sober and realistic way. At the same time, a critical perspective must seek to highlight the potentials for transformation. This means developing an intellectual framework that can capture the political movement of social and economic forces on a world scale and identify the capacity for political agency for different sets of social forces in the context of the making of history (Thompson, 1980).

Political agency involves struggles to constitute and to re-constitute the "limits of the possible" for a civilization at a particular moment in history (Braudel, 1979, Vol. I). These limits involve values, social and cultural practices and institutions, individual and collective identities. Yet these limits are transformed in struggles between old and new, over interpretations of tradition and myths of future possibility. So a key question for global politics today is how far and in what ways have democratic-popular forces created new processes and methods of collective action? How far can they create alternatives to the existing order in a more compelling way? Attempts to institutionalize the power of capital on a world scale provoke resistance—to the intensification of social hierarchy, inequality, alienation, commodification, and exploitation that is engendered. Resistance, of course, is not always associated with progressive politics, since "anti-systemic movements" can come from both forces of the left and from the reactionary forces of the nationalist and fundamentalist right. In other words, to more fully explore the implications of shifting geopolitics we need also to reflect on democratic potentials for transformative action.

One way to do this is to compare the situation today with that of the 1930s, when a crisis of capitalism was widely proclaimed and real alternatives emerged, in the form of Stalinism, Fascism, and Nazism. Of course, there are many differences between the inter-war period and the 1990s. However, for most of the world today there is a worldwide economic depression. This has been triggered in part by the collapse of a pyramid of risky investments, some of which have been in the so-called "emerging markets" of East Asia and the former Soviet Union. What is clearly different is that by contrast to the 1930s, the G7 exists—that is, capitalist states are more unified under U.S. leadership. Unlike the inter-war years of growing inter-imperial rivalry, the United States has constructed a set of organic alliance relations and its centrality in these arrangements has been consolidated in the 1990s. By this I mean the United States has primacy in its military alliances and in the G7 and other key economic organizations, and it seems to have had some success in incorporating the new Russia in the wake of NATO expansion. The United States and G7 and the international financial institutions have to a degree managed to institutionalize global economic relations. There is now a transnational system of surveillance and intervention in order to contain some of the contradictions of capitalist accumulation, which contrasts greatly with the 1930s situation. Moreover, despite the instabilities associated with the current phase of capitalist development, a general war among the most powerful states seems unlikely in the foreseeable future, although there are worrying trends in nuclear proliferation.

On the other hand, the world is, in both a formal and a substantive sense, much more democratic than was the case in the 1930s. So what seems to be more likely in the twenty-first century is an increase in conflict and violence associated with struggles linked to globalization and democratization. Under conditions of budgetary austerity to finance deficits and pay external debts, governments have reduced social provision of basic public goods. This has had gender as well as class-based effects. For many, globalization appears as a relentless Social Darwinism that increases inequality and political marginalization.[14] Thus dialectically, there is a growing disillusion with conventional organized politics and a politically unsatisfied desire for alternatives to the instrumental, irresponsible, unaccountable, and corrupt political elites and ruling classes that have presided over these developments.

In this context, there is a pervasive sense of structural crisis, a widespread sentiment of uncertainty and anxiety, of exhaustion of political alternatives, and in some manifestations, a yearning for "order": a new order or an attempt to reconstitute the old order. This is akin to the condition of disorientation and flux that Giovanni Arrighi (1993) associated with periods of "systemic chaos" such as the 1640s, the 1790s, and the 1930s, when the credibility and appeal of the old order and of a range of political alternatives was at a historic low. And, as in the 1930s, this may lead to Caesarism and fascism in some parts of the world, as well as a strengthening of the left in others. At the same time it would seem on the surface that there is little in the way of developed political alternatives to capitalism at the end of the twenty-first century. Is this really the case?

If we step back, we can see that there is a tripartite division in terms of the movement of social forces within world politics today. In many respects this division corresponds to the social hierarchy that is associated with neo-liberal patterns of accumulation. At the very top, at the apex of globalization as it were, sit its beneficiaries: the dominant or supremacist forces associated with the G7 state apparatuses and the big corporations and investors. Beneath this level are both democratic and reactionary forces that are not fully incorporated into the dominant projects or who are seeking in different methods to directly oppose neo-liberal globalization. In fact the reason that we have the incidence of both nationalist and fundamentalist movements, as well as increasingly democratic social movements opposed to globalization—as the research of Joseph Nye and his colleagues suggests—may be because conventional politics and government are at an impasse. Governments are seen by their citizens as either fully aligned with the forces of globalization or else offering no alternatives to globalization. And, as such, government statements read as a litany of impotence. This generates a crisis in terms of the representative institutions of the state and a crisis of government credibility. Citizens realize that governments are unable or unwilling to deal with basic issues of political identity or to solve common problems in the everyday lives of people. This second level of forces merges with a third. The third includes those generally marginalized from mainstream political life: new political forces consisting of feminists, indigenous peoples, minority groups, peasants, some trade unionists; some former members of left-wing political parties (many of whom have quit because the old parties are not proposing new solutions). While the links between peasants and other "anti-systemic" groups may not be highly developed, there is nevertheless some sense of movement.

The crisis of representation and legitimation is an often-ignored political dimension of globalization. Indeed it helps to explain why different kinds of agencies, church groups, and so on, are forming themselves in civil society and contributing to a democratizing process that in many respects is independent of formal state apparatuses and formal democratization (electoralism). One response from state elites is to try to repress these forces in civil society. But it seems unlikely that this can succeed. The forces involved are too numerous and scattered. They cannot be controlled or easily incorporated by the old political processes, and they do not accept the proposition that neo-liberal globalization is either desirable or inevitable.

So what is to be done? Clearly progressive forces need to reconsider their criteria of action and political agency to better synthesize and channel the potentials for resistance into a more creative political project. Their project should be the creation of a more powerful form of democratic collective agency in a new form of global political association.

Moreover, the forms of global democratic collective action that emerged at the end of the twentieth century cannot, in my view, be understood in the singular. There is no single "democratic" or "progressive" party with a single form of identity, nor should there be. What are emerging are collectivities that are plural and differentiated, democratic and inclusive. These new forms of collective action contain novel conceptions of social justice and solidarity, of social possibility, of knowledge, emancipation, and freedom. What we are discussing is, therefore, a very complex organism that is much more than a political party as it is usually defined. It is a set of social forces that includes educational processes and cultural movements. However, this organism does not act in the old sense of an institutionalized and centralized structure of representation. Indeed, this "party" is not institutionalized as such since it has a multiple and capillary form. Moreover, many of the moments and movements of resistance noted above are at first glance "local" in nature. Nevertheless, these movements involve a broad recognition that local problems may require global solutions.[15]

Thus although one can be pessimistic about globalization in its current form, this is perhaps where some of the optimism for the future may lie: a new set of democratic identities that are global, while being rooted in local conditions, problems, and opportunities. This needs to be understood as a set of forces in movement, with their own forms of mobilizing political myths. The new myths are both practical and critical and linked to the solution of shared problems— they involve critical problem solving. The historical outlook of these forces is not teleological. Nor is it linked to abstract utopias, such as those associated with the construction of Soviet Man (sic) or liberal capitalism-as-progress. These forces take distance from the relativism of the neo-Nietzschean dystopias currently fashionable among policy-makers and intellectuals in the United States: the "end of history" and the "clash of civilizations."

So what is the role and duty of critical intellectuals in the social sciences and humanities in the context of global crisis? Unfortunately too many intellectuals subscribe to or create orthodoxy that simply reinforces dominant power-knowledge structures. Others simply ignore fundamental problems of authority and violence and, as such, indirectly subordinate themselves to dominant power. By contrast, this chapter has been written from the viewpoint of a critical theory that seeks to develop a new transnational historical materialist approach. So, from a critical perspective, what is the role and duty of critical intellectuals? First, they must provide a clear and realistic analysis of the nature and logic of contemporary developments. Second, they must speak out critically on the basis of their freedom to demand respect for questions of justice. Third, they must oppose all patterns of domination that destroy the human creative spirit. And finally, they must find ways to develop new, critical perspectives. And at a time of social crisis, where social and political thought seems to be at an impasse as it stands transfixed before the dilemmas of globalization, intellectuals need to use their creative imagination. They need to help us to rethink the potentials in society that allow for creativity and greater human possibility—that is, rethink essential aspects of what it means to be human. This means that political thinkers need to return to the imaginative task of innovation that has been central for the human spirit since the beginnings of historical time.

NOTES

1. By contrast, some contributors to this volume have stressed that the major and most important issue of the twentieth century concerned social adaptation to pressures emanating from the European industrial revolution. Indeed, Daniel Chirot makes the claim that the optimum forms of adaptation have involved liberal forms of state and society.

2. Renato Ruggiero, Director General of the World Trade Organization, "The High Stakes of World Trade," *Wall Street Journal*, interactive edition, February 28, 1997.

3. *Financial Times*, March 18, 1998.

4. This way of posing the question of property rights might be contrasted with that of an earlier liberal. Adam Smith noted, "Civil government, so far as it is instituted for the security of property, is in reality instituted for the defence of the rich against the poor, or of those who have some property against those who have none at all." (Cited in Hill, 1967: 287.)

5. Evidence amassed by the UN and the World Bank over the past thirty years contradicts Chirot's unsubstantiated claim that Marx was wrong about rising inequality within capitalist societies.

6. See International Labor Organization, *World Employment Report*, 1998–99. Geneva: International Labor Organization.

7. A good example of this process is Microsoft, which had a market capitalization of about $271 billion in late January 1999. How much of the value of Microsoft is due to the productivity of its owners and workers? How much is due to the apparatus of production they control and have legal production for—that is, without copyright how much would Microsoft be worth? Probably very little indeed. Microsoft's products build on ideas taken from Apple, binary logic, mathematics, the English language, museums and art galleries, encyclopedias and draw on a massive social structure of generally public knowledge. This is converted into products protected by copyright—that is, private intellectual property rights. This protection is linked to marketing and other political and business arrangements, which allow Microsoft to create and in some senses to dictate our needs.

8. R. Gwyn, "Size matters to those laid off by mergers," *Toronto Star*, July 5, 1998.

9. Of course liberalization also means allowing foreign property holders a bigger strategic stake in the national economy.

10. Fiscal crisis is connected to globalization; financing fiscal deficits increasingly involves governments selling bonds in the global financial markets.

11. Gramsci's *Prison Notebooks* (1971) primarily analyzed historical blocs within the context of the construction of the hegemony of the bourgeoisie within particular nation-states, although he did give indications that historical blocs and forms of rule could become transnationalized. He did this, for example, in his analysis of the relationship between the spread of Enlightenment ideas and institutions and the onset of bourgeois

revolutions in the eighteenth century and in the twentieth century in his analysis of Americanism and Fordism.

12. However, it also includes many of the elites and emerging middle classes in the former East Bloc and the Third World, as well as many subcontractors, import-export, and other smaller businesses and small investors that are linked to the activity of transnational corporations and investment in stock markets.

13. Of course, the precise ways in which the political and the economic are separated or combined varies across different state–civil society complexes, that is, in forms of what Gramsci (1971) called the "extended state": the ways that political and civil society are inter-penetrated in the form of state.

14. One intense example is the predicament of the vast majority of women in the Third World. In many parts of Africa working-class and peasant women tend to have to bear more of the burdens of structural adjustment in, for example, caring for the young, the old, and the infirm. African public health care systems have been disintegrating due to a combination of maldevelopment, budget austerity imposed to pay external debts, and epidemics that are ravaging the continent (e.g., AIDS).

15. Elsewhere I have called this development the emergence of a "post-Modern Prince." What I have in mind is a form of transnational collective agency that goes beyond the association of leadership and collective action with a particular individual (à la Machiavelli's *The Prince*) or indeed with a specific political party, internationalist or otherwise (as in Gramsci's *Modern Prince*). The postmodern prince is not to be confused with postmodern philosophy since it has a universalist aspect. Although it operates in a localized and decentralized way, it seeks to mobilize and to create global democratic potentials in the twenty-first century. Stephen Gill, "Imagining a 'post-Modern Prince' in an era of global crisis," Toronto, Canada, Mimeo, 1998.

3

Stateness and System in the Global Structure of Trade: A Network Approach to Assessing Nation Status

Michael Alan Sacks, Marc Ventresca, and Brian Uzzi[1]

Global stratification of states and nations is a much debated feature of the contemporary world system. Business analysts and many international scholars have advocated comparative advantage as the tool for analyzing variations and dynamics of outcomes such as nation status. This type of analysis highlights the importance of factors internal to a nation and stresses factors such as modernization level, educational training of citizens, and investments in domestic capital as determinants of national prosperity. World-system theories stress a global embeddedness approach to investigating nation status, highlighting how historical contingency and position in the global political economy impact nation status and other outcomes of interest.

More recently, the argument that the structure of global trade patterns economic outcomes reinforces a central claim of contemporary economic sociology regarding the embedded nature of economic activity (Coleman, 1990; Granovetter, 1985). In this view, dynamics of behavior and relationships create a structure that at times helps or hinders actors' ability to be economically successful. Thus, two actors with comparable resources and internal attributes will receive different rates of return because of their positions in a web of exchanges that affects the process of trading (DiTomaso, 1982; Miller, 1980).

We apply this embeddedness approach to understand the trade dynamics of the world system. In this chapter, we test empirically these perspectives in three time periods, 1965, 1970, and 1980, to show the impact of system and stateness on standard indicators of national prosperity. This chapter reports original theoretical arguments and evidence about state and system-based factors affecting nation status, building on initial findings from our work on the contingent effects of social capital in the world system (Sacks, Uzzi, and Ventresca, forthcoming). We show how these effects have changed over time as the institutional conditions of the world system have shifted. Finally, we address the implications of our findings for nation status in the new millennium.

STATE VERSUS SYSTEM-BASED ARGUMENTS ABOUT CHANGES IN NATION STATUS

Theorists have articulated a variety of perspectives on how nation status changes in the world system (McMichael, 2000). Modernization theory asserts that all nations follow relatively uniform stages of development, and that less developed nations must "modernize" their economic, social, and cultural foundations in order to develop more quickly. Nations were seen as being in various stages of development, with those struggling seen as "less developed" than the more advanced Western nations. Differences in development are seen as manifestations of uneven modernization throughout the world, and modernization theorists argue that as "modern" features diffuse into the "underdeveloped" nations, they too will follow the path to greater levels of industrialization and economic prosperity (Chirot, 1986; Rostow, 1960a). This research focuses on the role of internal processes in the economic growth of nations (Delacroix, 1977) and proposes that the best strategic approach a nation can take in the global market is to enhance its own internal characteristics (Griffin, 1981). Recent work on "competitive advantage" advances modernization ideas and retains the same focus on factors internal to the nation (Porter, 1990).

Standard economic analyses of the strength of national economies are typically assessed through comparative advantage—using internal national economic indicators (i.e., inflation rates, unemployment figures, etc.) to compare economic statuses. This framework stipulates internal measurements as the units for analyzing nation status in the global economy, with any relevant external factors such as international aid incorporated into the endogenous analysis (Linnemann, 1966; Meyer and Hannan, 1979). Thus, national comparisons are often made irrespective of the roles of other global actors in the process of economic growth.

In contrast to comparative advantage approaches, world-system theories emphasize the importance of international economic, social, and political interdependencies in understanding nation status (Bergesen, 1980; Chase-Dunn, 1989). A key paradigm for analysis of global structure is Wallerstein model of core/periphery/semi-periphery status (Wallerstein, 1974b). In this view, national prosperity is an outcome of a nation's position in the stratified world system and the global processes that lead to these outcomes. World-system theory "challenges the assumption that national societies constitute independent units whose development can be understood without taking into account the systematic ways in which societies are linked to one another in the context of a larger network of material exchanges" (Chase-Dunn, 1989: 1). World-system theorists have argued that nation status cannot be measured with internal economic indicators alone because this framework neglects the process and effects of more fundamental structural relationships.

In this chapter, we develop Wallerstein's arguments in the context of international trade. In this view, nations positioned at the core of international economic activity experience advantaged interactions in global trade, those located in the semi-periphery experience somewhat disadvantaged interactions, while those nations in the periphery experience highly disadvantaged interactions in global trade. Despite the substantial impacts of this classic argument, efforts to test the theory have struggled to corroborate its empirical claims. Questions over stratum membership, number of categories, conflicting sources and consequences of the stratification, and methodological difficulties have all contributed to disagreements and confusion over exactly how to operationalize Wallerstein's model. Additionally, this approach focuses solely on the structure of the world trading network, without looking more deeply into the dynamics that reinforce and perpetuate it. World-system theorists argue that international roles and relationships are key in any causal understanding of national economic statuses and changes within particular nations (Chirot and Hall, 1982; Korllos, 1991). Despite general agreement on this idea, specific descriptions of the global social structure are a fairly recent development. Network analysis researchers have only recently begun to clarify the disparate views surrounding these questions (Su, 1995).

Network analyses of the world system provide an empirical framework for operationalizing theories of global structure and use international trade figures as the basis for constructing the world network. Early efforts to use network analysis of the global economy showed that nations more central in the world system in 1965 experienced faster rates of economic growth than those more peripheral (Snyder and Kick, 1979). Nemeth and Smith (1985) improved on Snyder and Kick's methodology by limiting the scope of analysis to exclusively international trade data and by developing more precise network analytic procedures to measure their data in relational terms. In an effort to examine the world system more dynamically, Smith and White (1992) performed network analyses for three periods—1965, 1970, and 1980—and made comparisons across these time periods. While the network structure remained fairly consistent during these times, nineteen nations shifted toward the center while three slipped toward the periphery of the world-system network. The authors did not address the causes of this network mobility; they simply demonstrated that some nations did in fact shift in the global network. Why nation status improves or declines in the world system remain questions only addressed at the theoretical level.

Dependency theory is a version of system-based approaches that seeks to explain how world systemic factors influence nation status change. This approach asserts that core nations exploit less developed ones for raw materials and resources (Munford, 1978; Roxborough, 1976). This process systematically alienates the less developed nations from the rest of the world and from full participation in the global economy, which is dominated by the few, rich nations in the core. In this view, peripheral nations need to overcome global trade alienation and assert their power as interdependent players in the international division of labor (Diamond, 1979). Through collaborating with one another, peripheral nations can form alliances to better negotiate for more favorable trading terms with the core nations (Gerami, 1985). The thrust of dependency theory focuses on the exploitation of periphery nations for the benefit of core ones. Accordingly, a nation's regional location is a prime determinant for its experiences in global relations and trade.

World-system perspectives suggest that nations with similar internal characteristics and production capabilities can gain unequal returns on their international trade because of the bargaining positions offered by their network positions. In this view, the global trade structure impacts nations' abilities to economically prosper, as some nations can gain better rates of return on trade based on their position in the global network. We apply Burt's (1992) theory of structural autonomy to test the impact of network position in the global structure of trade.

WHAT IS STRUCTURAL AUTONOMY?

Burt (1992) argues that attributes of individual actors (human capitals such as education and ability for individual persons; efficiency at the organization level) can determine the amount of value possible within economic transactions, but position in a social structure better predicts which actors get what portion of that value. Actors with higher structural autonomy—network freedom through reduced dependencies that allows actors greater negotiating power and access to resources—garner higher levels of desired returns. Higher autonomy generates more "structural holes"—disconnections between actors in a network. Structural holes between actors can be exploited by third parties who serve as the broker between them.[2]

Burt's argument turns on a crucial behavioral claim: that the allocation of benefits—and no doubt burdens (Northcraft et al., 1995)—in both economic and social contexts seldom works according to the principles of neo-classical markets. Instead, *social* capital conditions allocation and returns beyond what an assessment of attributes of individual actors—*human* capital—can provide. The structure of relationships itself comprises varied features that create the possibility for advantage (or disadvantage).

STRUCTURAL AUTONOMY IN THE WORLD SYSTEM

In our work on world trade, structural autonomy is the aggregate of a nation's constraint (both primary and secondary) and opportunity conditions with its contacts. Primary constraint refers to the amount of time and resources a nation's contacts invest in relationships with that nation's other contacts. Secondary con-

Figure 3.1
Pure Autonomy (Autonomy = 1)

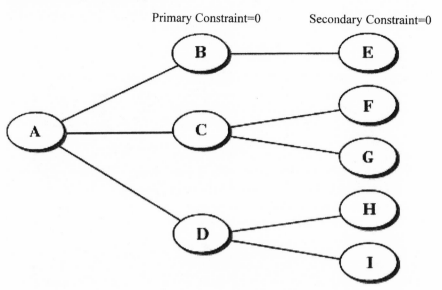

Primary Constraint=0   Secondary Constraint=0

straint is the redundant ties that the nation's contacts' contacts have with one another. Constraint varies from 0 (where a contact has no common connections, primary or secondary, with the nation's other contacts) to 1 (where a contact has ties to all the other contacts of its trading partners). Opportunity refers to the extent to which other nations are not trading with one another. Opportunity ranges from 0 (where nations in the network all trade heavily with one another) to 1 (where nations aren't trading with one another, allowing many chances for a nation to dominate the terms of trade in that network).

We present the structural autonomy argument visually in Figures 3.1 and 3.2. Figure 3.1 is a situation of pure network autonomy for actor A. A's three network connections (B, C, and D) are not connected with one another (no primary constraint), and they do not share other connections through which they could exchange information (secondary constraint). They have no ability to compare information that A gives them, nor can they collude in any move against A. Furthermore, A has a choice among the three connections for resources, while B, C, and D have no alternative to A for information or resources. These facts give A a great advantage in gathering information and negotiating the terms of exchange for trade. In this case, A has a structural autonomy measure of 1—the maximum possible score for autonomy.

Figure 3.2 shows the opposite situation. In this case, A's three network contacts (B, C, and D) all have connections with one another (primary constraint), and they have mutual connections in their networks (secondary constraint). A cannot play one contact off another, as their connection provides them with

Figure 3.2
Pure Constraint (Autonomy = 0)

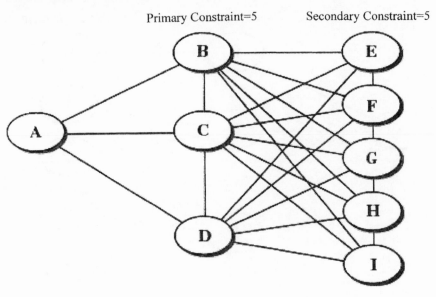

information on the actions of A on other actors in the network (i.e., pricing, terms of trade, costs, profits). Additionally, actors in the network can collude against A. A's information gathering and negotiating power has been significantly reduced through the highly constraining nature of the multiple ties within the network. In this case, A has an autonomy score of 0—the lowest possible autonomy score. A is in a highly disadvantaged position for trade.

ORIENTING ARGUMENTS

We argue that nation status is contingent on location in the structure of the world system; complex political, social, and economic phenomena in the world foster imperfect competition and help produce a stratified international economy. Specifically, we argue that nations that serve as brokers between international trading partners will benefit from this role. Furthermore, changes in the institutional features of global trade—regime governance, volume, composition, and participation—during the period 1965–1980 impacts the extent to which there are advantages to reap and for whom. Because the contingent value of social capital rests in part on the number of actors involved in the core of trade (Burt, 1997), we predict that the value of structural autonomy decreases over time as the volume of trade and number of nations actively involved increases.

Dynamic shifts in the world system over time dramatically shape the institutional conditions in which nations prosper (Chase-Dunn, Kwano, and Brewer,

2000). The structure of trade from 1965 to 1980 is a challenging empirical site in which to develop Burt's arguments for two reasons: (1) overall volume of trade increased dramatically and the composition of trade shifted; and (2) more actors came to participate and more varied trading relationships developed. Early in the period, 1965, hegemonic world economic (and political/cultural) relations and immediate legacy of colonial experiences maintained an effect on world trade structure. Regime studies of international trade show major shifts in the early 1970s, marked by the establishment of UN agency mandates that promoted trade in and among developing countries in the postcolonial period, the proliferation of multilateral trade agreements, and the initiatives of global financial actors like the IMF to regularize and monitor export/import activity and in effect to promote it (Krasner, 1985). By 1980, substantial differences in patterns and participation in world trade emerged, due in part to the role of global trade regimes in defining "rules of the game," meaning, and mechanisms of trade. We argue that these shifts in the governing regime describe important changes in the institutional context, redefining foundational rules of trading activity at the global level and having diverse effects on countries located at different positions in this system.

We predict that for each time period, higher scores on the structural measure will vary directly with increases in nation status, and we expect this to hold across the three periods. Second, we argue that other factors will vary in their effects on nation status due to changes in the international trade regimes that govern trade. We use the presence of a government trade ministry or similar bureaucratic agency to capture the effects of such changes. Institutional arguments and the contingency of social capital arguments combine to suggest that in the 1965 period, when trade is subject to fewer international regime arrangements and where trade remains the province of a relatively few countries, the presence of a trade ministry marks either state intent, capacity, or "modern state" status in the world polity understanding. The 1970 period is a time when more countries are participating in world trade, most states of the world have become independent, and there are beginnings of global trade regimes. This is a transitional period, but we would expect ministry age to still contribute to nation status. By 1980, the global trade regimes are well established and patterns of trade incorporate a wider group of countries in routine ways.

DATA AND METHODS

Dependent Variable

Researchers have focused empirical attention on a number of general outcome variables such as nation status, national prosperity, well-being, and even human misery (Ragin and Bradshaw, 1992). As such, many dependent variables have been used as proxies for these varying outcomes. We use GNP/capita as a proxy for nation status. The concept and its measures are much debated. We use it to be consistent with much prior world-systems research, including network studies (Nemeth and Smith, 1985; Smith and White, 1992).

Control Variables

We control for political-geographic region, population size, modernization level, and education quality in efforts to take into account the key features of the modernization/comparative advantage arguments. Our first three control variables capture effects of internal nation characteristics that figure in standard modernization models of nation status. These are industrial development, domestic investment, and education. We utilized kilowatt consumption per capita as a proxy for the level of industrial development or modernization for a nation. We took the log of this variable to control for the large range and skew of data within our sample. Second, we used domestic capital rates to control for internal expenditures that nations invest for the improvement and vitalization of their infrastructure. The distribution of this variable was relatively normal and required no transformation. Third, the secondary education variable captures the extent to which nations have a labor force with advanced training and expertise. It is measured as a percentage of the population that had been enrolled in secondary education during any particular year. This variable was highly skewed and required a log transformation for the purposes of creating a more normalized distribution.

The remaining two control variables represent features of the nation in relation to international location and commitment to global trade, which provide alternative explanations for nation status. The first distinguishes among countries by region and historical relation to international state systems. We used six categories to control for linkage type effects (Meyer, Ramirez, and Soysal, 1992): 1 = Sub-Saharan Africa; 2 = European Periphery; 3 = Asian and Pacific Rim; 4 = North Africa and Middle East; 5 = Latin America; and 6 = European and Anglo-Saxon Core. We omit category 1 as the reference category. The second is the presence and age of state ministries of trade or their bureaucratic equivalent (commission, trade council, etc.). This captures the effect that the existence and endurance of a trade ministry provides a formalized institutional link to the core of global trade and promotes international mobilization around trade (Kim, 1996). Note that the central role played by governments in economic activity and, in particular, trade in countries around the globe (Evans, 1995) is an additional motivation to incorporate measures of presence and experience of state ministries in this arena. In effect, it is a crude measure of state attention and intent with regard to trade. It is simply a count of how many years a nation has had a trade ministry prior to the year of study. No transformation was needed for this variable, as it was relatively normally distributed.

Constructing the Structural Autonomy Measure

Studies of international trade have used yearly import/export trade flows for a wide range of commodities compiled by the United Nations Commodity Trade

Statistics (Delacroix, 1977; Nemeth and Smith, 1985; Smith and White, 1992; Steiber, 1979).[3] These data report relational dyadic exchange matrices for each commodity, for example, the amount of wheat (in U. S. dollars) traded between France and Japan, and so on. They are widely considered the most accurate and complete among international trade statistics. We utilize data from years 1965, 1970, and 1980.

Our sample comprises only countries with a population of one million people or more. This reduces potential concern that smaller nations are disadvantaged simply by population size from being equipped to participate in international trade. In addition, nations that failed to report commodity trade data for any of the three time periods were eliminated from consideration. The sample of nations available for analysis is sixty-three.

The next step was to choose a sample of specific commodities from the thousands available in the dataset. Previous research on world trade patterns (Chase-Dunn, 1989; Hirschman, 1945; Rau and Roncek, 1987; Rubinson and Holtzman, 1981) finds a global division of labor where core nations export more processed commodities, whereas periphery nations export raw materials. Thus, following the logic of Nemeth and Smith (1985), we chose commodities that represent different levels of processing, from raw materials to "finished products." We used two-digit SITC (Standard International Trade Classifications) categories to capture a broader array of commodities. SITC codes vary from five-digit (very specific) to one-digit (very general) classifications; using two-digit categories allows for a more heterogeneous examination, without the complete loss of commodity flow homogeneity in the one-digit codes. This reduces the concern that a nation's strength in a specific commodity (through using five-digit SITC codes as the unit of analysis) would be overgeneralized in an analysis of global trade, as the two-digit SITC codes encompass many specific types of commodities within them.

Smith and Nemeth (1988) performed a factor analysis of all the bilateral exchanges between nations to find five bundles of commodities that tend to move together in the global economy: High Technology and Heavy Manufacture, Sophisticated Extractive, Simple Extractive, Low Wage/Light Manufacture, and Food Products and By-Products. Three commodities that "consistently loaded most highly on each of the five factors" were selected from each grouping (Smith and White, 1992: 866). These are the fifteen commodities for our investigation (see Appendix 1 of this chapter for a listing of categories and commodities). They represent the major types of global commodity exchange. The dataset compiled the dollar value of trade between nation dyads for each category for each of the three time periods. This resulted in forty-five commodity trade tables of size 63×63, with missing diagonals (the diagonals represent the point at which a nation's position on the vertical and horizontal axes meet). These tables served as the raw network data we used in generating the structural autonomy means.

The computations involved in a structural autonomy network analysis rest on the measurement of network constraint and opportunity. The structural autonomy calculation is often, but not always, weighted by an oligopoly measure.[4] In the present analysis, the oligopoly measure has been set to 1 throughout the computations. This follows the logic that as the number of actors increases in a network, the concentration ratio becomes less important in the overall autonomy measures, as they have multiple network contacts with whom to engage in negotiations (Burt, 1992). In the present study, the use of two-digit SITC codes—broad categories of a wide array of commodities—helps ensure that there are many producers and consumers in all of the commodities under investigation. Additionally, the factor analysis described earlier provided commodities that are traded most heavily in the world system. These facts lead to the conclusion that concentration ratios are less useful in the present case. This would be a very different situation if five-digit SITC codes were being used as the units of investigation.

Forty-five network analyses were conducted to produce a mean of structural autonomy for each nation in each commodity category (during each of the three time periods). Following the previously stated logic that these commodities are broadly representative of the larger patterns of global trade, we aggregated the specific commodity level autonomy scores to an overall nation-level autonomy score for each of the three years. After this, we began the fourth step, which was to add theoretically relevant control variables into the regression equations.

Modeling Strategy

To assess the arguments and claims we put forward, we ran three robust regression analyses to test the effects of autonomy and our control variables on GNP/capita as the dependent variable. A robust regression is similar to a regular regression, except that it does a better job controlling for the effect of outliers by testing around the median, not the mean, of a sample. It is wise to use a robust regression when theoretical concerns validate that outliers may overestimate the significance of the overall equation. We then took a closer look at the distribution of the autonomy score within each of the three time periods. This allowed us to contrast the overall autonomy changes with an explicit focus on which portions of the autonomy distribution were changing over time.

RESULTS

Table 3.1 presents the results from robust regression analysis of the factors affecting nation status. Model 1 provides robust regression results for the period 1965, model 2 for 1970, and model 3 for 1980. In Model 1, autonomy is positive and significant—that is, a relatively advanced position in the flow of world trade increments the nation status measure. The variables that would support modernization arguments post few significant results, with the exception of the overall industrialization measure, which is positive and strongly significant. Secondary enrollment rates have no effect; neither do the rates of domestic capital invest-

Table 3.1

Regression Estimates of Structural Autonomy in Trade as a Determinate of Nation Status, 1965, 1970, 1980

Year	1965	1970	1980
Model	Model 1	Model 2	Model 3

Independent Variables:

Autonomy	1.345**	1.123*	1.518
	(-0.531)	(0.53)	(0.84)
Ministry Age	0.014**	0.011*	0.005
	(0.005)	(0.005)	(0.004)
Domestic Capital	0.004	0.038*	-0.017
Investment Rate	(0.011)	(0.012)	(0.011)
Secondary	0.042	0.137	0.128
Education	(0.123)	(0.128)	(0.161)
Kilowatt/capita	6.392**	5.608**	9.29**
	(1.3)	(1.414)	(1.244)
Euro. Periphery	0.256	0.25	0.228
	(0.271)	(0.305)	(0.342)
Asia & Pacific Rim	-0.133	-0.546*	-0.396
	(0.251)	(0.27)	(0.287)
North Africa	0.221	0.243	-0.051
	(0.234)	(0.253)	(0.297)
Latin America	0.237	0.04	-0.093
	(0.203)	(0.235)	(0.26)
Euro. Core	0.726*	0.786*	0.452
	(0.295)	(0.333)	(0.392)
Constant	-4.045**	-3.061	-6.62**
	(1.5)	(1.61)	(1.504)
Pseudo R-squared	0.91	0.9	0.88

*p<.05; **p<.01

Model 1–3 = Robust regression estimates for years 1965, 1970, and 1980, respectively ment. We find the expected results for region/linkage in this period: being a country in the developed European core/Anglo-American world increases nation status relative to countries in sub-Saharan Africa, the omitted category; countries in other regions do not differ significantly from the omitted group. The effect of trade ministry age is also positive and significant, supporting our expectations.

We turn to Model 2, for the 1970 period. The results of Model 2 repeat the general pattern for the 1965 period, but with two exceptions. The autonomy measure is positive and significant, overall industrialization is positive and significant, the European core is positive and significantly different from the omitted category, and trade ministry age is positive and significant. The 1970 results vary in that the domestic capital investment measure produces a positive and highly significant effect, countries in Asia begin to return negative and significant results, and the autonomy measure is less significant than in 1965.

Model 3, for 1980, presents some striking differences from the earlier periods. First, the autonomy measure is positive but no longer significant. In addition, the European core no longer differs significantly from the omitted regional group, and the ministry variable no longer has an effect. Finally, among the modernization measures, only the overall measure of industrialization continues positive and significant; neither rates of secondary enrollment nor rates of domestic capital investment have an effect. As more nations have engaged meaningfully in trade, and as the volume of trade has grown, system-based factors seem to have dissipated in their influence on nation status.

The results for each period provide evidence for the overall importance of the autonomy measure for the first time periods, but not the final one. There is also support for the importance of the overall industrialization measure, which is consistent with much previous research on the determinants of nation status and development. The pattern of results for the region variables also confirms that in the early period, being among the developed countries of the core is beneficial for nation status, but by the 1980 period, being part of the European core no longer distinguishes countries in terms of nation status. The early importance of the trade ministry variable and its subsequent lack of effect provide evidence that the shifting institutional context of trade affects the benefits that can be reaped and who can attain them in the global structure of trade.

A more in-depth examination of the distributions of the autonomy scores for each year further reveals important shifts in the context of global trade over this time period. Table 3.2 shows the frequency distribution statistics for the autonomy scores within each year. The 1965 and 1970 autonomy distributions were not statistically different from one another, but both the 1965 and the 1970 distributions were statistically different from the 1980 distribution. However, the mean autonomy score rose (1970: 0.439; 1980: 0.480), while the standard deviation declined (1970: 0.118; 1980: 0.092). This suggests a trend of higher autonomy scores arranged in a more tight distribution than in 1970. The finding is supported by the range of the autonomy scores in the time periods (1970: 0.525; 1980: 0.442), verifying a tightening of the distribution in addition to its overall higher mean.

Table 3.2
Distribution Statistics for the Autonomy Variables

	AUTO65	AUTO70	AUTO80
N	63	63	63
Mean	0.44	0.44	0.48
St. Dev.	0.12	0.12	0.09

	AUTO65	AUTO70	AUTO80
Max	0.696	0.706	0.689
95%	0.6	0.597	0.608
75%	0.527	0.517	0.545
Median	0.458	0.449	0.495
25%	0.352	0.342	0.406
5%	0.247	0.245	0.328
Min	0.186	0.181	0.247
Range	0.51	0.525	0.442
75%-25%	0.175	0.175	0.139

Most revealing are the cumulative percentage points across the autonomy distributions. These show where most of the change is taking place within the distribution. There was very little change in the top 5 percent of the distribution of autonomy scores between 1970 and 1980 (0.597 vs. 0.608), but there was a significant change in the bottom 5 percent of the distribution (1970: 0.245; 1980: 0.328). Importantly, this finding suggests that nations with very low autonomy scores in 1970 had increased autonomy scores in 1980, while those with higher autonomy scores remained essentially constant. We initially suspected that this shift was due to an increase in the number of network ties among the poorer nations of the world. Any increase in the number of ties would almost certainly raise the autonomy scores of nations with very few ties to begin with. If this was a general trend among poorer nations during the 1970s, then this rationale was likely to be a big part of the explanation. However, the difference in the mean number of ties from 1970 to 1980 (a ten-year time period) was about twice that of the difference between 1965 and 1970 (a five-year time period). So the rate of increase in network ties remained relatively constant across the time periods. This suggests that while the autonomy scores of core nations remained somewhat stable over time, peripheral nations experienced an improvement in terms of network position.

CONCLUSION

The regression results provide substantial support for our claims about the general relationship between structural autonomy and nation status. In addition, the pattern of results across the three time periods offers evidence for the decreasing effects of social capital benefits and the consistent importance of industrial capacity. In this empirical case, these changes reflect the growing volume of trade as nations more meaningfully participate in that global exchange.

In 1965, when international trade was dominated by the central, prosperous nations, autonomy and trade ministry existence are significant factors in nation status. In 1970, which emerges as a transitional period, autonomy and trade ministry remain significant, though not as strongly so. By 1980, neither has a significant effect on nation status. To make sense of this pattern, we apply Burt's arguments (1997) about the contingent value of social capital. Burt argues that as networks comprise more and more participants in dense network relations, social capital effects are contingent. The history of the time periods within this study encompasses just such shifts: more and more countries participate in global trade as standard state members; trade itself expands and more countries trade in more complex ways. By 1980, autonomy and trade ministry establishment do not return significant advantages to any group of countries. As more nations "do" international trade, the advantages from network position or formalized trade ministry dissipate.

This study generally validates arguments about the positive value of structural autonomy, but shows that this value is clearly contingent on: (1) positions within a social structure, and (2) the nature of that social structure itself. Actors within a social structure are differentially able to reap benefits based on their network position, and unique social structural conditions provide different types of benefits to distinct kinds of actors. This study of the structure of world trade shows how changing contexts within the global economy affect what the broader social structure has to offer and who benefits from those structural arrangements.

Our results suggest important trends for the structure of global trade in the new millennium. The shift in number of nations trading and the quantity of trade between 1965 and 1980 had grown even more substantially in the 1990s. Additionally, international trade has become increasingly systematized as global regimes routinize the ways in which trade is conducted. Our results imply that as these trends continue, the benefits of social capital are likely to further diminish. This project supports the continued use of novel methodological and social network theory to examine future trends in global trade. One such avenue for this would be to explicitly study how changes in composition and content of trade affect nation status outcomes. Our work aggregates various levels of trade into a larger trading category per nation. Future studies can disaggregate this data to examine how *what is traded* changes over time, and how these changes are experienced by different nations.

The evidence that benefits of structural position are dissipating also argues for conceptual attention to identify new sources of global advantage, in a world system marked by substantial political and cultural redefinition of opportunity and constraint. Trade itself may change in its value as an indicator of relevant world system position. Research attention to these issues—changes in the composition of trade, the social structures at the international level that organize and routinize trading, and the participants in global trade—all point to new contingencies that will reshape the value of social capital and its impact on nation status and prosperity. The political and policy consequences of such research are vivid in contemporary press accounts and policy discussion about issues as disparate as contested membership in the WTO, IMF funding criteria and debt-forgiveness schemes, emerging conventions that guide global capital flows, the integration of new economic enterprise zones, and the cultural redefinition of trade activity by international experts. These are some research opportunities that deepen our understanding of linkages between structure of trade, economic outcomes, and nation status in the emerging twenty-first century world-system.

NOTES

1. Portions of this chapter are excerpts and selections from an article forthcoming in *American Behavioral Scientist*. We gratefully acknowledge grants in support of our work from the Center for International and Comparative Studies, the Institute for Policy Research, the Department of Sociology, and the Department of Organizational Behavior, all at Northwestern University. We thank Cindy Aitken and Michelle Nattziger for editorial assistance.

2. A structural hole does not imply the complete absence of a relationship between two actors. Rather, a third party can serve as a broker between two moderately connected actors by forming a stronger tie with each actor than they have with one another.

3. We benefit from the generosity of David Smith and Douglas White, who have made available for us the dataset they analyzed in Smith and White (1992).

4. This is important in assessing the competitiveness of the network, as a network with a high oligopoly measure is one where a few players have a high amount of control within the network. This oligopoly measure is often described using a concentration ratio, which describes a nation's freedom in their network as measured by the extent to which they are central and not easily replaced by another contact. Specifically, this is operationalized as the extent to which a proportion of all network exchanges comes from a limited number of sources within the network. The fewer the sources and the higher the degree to which a resource is concentrated in these few sources, the higher the concentration measure.

APPENDIX 1: COMMODITY BUNDLES WITH SPECIFIC COMMODITIES

SITC Code	High Technology & Heavy Manufacture
46	Machinery-nonelectrical
35	Artificial resins, plastics, cellulose esters and ethers
45	Manufactures of metal, not elsewhere specified

SITC Code	**Sophisticated Extractive**
40	Paper, paperboard, and articles of paper pulp
16	Pulp and wastepaper
23	Gas, natural and manufactured
	Simple Extractive
13	Oil seeds and oleaginous fruit
25	Animal oils and fats
04	Cereals and cereal preparations
	Low Wage/Light Manufacture
52	Articles of apparel and clothing accessories
53	Footwear
51	Travel goods, handbags, and similar containers
	Food Products and By-products
01	Meat and meat preparations
02	Dairy products and bird's eggs
20	Crude animal and vegetable material, not elsewhere specified

APPENDIX 2: FULL DESCRIPTION OF STRUCTURAL AUTONOMY NETWORK ANALYSIS

Entrepreneurial opportunities are constrained to the extent that one of a nation's (i) contacts (q) has invested in a relationship with another of the nation's contacts (j). This can be expressed in the following manner:

$$P_{iq}P_{qj}$$

where P_{iq} represents the proportional strength of i's relationship with j (in terms of time and resources spent in the maintenance of the relationship), and P_{qj} represents the proportional strength of q's relationship with j. A high product of this equation represents a high degree of constraint that j's relationship with q places on i's relationship with q, making it harder for nation i to serve as a bridge between q and j. An aggregate of the product of the above equation across all of the contacts in the network (excluding nation i) shows the overall extent to which nation j constrains nation i in the network. Adding this to the direct connection i has with j produces a figure that defines the constraint that nation j places on nation i directly and indirectly:

$$P_{ij} + \sum P_{iq}P_{qj}$$

The sum of the above equation across all contacts j measures the aggregate constraint on nation i's entrepreneurial opportunities within the network:

$$C = \Sigma \, (P_{ij} + \Sigma \, P_{iq}P_{qj})$$

The second part of the structural autonomy computation involves the opportunities other nations have to exploit disconnections between nation i and its contacts within the network. This is because i must also spend time protecting itself from other nations that wish to serve as the bridge between i and its contacts. We begin the process of deriving the sum opportunity for other nations to exploit the relationship between nation i and its contacts by examining the extent to which another nation (j) is able to fill a structural hole between i and another of its contacts (q):

$$P_{ji}P_{iq}$$

where P_{ji} represents the proportional strength of j's relationship with i (in terms of time and resources spent in the maintenance of the relationship), and P_{iq} represents the proportional strength of q's relationship with j. When the product of this equation is high, nation i would have to spend more time and resources connecting with j and q in order to counteract the efforts j maintains to serve as a broker between them.

The next step is to measure the extent to which nation j can exploit the relationship between nation i and its contacts with other nations in the network. To do this, we aggregate the product of the above equation across all of i's contacts in the network (excluding nation i) and add in the direct connection that j has with i:

$$P_{ji} + \Sigma \, P_{jq}P_{qi}$$

The resulting sum is the total extent which j can exploit the disconnections between nation i and its contacts. The last step is to determine the extent to which all nations j can fill structural holes between i and its contacts. This is done by aggregating the above equation across all of the other nations in the network:

$$O = \Sigma \, (P_{ji} + \Sigma \, P_{jq}P_{qi})$$

Thus, O represents the total opportunity other nations have to exploit i's connections with other nations in the network.

Understanding the components of O and C, we can now turn to the overall structural autonomy calculation. The functional form of structural autonomy is:

$$A = \alpha(1 - O)^{Bo}C^{Bc},$$

where O is the sum of other nations' opportunities to fill structural holes between the focal nation and its contacts, and C is the sum of the focal nation's constraints. Estimates of Bo and Bc are negative fractions, which illustrates that structural holes are most effective at lower levels of constraint.

4

Predictions of Geopolitical Theory and the Modern World-System

Randall Collins and David V. Waller

In this brief overview, we will summarize the main points of geopolitical theory in relation to world-system theory. The aim is to see where there are problems within each model, disagreements between them, and finally where they might be integrated. The starting point of geopolitical theory is that the center of the state is its military apparatus. The geopolitical line of argument is that the behavior of states (and to a considerable extent their structure as well) is determined from the outside in; states act and react in relation to the military capacities of those around them. This rather forbidding view of the state is consonant with Max Weber's approach, and with a major theme of historical sociology of the past two decades. The history of states is the growth, transformation, and crises of their military apparatus, and of the organizational machinery constructed to support it.

Geopolitical theory thus meshes with what might be called the military-centered theory of state development. The latter has been formulated by a number of scholars, from which the leading statements are perhaps those of Charles Tilly (1990) and Michael Mann (1993). In brief, the modern story starts with the so-called military revolution that began around 1500, a series of large expansions in the size and expense of armed forces. The result was that rulers embarked on a program of revenue extraction to support the ever-increasing numbers of battlefield troops, the shift to centrally supplied gunpowder weapons, the parallel expansion of naval armaments, and the logistics costs associated with all of these. The effort to extract greater revenue for the state led to a chain of consequences: It fostered a bureaucratic organizational apparatus, increasingly penetrating society, tabulating information and inscribing the population as tax-paying citizens. This bureaucratic apparatus might subsequently be turned to other purposes, including public education, welfare, and control over the economy. State penetration into society also had the effect of mobilizing the population for political action: above all by creating a national arena or stage on which contests for power could be carried out; thus a (very much unintended) consequence of state penetration was to crystallize formerly localized and inchoate interests into class, ethnic, gender, and other kinds of mass mobilization. Yet another consequence of state revenue extraction and societal penetration was to evoke resistance; in the early modern period of Europe, under some local conditions the aristocracy—the rival form of the organization of military power, carried over from the period before the revolution in military expenses—was able to obtain concessions of shared power from the ruler that became institutionalized in parliamentary democracy. (Tilly, 1990, argues also that the varying local economic environments of military regimes made it easier or more difficult for some of them to extract revenue from trade or from agricultural production, thus shaping different state pathways.) To round out this list of consequences of rising military cost/revenue extraction, we may include revolutions. In the model made prominent by Skocpol (1979), it is conditions of extreme strain on the military apparatus, and especially on its resource extraction capability, that leads to the breakdown of state power from above, unleashing revolutionary movements from below.

Such, in brief compass, are the chains of consequences of the military revolution. Generally this analysis has taken the escalation of military size and expense as its starting point, and focused attention on what followed. The initiating process, the spread of the military revolution from one state or would-be ruler to another, was a geopolitical process: states leading the military revolution tended to defeat or even to swallow up those who lagged (although we can specify as well certain geopolitical niches or protected circumstances, and conversely especially vulnerable circumstances that allowed some states to deviate from the pathway of military emulation). Many important structural changes have flowed from geopolitical relationships. What, then, are geopolitical relationships themselves? In what sense is geopolitical theory a theory, such that it helps explain variations in what states do and have done to them? We may note, in setting out, that whereas the military revolution/revenue extraction theory of the state is a generalization about the modern European state, geopolitical theory is applicable throughout world history. That is, synthetic formulations such as Collins (1978, 1986) and various predecessors (e.g., Boulding, 1962; Stinchcombe, 1968; as well as classical antecedents) have attempted to fit generalizations to wide swaths of human history, including the earliest ancient states. (Collins, 1986, presented evidence to support the point that changes in military technology and in transportation, enormous though they have been, have not altered the analytical principles of geopolitics, but have only introduced some quantitative extensions of them.) In this respect geopolitical theory resembles world-system theories in recent incarnations (e.g., Chase-Dunn and Hall, 1997;

Frank, 1998). A synthetic formulation of geopolitical theory also sets our approach apart from the organicism of the German geopolitik tradition that runs through the works of Friedrich Ratzel, Rudolph Kjellen, and Karl Haushofer as well as the American realist tradition running from Mahan, Mackinder, and Spykman through the contemporary grand strategists such as Zbigniew Brzezinski, Edward Luttwak, and Colin Gray for whom geopolitics is an extension of statecraft.

Geopolitical theory, in our understanding, is primarily a theory of the dynamics of state control over territories. It gives a small set of principles that, operating in conjunction, predict the extent to which the borders of states will be stable, expanding, or contracting (or to put it more precisely, the shape of the territories over which military control of varying degree is exercised from a given center). From these too may be derived several corollary principles regarding the consequences within states as the main principles are played out in time. Such corollaries concern the character of conflict among states, the consequences of showdown wars for the reordering of geopositional vantage points, social movement mobilization in opposition to the state (see Collins, 1995; Waller, 1992) and the shifting boundaries of ethnic groups in relationship to the power-prestige of the state (see Collins and Waller, 1994). The main geopolitical dynamics may be summarized in five principles:

(1) Territorial resource advantage. States with greater resources on their territory in economic productivity and in population size tend to expand territorially at the expense of states with fewer such resources.

(2) Geopositional advantage. States that have military rivals on fewer borders expand territorially more those that are circumscribed by enemies in more directions. Historical scholars such as McNeill (1963) have noted this as a marchland advantage: states on the edges of "civilized" (i.e., populated, economically developed) areas tend to expand at the expense of those in the center.

(3) Balance of power and fragmentation of the middle. Closely packed, multiple states in a geographical area tend to produce a stagnant situation, to balance each other off and prevent any from expanding. This is particularly so if the states are approximately equal in resources; but, even when they are not, balance of power theory (one of the earliest segments of geopolitical theory to be formulated, Morganthau, 1948) holds that the strongest state will provoke a coalition of the rest to oppose further expansion in its power. This also implies that a balance of power situation (multiple states with multiple common borders) is a shifting network of alliances. Synthetic geopolitical theory has extended the argument by combining balance of power logic with the geopositional principle in #2 (in a sense #3 is an analytical corollary of #2): in a balance of power situation, not only is a marchland state the only kind that can expand, but the other states, especially those in the middle of a contested zone, tend to fragment over time into smaller units. This fragmentation of the middle (a prime example of which is the fragmentation of the German Empire in the late Middle Ages) comes about by the interference of consolidating marchland states from the

edges, and by the shifting pattern of unstable conquest and alliance in the central zone.

All of these processes so far considered take considerable amounts of historical time; they operate at the level of state time or geopolitical time, which is considerably more slow-moving than the episodes of human lifetimes. From historical atlases on which Collins based his formulation of geopolitical theory, he estimated that about thirty to fifty years is a minimal unit of geopolitical time, in the sense that states act to take advantage (or suffer the consequences) of their geopolitical position, not immediately, but within this time frame. The slice of history, thirty to fifty years, may be regarded as the window of indeterminacy within geopolitical theory, the resolution of the microscope below which patterns cannot be seen. At the upper limit, something on the order of 500 years seems to be the period within which full concatenations of geopolitical processes work themselves out. Since the interaction of geopolitical principles is, by definition, a multicausal process, we do not expect a simple repetition of historical phases; but there are major inflection points or turning points that operate at the scale of several centuries. Below we will compare this to the double Kondratieff waves that have come to figure so largely in recent macrohistorical world-system theory.

(4) The first three principles are cumulative and interacting. Principle #1, resource advantage, seems banal: other things being equal, big states beat little states in wars. But it is a deadly banality and one that figures largely in the synthetic model that emerges when the analytical principles are allowed to operate throughout time. Over time, big rich states grow still bigger and resource-richer by absorbing smaller and weaker states. At the same time (a process analytically distinct but sometimes empirically overlapping) marchland states expand at the expense of the fragmenting middle. The analytically separate geopolitical principles are cumulative over time; through a series of feedbacks, big states swallow up smaller states (or incorporate them into their sphere of influence, drawing on their resources and military manpower); and marchland states expand from the edges into the center of a militarily accessible region. Principle 1, if taken exclusively, would lead to the extrapolation of one huge empire eventually swallowing up all the rest (Boulding, 1962, suggested this extrapolation). In the multicausal situation, however, this need not come about, since there are marchland states expanding from opposite sides at once. The long-term result of these feedbacks is to simplify the geopolitical arena down to two huge states or power blocs, expanding toward a common frontier. Thus we may say that the long-run tendency of a geopolitical arena is periodic simplification and showdown war between rival great powers.

A corollary of principle 4 is that the ferociousness and destructiveness of wars increase to their heights at the time of showdown wars. Conversely, in balance of power situations, war is carried out in a "gentlemanly" fashion, restrained by rules and codes of honor; this is fostered structurally by the circumstance that significant victories are unlikely, and that rapidly shifting alliances

will move professional soldiers into their enemies' camps. Geopolitical "show-down wars" are the "world wars" of common parlance and are equivalent to wars of hegemonic transitions in world-system parlance. A second corollary of principle 4 is that a showdown war is a turning point, leading to diverging outcomes. One of the contenders may be victorious, thereby creating a "world" empire. This has happened many times in the history of China, following periods of multistate fragmentation, and eventual simplification. Another possibility is that the two great contenders mutually exhaust each other's military capabilities. In this case, the long-term process turns toward renewed fragmentation, with geopositional advantage passing to newer and more distant marchlands. This is what happened in the case of the Roman empire vis-à-vis the Persian empire; their fruitless confrontations of the eastern Mediterranean eventually created a power vacuum into which swept the Islamic movement from the marchland of Arabia. Similarly, Collins (1986) suggested that if the United States and the USSR were to proceed to nuclear war, it would not be unprecedented but a typical showdown war, mutually destroying the rival marchland-based empires and opening the way to a new round of multiple states and eventually new great powers expanding from elsewhere on the globe.

(5) Logistical strain or overextension leads to episodes of rapid territorial loss. Consider one of the branches of the cumulative process in principle 4: if a unified world empire is produced by a victorious state subordinating or absorb-ing all the others, what could keep it from lasting forever? This situation was often repeated in the history of China, during the long period when it was effectively isolated from large-scale military threats from other parts of the globe; completely dominant unifying empires were repeatedly established, ruling "the middle kingdom" at what was regarded as the center of the civilized world, taking homage from peoples on its peripheries. Under what geopolitical prin-ciples could such a hegemonic state decline? Principle 5, logistical extension, fits every case of Chinese dynastic decline and also has a much wider applica-bility. The greater the distance military power is projected from its home re-source base, the greater the proportion of resources that are used up in logistics, the costs of transporting and supplying troops at a distance. At some point, as Stinchcombe (1968) noted with mathematical precision, the proportion of re-sources actually used for fighting rather than for supplying the logistical orga-nization diminishes to the vanishing point. Thus there is an economic limit, under any existing system of production and technologies of distribution, for how far military power can be projected geographically. What makes this prin-ciple generalizable is the fact that opposing forces have resource bases some-where else, on the other side of the frontier or battle line; the side that is closest to its resource base can use a higher proportion of its resources for fighting rather than for logistics costs. A previous publication (Collins, 1986) indicated how to calculate a gradient of vulnerability of any particular territory to military forces impinging on it from varying distances; the resource advantage or dis-advantage of one army vis-à-vis another (principle 1) is weighted by its degree

of logistical cost. High levels of logistical cost (multiplied by resource level), relative to the logistical cost (times resource level) of opponents, constitute over-extension. Thus even the biggest, wealthiest states can be brought down geo-politically, by what Kennedy (1987) has called "imperial overstretch." Collins (1978) argued, additionally, that the degree of resistance to control as military forces move farther from home is caused not only by logistical costs, but by cultural resistance, as the distance or degree of familiarity among ethnic groups becomes more extreme; this colors the terms in which the experience of being "too far from home," "on alien ground" is experienced by imperialists and re-sisters alike.

Here too are several corollaries. First: logistical overextension typically leads to sudden reversals in the fortunes of a state. Empires come apart much more rapidly than they are put together; the growth period may take centuries, the disintegration a decade or less. The giant does sometimes stumble, and David defeats Goliath. This happens, not as the typical outcome, which is quite the opposite (as principle 1 indicates), but in the special circumstances when logis-tical costs have reduced and even reversed the effective resource advantage of troops on the spot. And since a state in a condition of logistical overextension is experiencing problems raising enough resources to support its military ma-chine, the result is usually a crisis in domestic politics as well. Logistical over-extension is one of the most common background causes of the state breakdown that ushers in revolution (best formulated in extension by Goldstone, 1991; and Skocpol, 1979; see Collins, 1995, for a synthetic model); the intervening pro-cesses include loss of the state's power prestige and of the legitimacy of its rulers, fiscal crisis, and splits among elites over whose privileges are to be sacrificed in order to overcome the revenue shortfall. Depending on the severity of overextension and the overall state resource strain, the military reversals fol-lowing from logistical overextension lead, at the least, to loss of territories and spheres of influence, and at the extreme to state disintegration and regime over-throw.

A second question arises here: If overextension is so fatal to a state, why would any ruler risk it? A glib answer would be the arrogance of power, the blindness that results from orchestrated adulation of persons at the top of large hierarchies. Sociologically, the dynamics of legitimacy in domestic politics are strongly influenced by the power and prestige that come from military activities; military action against foreign foes typically generates national solidarity while it is going on, and especially if it is victorious. Rulers of states that are still on the favorable side of the contest of resources and of geopositional advantages vis-à-vis their neighbors become spoiled with a steady diet of legitimacy-enhancing victories. In a more constricted orbit of action, field commanders also feel the emotional dynamic of successful advance as more appealing than stable borders. Together, these social-emotional processes tend to make commanders at almost all levels overly optimistic about their prospects for success on distant frontiers. It seems difficult for states to disengage themselves from a trajectory leading to overextension, even if they are consciously aware of the danger.

We will wind up this brief exposition of geopolitical theory by noting two ways that strong states can be destroyed, which is to say how states that have grown through previously favorable geopolitical circumstances enter into a period in which their geopolitical favors are reversed. One path is that the state can expand, taking advantage of local resource matchups and geopositional advantages, until its borders come up against a state that is equally strong; typically this is the situation of two rival marchlands accumulating resources and chewing up the smaller states in the middle (like the Roman empire expanding east to encounter the Persian empire moving west; or the United States and USSR meeting in central Europe in 1945). This confrontation then may result in stalemate and resource exhaustion, either through violent (and often inconclusive) conflict (the Roman/Persian case) or through the "Cold War" problems of a prolonged arms race (which ultimately was behind the collapse of the Soviet empire: Collins, 1995). The other path is for a state on the upward slope of the resource curve to expand against weak opponents, until it reaches the point of logistical overstretch. Then it seems to fall into problems vernacularly characterized as "old age," "corruption," and the like, but that are specifically connected to the ramifications of logistical strain. Geopolitics is not a moralizing science, but if we wished to point out a moral, it would be: there are limits to military greatness, and surpassing them humbles even the greatest of states.

WORLD-SYSTEM THEORY AND GEOPOLITICAL THEORY

The analytical core of contemporary world-system theory, we suggest, is the pattern of economic long cycles, their correlation with military hegemonies, and with systemic wars at cyclical crisis points. If the long cycles are double Kondratieff waves, the dethroning of a hegemon and replacement by another happens in the down phase of the second K-wave and upturn to the next round. In world-system theory, this is interpreted as an economically driven process; the causal dynamics come from the expansion and contraction/stagnation of world production and distribution. Implicitly, world-system theory does incorporate some geopolitical principles. First, it seems to imply principle 1, cumulative resource advantage: the resource-rich state at the core becomes geopolitically dominant over peripheries, thereby extracting more resources that make it progressively richer and more capable of geopolitical dominance. The upsurge of warfare within the core that occurs during the cyclical down phase can be explained as a squeeze on economic resources at just the time when the military machinery needs increased revenue to keep up with increased tension; that is, the escalation of jealousies as core states try to divide a shrinking pie; and also (the overextension principle 5 may be implied here) the previous hegemon appears visibly weakened in its military resources, motivating new contenders.

Second, various formulations of world-system theory (e.g., Arrighi, 1994; Wallerstein, 1974b, 1980, 1989) introduce in a somewhat ad hoc way the notion of geopositional advantage: for example, that the locations of Portugal and England on the edges of Europe favored their expansion as overseas empires, at just the time when the continent was a cockpit of resource-richer but mutually stalemating land powers. From the point of view of geopolitical theory, what world-system theory interprets as economically driven cyclical decline of hegemons could be the result of geopolitical strains: overextension via logistical strain (principle 5), or mutual destruction of resource-rich states in showdown wars (principle 4) leads to relatively sudden collapse, thereby creating a power vacuum, an opening to new would-be hegemons. The alternative explanations here need closer examination in specific historical cases. Here we will make only two suggestions.

First, world-system historians may overstate the generality of the model that there is always, at the appropriate cyclical peak, a hegemon in the full sense of the term (i.e., both as center of economic networks, and also clear-cut military dominant). The international relations theory of hegemonic stability (Gilpin, 1987), although it lacks the economic model of the capitalist world-system, similarly shares this analytical preference for the existence of a hegemon. But geopolitical theory suggests that simplification down to two major contending powers is rare enough, let alone further simplification down to a single overarching state power. Geopolitical theory suggests that for large portions of history, there are a plurality of states, most of which are blocked in a balance-of-power situation, while there exist only incipient dominant powers moving up through the cumulative feedbacks of resource growth and marchland advantage. World-system theory concedes this in a sense, since the very notion of a world-system is distinct from a situation of world-empire that is antithetical to the space for capitalists to maneuver in the first place. Hence a world-system hegemon may be no more than "first among equals," although there seems to be a tendency of world-system theorists, especially in schematically laying out the political correlates on long cycles, to exaggerate the extent of hegemonic domination in a given period. (This tendency is most explicit in the world leadership version of long cycle theory represented by Modelski and Thompson, 1988, 1996). Thus we are doubtful that the Netherlands was ever a military hegemon at the time when it was the economic core of the world-system; it might be more accurate to describe the mid-seventeenth century as a balance of power situation in which the biggest military powers, Spain and France, blocked and exhausted each other, allowing specialized niches for military expansion by smaller powers, provided they did it offshore.

Second, we need to rethink the place that geopolitical processes have in bringing about cyclical decline. Is it possible that without the geopolitical process of overextension (principle 5), or the culminating long-run military feedbacks into showdown wars (principle 4), that cyclical crises and hegemonic declines would not occur? Or more mildly, that without these geopolitical processes, the economically driven processes of cyclical decline would happen more slowly? These questions imply that if states could learn to restrain their military activities (perhaps by explicitly attempting to avoid provoking the negative consequences of geopolitical principles 4 and 5), the world-system cycle would either come to an end or be retarded. This is worth thinking about for scenarios of the twenty-first century and beyond.

A more apparent lacuna in world-system theory is in explaining who will be the challenger to the hegemon; or, to say it a different way, since we have just suggested that the concept of "hegemon" may be too idealized, the question really is, who will move up and down geopolitically within the core? World-system theory is a structuralist or system theory; it posits a set of positions in economic/political relationships. As such, world-system theory does not give analytical emphasis to who is in the core at any given time, but to the structural point that there is always an economic core, and that there is only limited room in it; hence there is a structure of inequality in the system as a whole, although there is also a process of upward and downward mobility in this game of musical chairs. Thus within the framework of world-system theory, there is room for an application of full-scale geopolitical principles, to specify who moves up or down geopolitically.

In effect, we are suggesting that the notion of world-system hegemon be deconstructed. Let us make the primary criterion of core position economic centrality in the structure of world economic relations; and let us see the degree of military dominance ("hegemony") as multiply determined, deriving in part from world-system economic position (via the inflow through principle 1, economic resource advantage), in conjunction with the rest of geopolitical principles (2–5). A step toward this analytical deconstruction of the hegemon has been taken by Arrighi (1994), when he suggests that the world-system financial core may externalize its protection costs to a geopolitical power, by alliance, or other out-franchising arrangements ranging from hiring mercenaries to writing off loans to military overspenders (as Arrighi suggests Genoa did in relation to Spain). Thus the economic core can reduce some of its own liabilities, letting the military franchisee take on the danger of imperial overstretch; the military "hegemon" can thus decline through geopolitical processes (including its own fiscal crisis of military revenues) while the economic center remains protected, at least for a time. In other words, the "hegemony" of the military franchisee is a kind of fiction that in the long run favors the relative position of the franchisee's core rivals.

CONTRIBUTIONS OF WORLD-SYSTEM THEORY TO GEOPOLITICAL THEORY

Geopolitical theory is an ongoing enterprise and would benefit from incorporating parts of world-system theory. The concept of resource advantage (in principle 1) has been presented baldly. One elaboration points to the efficiency of resource extraction. Thus Hobson (1997) shows, in the case of antecedents to World War I, that not only the overall level of economic resources within state boundaries contributes to military power, but also the efficiency of the state apparatus in extracting these resources; in a development of Mann's point (1993), Hobson argues that parliamentary democratization makes a state stronger because it co-opts private economic resource holders into taking responsibility for the fiscal soundness of the state that they control. Geopolitical theory also needs a better model of what determines the level of economic resources in the first place. World-system theory fills an important part of this gap by deriving economic resources from world-system position. In earlier periods of the world-system, economic resources came primarily from the core's position on the market for exchanged goods and services and through economic efficiencies generated by the core's direct or indirect administrative control over resource extraction and commodity production.

Analytical work is going on within the world-system school over just how these mechanisms operate in time, over the course of the economic cycle. Arrighi (1994) argues that the superior financial liquidity of the core enables it to bide its time for advantageous investments, as well as to ride out crises and accumulate the assets of those who are forced to sell in a pinch. Arrighi provides a mechanism: A phase expansion generates core profits by lowering costs on volume of trade, while B phase brings declining returns because of increased competition, which in turn motivates holders of capital to move from investment in production to financial speculation. Such a model suggests, for geopolitical theory, that the availability of economic resources that can be turned to support the military state will vary with phase of world-system cycle; it is worth investigating whether the increased liquidity of the B phase (greater holdings in purely financial assets) might not lead to the greater propensity to military buildups at this time. One might analytically overlay world-system economic cycles on the geopolitical model of long-term cumulating advantages and disadvantages of interacting states, periodic simplifications and showdowns, and the dynamic of logistical overextension. (This may be easier to do conceptually than empirically, as there is a data analysis problem of how to decide what is evidence for which theory.) In such a synthetic geopolitical/world-system theory, both theoretical branches give mutually reinforcing processes by which core states promote expansion into the periphery. In both branches, cumulatively self-enforcing feedback processes are at work: increased resource extraction occurs by imperial conquest, as well as by market advantages in world-system flows. Over the course of the expansionary cycle, these resource advantages for the geopolitical position of leading core states accelerate.

But this is only a partial picture of the overall geopolitical situation; the particular geopolitical position of rival states within the core are also determined by the full range of geopolitical principles. Thus during the time when England was both economically and geopolitically dominant in the world-system, it was unable to exercise hegemonic influence on the Continent, and indeed played the diplomatic game of traditional balance of power alliances in that arena—in fact, it is precisely England's continental strategy that gives the classic instance of balance of power. Geopolitical principles, in fact, are geographically and temporally very specific in their application; a state is not geopolitically powerful as a diffuse quantity, but has a particular geopolitical level of advantage or disadvantage for every particular spot on the globe where military power might be projected; and the advantages or disadvantages shift over time following the interplay of geopolitical principles for multiple states.

Consider now the possibilities of downturn for dominant states in the world-system. There are two broad possibilities: (1) geopolitical rivalry itself can produce a reversal in both military dominance and economic transfer advantages. Because of showdown wars or logistical overstretch, a major world power may decline on its own geopolitical momentum. A related possibility worth considering is that such a geopolitical decline may further affect the ability of such a world-system "hegemon" to dominate world market relations; thus a geopolitically driven decline might trigger what appears to be a world economic decline. (2) Or the line of causality might run the other way. The B phase of the world economic cycle leads to a downturn in resource extraction, which in turn weakens the resource base of the military. There are, of course, other geopolitical principles besides #1; but there may be cases in which the sheer quantitative loadings on one particular geopolitical process are so much more extreme than on other geopolitical processes that they drive events. (For instance, if the difference in resource advantages between states [principle 1] is quite extreme, whereas the other geopolitical advantages and disadvantages are more evenly matched, principle 1 will make most of the difference; similarly if the level of resource advantages of states [principle 1] is shifting very rapidly, while the other geopolitical factors are changing slowly, principle 1 will appear to be driving all the action. In this way concentrating on a particular historical case can obscure the range of analytical principles involved.)

There is a lot to be investigated here. A small number of analytical principles can generate quite a range of empirical situations, depending on quantitative levels of each and the combination of processes. Elsewhere, Collins, Hanneman, and Mordt (1995) showed by computer simulation that differences in quantity, within an analytical model of feedbacks among multiple processes, can produce a wide variety of historical patterns. The combination of geopolitical and world-system schematic principles can move both of them toward closer meshing with the branching pathways and sudden reversals of actual history.

SOME APPLICATIONS TO THE TWENTY-FIRST CENTURY FUTURE

The elegant schematics of world-system theory lend themselves to extrapolation in a general way: one can anticipate the inflection points of the cycles and foresee a shift in world hegemony. Wagar (1989) provides a version that is both plausible and imaginative. World-system theory mainly concerns a set of structural limitations within which economic and political-military actors maneuver for advantage, subject to long-run shifts that for a while amplify advantages and eventually turn into disadvantages; but exactly who figures in the shifts and how transitions come about calls for further considerations. Wagar describes a scenario in which the United States falls out of the core, due to the buildup of immigration from the Third World, and fights a nuclear war against the UN, which has become the military enforcement arm of the transnational corporations. This has a certain amount of geopolitical plausibility, but more explicit considerations of geopolitical theory lead us to put it another way.

The Cold War of the latter half of the twentieth century between the United States and the USSR was the kind of long-term simplification that comes from the cumulative working out of geopolitical processes. The threatened nuclear war was a showdown war. Logistics costs are determinative in an arms race as well as in hot combat, and surrogate confrontations drain resources in much the same way that war between Great Powers do, although more slowly. The USSR collapsed, not because of the intrinsic economic inferiority of socialism to capitalism (or at least not principally for this reason), but because of its combination of geopolitical disadvantages. As Collins (1986) noted in anticipation of a future collapse of the "Russian empire," the expansion of Russia over the centuries had moved it into an arena in which all geopolitical principles had turned to negative values during the twentieth century. The USSR came apart under military resource strains from its overextended, outproduced, and multi-fronted military position (see Collins and Waller, 1994, Waller, 1992). In classic fashion, these led to a domestic struggle to increase military resource extraction, splits within the elite over who would have to sacrifice in order to set things right, opening the way for popular discontents to become mobilized (see Waller, forthcoming).

Since we want to look ahead at the post-collapse period, let us first concentrate on the position of the United States. The collapse of the USSR clearly leaves the United States without a militarily comparable rival, but it does not make the United States a "hegemon" in the strong sense of the term. The USSR first reached the breaking point in its resource strain over the arms race and Cold War maneuvering generally, but the United States paid a considerable cost: the budget crisis that dominated domestic politics in the 1990s was due largely to the huge military buildups of the Reagan administration. One might say that these expenditures paid off by bankrupting the Soviets, but the United States has similarly been at least partially hamstrung by its debts and the resulting move to reduce military expenditure. The United States also faces, not just the temptation to act as the Great Power that can project force anywhere on the globe, but also the real limits of logistical overstretch fostered by this temptation. As the example of successive Chinese empires demonstrates, a state without rivals in absolute resources nevertheless can collapse militarily and in revenue crisis if it follows the apparent lines of geographical least resistance far enough.

Similarly, the Gulf War between the United States and Iraq may be a harbinger of future dilemmas for the United States that follow from the collapse of the USSR. With the USSR on the decline, the position of middle states changes. In geopolitical terms, the territorial conquest of Kuwait by Iraq was one of the first geopolitical shifts among middle states outside of Europe resulting from a weakened Soviet Union. Rapidly, because of the absence of Soviet power in the region, logistical advantages go to stronger states in marchland regions and the logistical costs increase for big states that must project even more force into distant regions against emerging regional rivals. In this context, the war possibly could have produced more fiscal strain and internal political turmoil at home if the United States had to go it alone. But the real coalition of the Gulf War was the financial coalition lead by Germany, Kuwait, and Saudia Arabia, who together paid a majority share of the cost of the war. The further we get from the turning point of the Cold War, the more difficult it becomes for the United States to project power, especially as an occupying force, at great distances from the North American homeland and into the territories of former middle states.

The decline of the United States's former rival and the favorable logistical loads for local powers only account for part of the new geopolitical climate. The third factor results from the costs of the showdown war for the United States. The United States military is at approximately 80 percent of Cold War era spending levels and has reduced forward troop deployment, especially in Europe, begun closing bases abroad and at home, and downsized personnel and hardware. At the same time, the tasks of the U. S. military are expanding; they may also be changing fundamentally because the United States must put together coalitions to share the financial burden of projecting power abroad.

We now turn to the position of states formerly in the middle between the United States and the USSR. On the one hand, the number of such states is greater due to the collapse of the USSR's formal empire and the fracture of some of the middle states. The first series of new geopolitical actors arrived on the scene as the Soviets withdrew from Eastern Europe. The second series of new geopolitical actors formed as the USSR became the Russian Federation, roughly occupying its pre-World War I territory. A third series formed out of the fracturing of some of the middle states such as Yugoslavia or Czechoslovakia. Few of these states are likely to become significant regional contenders anytime soon, though they may well become the battleground of conflicts among more significant regional and global contenders. What is most interesting about these states is how there appear to be unique geopolitical trends specific to their geoposition. Nearly every northern European country is seeking to become aligned to one degree or another with the European Union (EU). The new countries in central Asia, when not in conflicts with one another, are ethnically and culturally more connected to the regional powers to their south—Iran and Turkey—than to the Russians. The third group, states in and to a lesser extent around the former Yugoslavia, continue as an ethnic checkerboard; and they are now reproducing the centuries-old conflicts among rival contenders for control of state power. There is some evidence of fracture elsewhere too; the uprisings among indigenous peasants in the southern state of Chiapas, Mexico, coincided with Mexico's tumultuous transition to a market economy; the ethnic rivalries in many African states threaten the stability of several state's boundaries in that region as well.

On the other hand, among other middle states there are trends running in the opposite direction of consolidation; the most spectacular instance of consolidation among middle states and rapidly escalating geopolitical advantages is ongoing in Europe with the formation of the EU. Though on a different scale, the transfer of control of Hong Kong from England to China is interesting geopolitically because it is timed with the rise of China as a capable regional actor and a potential counterweight to Japan's regional economic domination. The territorial expansion of China is a marked contrast to Japan's informal financial and production empire elsewhere in Southeast Asia.

Another potential basis of consolidation among middle states is religion, especially Pan-Islam. The spread of Islam against the backdrop of the global geopolitical rivalries among Western countries has at times created conditions favorable to the development and spread of Pan-Islamic ideologies; under just the right conditions ideological movements can serve the geopolitical interests of rising states. The spread of Islamic religion has been ongoing for many centuries out of the Middle East and into Africa, Europe, Central Asia, India, and Southeast Asia. But this expansion is not uniform; it has an historical and geopolitical character to it. As religious organizations spread from state to state, the religious organizations that become established within a particular state's boundary are uniquely linked to that state, establishing fealty bonds with it. Such bonds are significant in the case of supranational religious movements because they create organizational fissures or administrative boundaries that define potentially rival groups; these in turn may become flash points for conflict among such groups. Pan-Islamic ideologies, or Pan-Christian ones for that matter, are ideologies of the religious elite; and because the theocratic class expresses specific loyalties to the state, the success of Pan-Islamic ideologies as a basis of international political consolidation is limited by the power-prestige of the state. Moreover, such ideologies are likely to be recognized as threats among rival national theological centers. At best, religion can function as a rallying point for members of coalitions united against an opponent. Thus, when powerful opponents fall, it is not the ideology that fills the vacuum left behind; rather it is the state or states strong enough to expand into new territory directly or indirectly.

The next geopolitical challenger to the U. S. position will come from either the East-Asian region or the European Union. Let us examine each of these in turn. In the 1980s the leading candidate for hegemonic successor was Japan. In the 1970s and early 1980s the escalation of the Cold War lead many observers to conclude that the United States and the USSR were exhausting themselves of their resources, thus enabling Japan to move ahead. The plausibility of such a scenario came to an abrupt end as state breakdown and revolution spread among states within the Soviet sphere of influence in 1989–1991. Of particular significance to perceptions of Japan's immediate and long-term fortunes are what did not happen during this wave of political turmoil in Japan's chief regional rival, China. That China did not collapse, that the Chinese Communist Party (CCP) did not surrender power in the aftermath of the spring uprising and Tiananmen Square, surprised many observers. Today, one is more likely to hear about China's rise to "Great Power" status than one is to hear "Japan as number one." Indeed to many observers China looms as the long-term threat to U. S. hegemony. What is the relationship between the collapse of the USSR and the stability of China? The declining geopolitical fortune of the Soviet Union created a more favorable set of geopolitical conditions for China. How ironic it must have been to the leaders of the former Soviet Union to have negotiated a mutual demilitarization of the Sino-Soviet border only to watch China's star rise while the sun set on their own.

It is precisely on this point that the Soviet Union and China took different paths. Leaving aside the question of how well one extrapolates the trend in economic resources, we may examine the situation of China and Japan over the next fifty years in narrowly geopolitical terms. In our estimation, both China and Japan are local geopolitical powers. Both have the advantage of a relative power vacuum in one significant direction: the greatly weakened Russian Federation, which may well undergo still more fragmentation; if so, there would be opportunities for both China and Japan (possibly also Korea) to make alliances and patronage arrangements with ex-Russian fragments. The trouble with the popular extrapolations of future Great Powers is that in effect they attend only to principle 1, relative economic size. But states expand contiguously, and China and Japan as Great Powers immediately come up against each other. Unless they carefully engineered separate spheres of interest, they would check one another; and even the successful manipulation of spheres of interest leads eventually to a point where two strong (pseudo-) empires meet at a contested border.

In this East Asian arena, let us also suggest one fairly immediate development. The reunification of North and South Korea would increase the chance of military tensions with the other local great powers. As the situation has stood for the past sixty years, the divided Korean peninsula has been a buffer zone, a fragmented middle where client states of the big power blocs engaged in surrogate confrontation, a limited war substitute for showdown war. The collapse of the USSR has changed all that. Reunification (impelled perhaps by the economic plight of the North) would make Korea into quite a respectable military power—in part, because of the relatively high level of military mobilization of existing resources. The missiles and nuclear weapons of the North combined with the economic production, population, and troop size of the South would likely give politicians in a reunified Korea a boost in their claims for international power/prestige. This is far from saying that Korea should be our candidate for new hegemon, even in the East Asian arena; but rather that that regional geopolitics would be at least a three-sided situation, among states of varying geopolitical advantages and disadvantages. On the whole, we are inclined to think that these will balance one another out and that East Asia will see something like classic balance of power politics.

The chief geopolitical challenger to the United States on the horizon is the European Union. It is not clear, of course, that the EU will actually turn into a real state, with a European army actively playing the part of a Great Power. Or rather, given the estimate of geopolitical time as moving in approximately fifty-year units, it may be some decades before the EU takes advantage of its geopolitical opportunities. These include the power vacuum that exists on its eastern and southeastern borders; one can foresee a combination of peace-keeping interventions, extension of alliances, and expansion of the federation that would move the EU along the path of expanding states in previous history. When and if this happens, one might expect a growth of tensions, possibly even conflict, between the EU—the rising geopolitical power, full of resources and without accumulated disadvantages of having financed the dominant role in the past—and the United States, the declining geopolitical power suffering from the costs of accumulated overstretch and other sunk costs limiting its sphere of action. Against this possibility of future confrontation, there are arguments that cultural ties make such a war unthinkable or that democracies do not fight one another; neither of these objections fits well with the historical record. Ideology follows geopolitics more than vice versa.

II

REDEFINING WORLD CULTURE

5

Why Must There Be a Last Cycle? The Prognosis for the World Capitalist System and a Prescription for Its Diagnosis

Daniel Chirot

CRISIS AND SOCIAL THEORY IN THE TWENTIETH CENTURY

The major social, political, and economic issue of the twentieth century has been this: How well did various societies adapt to the immense, rapid set of changes forced on the entire globe by the industrial revolution that began in Europe in the late eighteenth century? These changes have now encompassed every corner of the globe, but now, as one hundred years ago, the most important question to ask about any society for the future is the same: How well will it continue to modernize and cope with all of the upheavals associated with modernization?[1]

The term "modernization" has been in disrepute for twenty-five years because of the attack in the early 1970s against liberal "modernization theory" (Wallerstein, 1974a). Whatever the merits or demerits of this theory, and whatever partisan use may have been made of it to support American foreign policy during the third quarter of the century (Rostow, 1960a,1960b), its eclipse has left us without an adequate word to describe a continuing phenomenon, whatever we may choose to call it. Why not go back to the old term and call it by its true name? The phenomenon encompasses urbanization, the rapid increase in productivity, the increasing mechanization of every aspect of our lives, drastic improvements in standards of living, increases in average life spans, a growing ability to travel and transmit information ever more rapidly, and the spread of education. All these changes are far from being finished. Even in the most advanced industrial countries such as those of Western Europe, or in the United States, rapid transformations continue as a result of accelerating modernization.

In France, as recently as two generations ago, peasants were the largest class of inhabitants, and women obtained the vote only fifty years ago, in 1946. In the United States, before World War II, the South, its largest region, was still a largely agrarian, caste-based, quasi-feudal, poorly educated, traditional society. Japan, for all its bristling militarism in the 1930s, was also a society dominated by an agrarian-feudal ethos and deep traditionalism. Only now, and as yet very incompletely, has rapid modernization begun to alphabetize the majority of peasants in South and East Asia and begun the process of mass urbanization. In many ways, we have hardly begun the modern age, and we barely understand its social ramifications. Only those with no sense of history, no awareness of technology, and no understanding of how incomplete our adaptation from agrarian to modern industrial society still remains could use silly terms such as "postmodern" or "late modernity" to describe late twentieth-century social reality. It takes an even greater lack of realism to claim that nothing important happened in Europe in the eighteenth century to change the course of world history. Modernization has occurred, is continuing, and will for a long time to come.

The debates about the best way of coping with rapid change are also very much alive. Nothing is firmly settled. This has been the condition of modernity for two hundred years and will remain so into the foreseeable future.

The two most successful and original ideological movements in the twentieth century were both attempts to cope with the disruptions and pain of modernization: revolutionary fascist corporatism and revolutionary Marxism. Each had an accompanying set of social theories that preceded its coming to power. Both political movements came originally from social theories produced by intellectuals in the nineteenth century, and they were later disseminated and popularized by activists. As social, economic, and political systems, however, both failed catastrophically. Yet the problems they were meant to address remain, and therefore, despite their failures, both these revolutionary movements continue to have adherents who accept many of their core beliefs, particularly Marxism.

The two other major ideological movements of the twentieth century have somewhat older origins than fascism and communism, though both have also been transformed to cope with the same problems that fascism and communism tried to address. One came from the European Enlightenment of the eighteenth century and emerged in the nineteenth as what is broadly called liberalism. This called for respect for individual over collective rights, a firm faith in human rationality, a conviction that on the whole individual choice expressed in open markets of opinion and economic goods (i.e., political democracy and capitalism) should determine most of the direction of both political and economic activity, and finally, a belief that it is impossible to devise perfect answers to social problems. It appeared, first, as a set of rather abstract philosophical principles in the seventeenth and eighteenth centuries, but eventually became the basis for some powerful political movements. In the first three-quarters of the twentieth century the theoretical view of society that is linked to political liberalism seemed to be in decline, but in the last quarter of the century, the success of the liberal, democratic capitalist systems has reversed this trend.[2]

Then, there has been nationalism. But nationalism may be consistent with either fascism, communism, or liberalism, and with sentiments of ethnic and religious communal solidarity that are older than any of the modern ideologies. Yet it too has been transformed and offered as another solution to the problem of how to cope with modernization. Nationalism has to be worked into any discussion about the major ideological trends in the twentieth century, but case by case rather than as a complete ideology by itself. This is theoretically awkward, but unavoidable. One thing that can be said about nationalism, however, is that in one important way it is like the other main ideological movements that have so dominated our century. Modern nationalism originated as a set of ideas among intellectuals and has spread from there to the general population.[3]

THE SHORTCOMINGS OF LIBERAL THEORY: PROBLEMS AND ANSWERS

In a fascinating recent book, the world's most eminent Marxist historian, Eric Hobsbawm, revealed his feelings in a way few of his readers had seen before. In his chapter entitled "The Crisis Decades" in *The Age of Extremes*, he suggests that the moral and economic decline of Western liberal societies marks the failure of free market liberalism just as surely as the fall of communism in Eastern Europe and the USSR marks the failure of socialism. And in his concluding chapter, he remarks that liberalism failed badly when it was actually practiced in its extreme form, with post-communist economic shock therapy in places like Poland, or by Mrs. Thatcher's attempt to impose it on Great Britain. This shows, he claims, that liberalism is practically impossible as well as theoretically bankrupt (Hobsbawm, 1994).

It takes a socialist like Hobsbawm, or in a somewhat different context, a communitarian like Robert Bellah to come up with the strange conclusion that liberal, democratic, market societies are in a state of collapse (Bellah et al., 1992). Aside from the fact that Poland was already doing quite well by the mid-1990s, as Hobsbawm was writing his book, and that other post-communist economies growing rapidly are the ones who have undergone the most liberal reforms, there is very little evidence that either Great Britain or the United States have been ruined by the revival of, and recent dominance of, what are now called "neoliberal" economic policies. On the contrary, all the evidence points to the remarkable revival of American productivity and competitiveness in the world economy, and the continuing, rapid spread of liberalizing measures throughout the rest of the world. What offends the Hobsbawms and Bellahs is the amorality and impersonality of markets, be they economic, cultural, or political. Measures of economic performance could hardly convince them to change their minds, though as long as there exist any signs of economic difficulty (which are always pretty easy to find in any system) the critics of liberal capitalism will use these to support their criticism.[4] Certainly, those who dislike open markets, increasing world trade, and liberalization now take heart, for the first time since the collapse of European communism between 1989 and 1991, because of the seeming failure of the East and Southeast Asian economic miracles. Of course, just as surely, the liberals interpret the economic depressions of East Asia as proof that these economies were not open enough (Zakaria, 1998).

If modernization proceeded smoothly and without much pain, there would, of course, be few theories around to attack it. If, on the other hand, it were an unmitigated social catastrophe for all but the elites in a few rich countries, and their handful of compradore allies elsewhere, there would be few who would deny the validity of an approach such as world-system theory. But unfortunately, reality is too complicated to satisfy the extreme variants of either approach.

It is possible to claim, as David Landes has in a recent book, that not only is a liberal interpretation of modernization correct, but that liberalism has long offered the best and surest path to modernization (Landes, 1998). In making such a statement, he is backed by a long and distinguished series of theorists and ideologues, but he runs directly into at least as long a list of opponents, ranging from (to name only a few of the most prominent) Jean-Jacques Rousseau, Johann Gottfried von Herder, Karl Marx, Martin Heidegger, Karl Polanyi, Immanuel Wallerstein, and Michel Foucault. The opponents of liberal theory, in one way or another, believe that its application leads to disaster, that the material progress of capitalism is bought at too steep a price, and that, in any case, it is bound to fail and be replaced by a better, less competitive, and more "natural," less repressive type of social organization.

Let it be noted that the anti-liberal approach to the study of social and economic change highlighted in this and other volumes in the series on the "Political Economy of the World System" is as compatible with right-wing as it is with left-wing critiques of liberal capitalism. The great Romanian economic theoretician Mihail Manoilescu, whose works inspired much of Latin American dependency theory in the 1920s and 1930s, was an unabashed corporatist fascist, whereas his American disciples laid the intellectual foundation for several generations of leftist theories.[5] The analysis remained the same: The world capitalist system will not allow competitors to develop, except with rare exceptions, and will stifle growth in most of the less developed world. The remedy, economic autarky and self-reliance, also remained similar in both the right-wing and left-wing versions. In fact, a reasonable argument might be made that fascist and socialist corporatism created quite similar blueprints for the societies they ruled, except that the socialist version lasted longer and corporatized societies much more thoroughly (Chirot, 1980; Cumings, 1982–83).

CYCLES AND THE ANTI-LIBERAL RESPONSE

One of the main shortcomings of liberal capitalist theories of modernization has been that they have tended to assume unilinear and smooth progress, without reversals and crises. The reality has always been that capitalist development is subject to cyclical reversals. Along with countless localized depressions and recessions, there have been five broad technology cycles since the start of the Industrial Revolution, and each one has been accompanied by what are now predictable, large-scale, global swings of prosperity. Each one has produced what was for its time an unprecedented boom and rise in productivity, and that has been followed by a downturn in which competition from new entrants into leading industries crowded the field, lowered profits, and led to economic, social, and political crises. Furthermore, in some cases adaptation to the new cycle has proved to be very difficult. These five cycles have been:[6]

1. The textile industrial revolution, from about the 1780s to the 1830s and 1840s, led by Great Britain.

2. The railway and iron revolution, from the 1840s to the 1870s, still led by Great Britain.

3. The organic-chemical, steel, and then electrical machinery revolution from the 1870s to the 1910s, in which industrial dominance shifted to Germany and the United States.

4. After World War I, and into the 1970s, the economic revolution dominated by the automobile and petrochemicals, but also by the spread of household electrical goods and the development of very rapid transport by air, an age that was dominated by the United States.

5. And finally, since the 1970s, and probably into the second or third decade of the next century, there is the latest industrial revolution, the fifth one, dominated by electronics, computers, and increasingly, biotechnology. The United States still seems to be the leading industrial power in this age.

It is unnecessary to go into detail about the disruptions each cyclical change has created. There have been vast migrations as obsolete forms of production have forced millions of peasants and, later, various kinds of workers off their lands and out of their jobs, or attracted millions into new boom areas because of new opportunities. There have been great shifts in the international balance of power that were poorly understood by statesmen and generals who responded to the rise and relative decline of great powers by entering into arms races and wars in order to reverse these shifts. The most notable error of this sort occurred in 1914 when hardly anyone understood that Germany's rise and Great Britain and France's relative decline had more to do with technology, education, and research than with the construction of vast military machines and the conquest of economically useless empires. There have been great depressions at the end of some cycles because previously leading sectors were decimated by competition, or at the beginning of others because political and financial institutions failed to adapt to higher levels of productivity. The most obvious example of this kind of maladaptation almost destroyed liberal capitalism at the start of the fourth industrial age, when the modern capitalist age experienced the biggest of all, the Great Depression in the 1930s (Kindleberger, 1973). Each of these upheavals resulted in significant political changes, revolutions, vast ideological shifts, and wars. In some ways, the collapse of communism in Europe had as much to do with its failure to adapt to the fifth industrial age as with its prior record of brutality and the suffering it had imposed on its populations (Chirot, 1991).

The first of these great reversals, at the end of the textile age and the start of the age of railways and iron, inspired Karl Marx to describe a plausible scenario for the end of capitalism itself. Of course, it did not happen as he predicted, or as the prophets of socialism foresaw in the 1870s, or in the 1920s and 1930s, or in the 1970s, because each old cycle has been replaced by new technologies, new growth, and a new adjustment of societies to what has invariably turned out to be an ever higher level of prosperity.[7]

In his elegant summary of Marx's economics, Joseph Schumpeter explained that up to a point, Marx was perfectly right. Improved technology cannot provide a secure long-term basis for profits because competitors obtain the technology. Thus, after a set of innovations, the firms possessing them reap giant profits, but with time, these erode. As Marx predicted, this puts downward pressure on wages, makes competition become more ruthless, and destroys all but the most efficient firms, so that the others fail. If that were the end of the story, capitalism would have disappeared a long time ago. But each time there have been more innovations, new firms, new products, and, eventually, whole new industrial ages that begin the story all over again. Only if innovation were to stop would Marx's predictions be borne out. That was Schumpeter's great fear, because he believed that political pressures against unregulated markets would indeed produce socialism, and this, combined with increasing bureaucratization, would crush the entrepreneurial spirit, and thus stop innovation and end industrial progress (Schumpeter, 1942). Schumpeter was right, at least in relative terms, about the capacity of socialism to bureaucratize innovation and therefore slow it down. That was precisely why the most advanced communist economies were unable to keep up with the more dynamic capitalist ones. But so far Schumpeter has been proved wrong in his prediction that socialism would conquer the advanced democratic capitalist societies of the world.

Yet, because dramatic shifts as industrial cycles continue will cause considerable disruption and suffering, theorists who either reject the value of modernization or believe that it can be better managed by anti-liberal policies will continue to thrive. This means that with every crisis there will continue to be sophisticated theoretical arguments against liberalism, either in the form of socialism, or in some other autarkic, anti-market, authoritarian form.

Surely by now, at the beginning of the twenty-first century, we must recognize that the only way to end the cycles of progress generated by capitalism is through some kind of political system that crushes entrepreneurship, scientific advances, and technological innovation. It is possible to create such political systems, but it remains unlikely that they could win power in the world's most advanced societies. Thus, critics of liberal modernization theory such as world-system theorists are left with a dilemma. How is it possible to reconcile the history of the twentieth century with the theory that interprets liberal capitalism as a cruel, wasteful, and ultimately doomed industrial and political system? This has been a century in which anti-liberal and anti-capitalist political ideologies, notably fascism and communism, have turned into anti-utopias far less able to adapt to the changing modern world than supposedly obsolete liberal capitalist societies. When will capitalism finally destroy itself?

INEQUALITY AND UNEVEN DEVELOPMENT

The second main cause of discontent with the liberal theory of modernization is that it does not take into account the fact of rising inequality. It is possible to argue that in the long run industrialization decreases inequality within advanced societies, though, if it does so, the decrease occurs unevenly, very incompletely, and with some reverses. Complete equality can never be approached by purely market mechanisms for the obvious reason that individual ability, background, and circumstances vary so much that markets are bound to reward some more than others. This hardly means that Marx was right about rising inequality within capitalist societies, but continuing inequality will always prove to be a fertile ground for his theories.

International inequality, unlike inequality within capitalist societies, has clearly and dramatically increased since the start of the first industrial age (Bairoch, 1993: 95). Nor is this spread decreasing in any sense, especially if the poorest parts of the world, notably in Africa, are compared to the richest societies in Europe, East Asia, and North America.

There are two explanations for the increase of inequality between rich and poor societies in the past two centuries. One version would have it that those societies that have successfully modernized have become much richer, and the others have stagnated because of their failure to modernize. The other theory is the exact opposite. It claims that the rich have grown fat at the expense of the poor, by exploiting them, and that economic development under capitalism is a cruel hoax because it enriches a few societies while immiserating the majority. Who is right?

The world-system theoretical perspective, which is, at its core, an argument about how the few core societies in the world enrich themselves by exploiting the majority in the periphery, is immensely appealing to intellectuals in poorer countries because it explains their societies' failure to become rich in terms of exploitation rather than because of domestic failures. Therefore, even if we could prove that such a theoretical view is erroneous, that would hardly diminish its emotional appeal. Part of the success of world-system theory and its many related viewpoints, including dependency theory, is that it deeply appeals to the nationalism of poorer societies. Aggressive external forces are to blame; they have dishonored and subverted "our" national honor and culture, and by reclaiming "our" rightful place "we" will not only salvage our pride but also "our" looted wealth. One may be a Fidel Castro or a Kim Il Sung, a Benito Mussolini or a Juan Perón, or for that matter, an Ayatollah Khomeini and agree with this view.

Unfortunately for those who agree with the theory that modernizing economic

development has occurred in the West primarily because it has looted and impoverished the rest of the world, and that therefore, the best solution is to be
both anti-liberal and anti-Western, the historical and contemporary evidence supporting such a position is not always comforting.

There is ample historical evidence that increasing contact with the core of the
capitalist world economy has stimulated modernization, including economic development, not retarded it. This is notably the case in Eastern Europe, which,
by some accounts, was the first "peripheral" part of the world. Thus, the northern
parts of Eastern Europe, what is generally called Central Europe, including Poland, the Baltic countries, the Czech lands, and Hungary emerged in the nineteenth century as more advanced in every respect than the Balkans. This was
not because the Ottoman Empire was a particularly backward agrarian empire,
but because it was an ordinary one. That is, every part of the world was relatively stagnant compared to Western Europe and North America in the nineteenth century, so the less exposure to capitalism and trade with the dynamic
core, the less economic development there was. The theory that Eastern Europe,
particularly Poland and Hungary, became "peripheral" because of their trade
with Western Europe reverses causality. These were thinly populated, technologically backward areas when they entered into closer economic relationships
with the more advanced parts of Western Europe, and it took a long time for
them to progress out of that condition, but it was not the contact as such that
made them backward. On the contrary, it has only been through contact that
they have progressed compared to adjoining regions with less contact.[8]

There is much debate about the effect of colonialism and how debilitating it
was. Can one argue that most of Asia, Latin America, and Africa had their
economic progress slowed or reversed by European conquest? There is no serious evidence that any of these places was headed for the kind of dynamic,
self-sustaining growth that might have produced the explosive growth that
occurred in the West after the late eighteenth century. On the other hand, there
is little question that in some cases, colonial policies either did little good or
actually retarded the adaptation that might have occurred through contact with
the West (Bairoch, 1993: 88–93). But can historical evidence, even if it were
to be conclusive about the ill effects of colonialism, be interpolated to apply to
the contemporary world? That is, can historical evidence support claims that
anti-liberal, anti-capitalist, and autarkic policies that remove poorer economies
from the world capitalist system work to stimulate healthy economic development and modernization?

Theoretical prescriptions, demanding closure, import substitution, and generally eschewing the world market have actually been turned into functioning
policies in many places in the second half of the twentieth century: all the
communist countries, Italy under Mussolini (his failures in foreign policy have
obscured his regime's dismal record in promoting economic growth), Argentina
from the 1930s to the 1980s, Peru in the 1970s and 1980s, Burma, India, from
independence until the late 1980s, and others. All have been long-term failures.[9]

It has not just been the communist and some fascist-corporatist attempts to modernize that have resulted in catastrophe. Looking across Africa since the establishment of independent states some three to four decades ago (but only two decades for the former Portuguese colonies), one sees an almost unbroken pattern of failure. Harsh communist regimes such as those in Guinea or Ethiopia, milder socialist ones that prevailed throughout most of the continent as, until the late 1980s, in Ghana, Tanzania, or Zambia, or even relatively nonsocialist governments such as in Nigeria, Zaire, and the Ivory Coast (once black Africa's most promising experiment with capitalism) have little to boast about. Immense, almost unbelievable corruption in places where there were valuable natural resources to be looted, as in Nigeria and Zaire/Congo, very weak loyalty to existing state institutions and boundaries, a virtual absence of strong bureaucratic traditions to guide civil servants, low levels of modern education, and autocratic but inept political elites have made most of the continent inhospitable to outside as well as domestic investors. Despite very low standards of living, African economies have been unable to take advantage of their low wage rates.[10]

There are other cases around the world of weak, corrupt states that have caused economic havoc. Pakistan comes to mind, and there are many candidates for this kind of failure among the post-Soviet states, particularly Ukraine, Belarus, and in Central Asia. An inability to maintain a stable currency, enforce contracts or even basic law and order, and systematic corruption made many Latin American economies perform anemically for long periods of time, and we cannot be sure that even substantial economies such as Mexico can avoid falling back into this kind of calamitous spiral in the future. Indonesia's immense corruption and nearly total absence of democracy under the Suharto regime was at least partly responsible for the fact that its economy has suffered far more than any other in the recent East Asian economic crisis.

Even within otherwise prosperous and successful modern economies we can find the same phenomenon at work at the regional level. Southern Italy, for all of the billions of dollars' worth of subsidies poured into it by the Italian government, remains far poorer than it should be because of corruption and a local social system unable to enforce basic norms of honesty. Corruption and the fact that government subsidies have been used inefficiently keep Southern Italy relatively backward to this day.[11]

All this suggests that it is not simply closure to the world economy that can delay economic progress and modernization, but, more fundamentally, policies antithetical to liberalism. Restrictive, closed economic and political practices may be practiced just as thoroughly by ostensibly "capitalist" regimes as by communist or fascist ones. Most European colonial regimes, even those run by nations that were liberal at home, were systematically guilty of such practices, and therefore often did serious damage to the colonial economies they were running. They may not have gained very much by such practices, but they certainly did a lot of harm (Bairoch, 1993, pt. II).

Economic growth, as Douglass North has been arguing for several decades, requires institutions that lower transaction costs, secure property rights, and make information widely available (North 1981; North 1990; North and Thomas 1973). States unable to carry out these functions or ones that deliberately block them, either for ideological, anti-market reasons, or for corruption's sake, to be better able to steal, will slow economic progress. No reasonable observer would deny the important tasks that governments have to be able to carry out. But in the absence of market mechanisms, even governments that build infrastructures, educate their populations, and maintain law and order will fail. This is what happened in European communist states. They did everything more or less right except that they were socialist and disregarded both internal and world markets, or at least they tried to ignore markets until it was too late.[12]

A PROGNOSIS: THE NEED FOR LEGITIMACY

Without claiming to have resolved any of the theoretical disputes about whether or not liberal capitalism is essentially predatory or progressive, or whether its continuing spread will produce ever-increasing global inequality or finally allow the entire world to be satisfactorily modernized, we can come to some conclusions about the immediate future.

Liberal capitalism may not be immortal, but as a system, it will continue to become ever more powerful for some time to come. In the twentieth century it was strongly challenged by fundamentally anti-liberal ideologies and great powers, and it survived. Today it is challenged only by weak and disparate ideologies. It has turned out that nationalism, not Marxism or corporatism, was the only lasting basis for challenging the ascendancy of liberal capitalism, and that will remain true into the foreseeable future. It is unpleasant for the intellectuals in poorly modernized societies to face their failures, and it is relatively easy for them to tap into the mass discontent produced by the economic fluctuations and inequality produced by modernization.

In a technical sense, there is no reason for the cycles of improving technology to ever end unless scientific progress and entrepreneurship are forbidden. There is no automatic economic mechanism such as that found by Marx that can predict theoretically how and why capitalism might come to an end. Quite simply, any social, political, or economic system that allows experiments to occur, and permits signals about the failure and success of these experiments to circulate and influence future decisions, will be able to adapt. It is the messiness of open politics and market economies that provides their strength, just as it was the hard-fought establishment of key corners of intellectual freedom that allowed the scientific and technological revolution in Western Europe to flourish in the early modern age. Immanuel Wallerstein, no matter how wrong he has been about many other aspects of the modern world system, was right about this: The very disunity of capitalist world economies was the key to its success (Wallerstein, 1974a). Competition and the inability to impose monopolies, despite the many attempts to do so, have remained the ultimate strength of liberal societies.

In the long run, the centrally planned, ideologically dictated, politically unfree societies that have competed with the liberal democracies in the twentieth century have proved unable to maintain the flexibility required to adapt to changing circumstances. Messages about failed policies do not circulate well enough; free thought, and therefore innovation, are partially or entirely stifled; popular discontent does not surface until it has become explosive; failure in the international arena, be it economic or political, is not permitted to affect central institutions or policies until it is too late and the failure has become catastrophic.

All this has been know for a very long time, but enemies of liberal, market societies continue to insist that there must be a better, fairer way than open competition, that there must be an absolute truth in some ideology or religion, and that open societies are too corrupt, dissolute, and disorganized to survive much longer. The same sentiment that makes so many opponents of modern capitalism say that there must be something more than a bottom line do not recognize that bottom lines are not simply matters of profits, at least not when it comes to whole societies, but of how well a society functions. The advantage capitalist businesses have is that they can sometimes see something measurable going wrong with their bottom lines before the company has collapsed. Closed monopolies, whether they are businesses or political systems, lack this adaptive capacity.

This is not, however, a particularly useful prognosis, because such a statement would have been just as correct in the year 1900 as in 2000, and yet liberal capitalism came very close to being destroyed by both fascism and communism. Economic resiliency does not assure survival as long as there continue to be economic cycles, inequality, and nationalist discontent against the effects of globalizing capital. Even in rich and powerful countries such as the United States, there are hostile reactions to liberal capitalism at any sign of economic trouble or relative decline in national power. The effects of such discontent in poorer parts of the world will not disappear, but will continue to produce antiliberal ideologies and regimes.

Markets, like all uncontrolled evolutionary processes in which the successful survive and others perish or fail to reproduce, have nothing inherently fair about them unless one considers utilitarianism the basis of an ethical doctrine. This is the principal reason for which almost all civilized societies in the past looked down on commercial activity as unclean money grubbing. Honor, noble bloodlines, gracious comportment, learning, or at least skill in some obvious physical endeavor rather than the mere ability to manipulate goods and financial instruments always struck upper classes in agrarian societies as more appropriate ways of assigning rank and prestige. And at the bottom of agrarian societies, there persisted for most of their existence a strong inclination to demand equality and disapprove of those who tried to get ahead too quickly. All of this may have been quite functional in agrarian societies, and perhaps much earlier than that when humans lived in small bands that had to stick together in a friendly way in order to survive. But market societies are in flagrant violation of all the old virtues, whether of nobles, learned officials, or egalitarian peasants. This is why, as Ezra Vogel has pointed out, it was necessary for the old Confucian order to be thoroughly discredited in East Asia before economic growth could take off.[13] Albert Hirschman reaches a similar conclusion in a different way in his examination of why Enlightenment philosophers had to legitimize capitalism before it existed in order to make a capitalist order possible in Western Europe (Hirschman, 1977).

In a peculiar way, many of the intellectuals who defend anti-liberalism throughout the world, especially those who make their living in state-supported educational institutions and as higher level brokers of culture, are like the Confucian literati who held back East Asia for so long. This includes the learned clerics who form the backbone of the fundamentalist Iranian Islamic regime, but also university professors throughout the world. In moments of economic and social crisis, if they gain political power, they can once again threaten liberal capitalism.

Intellectuals can play a particularly important role, either in blocking or in accelerating successful modernization. Many of the theories of change popular among intellectuals, whether of the fascist-corporatist or of the socialist variety, have contributed mightily to slowing modernization insofar as they have been taught in school systems. The successes of leftist and rightist revolutionary parties in mobilizing students and intellectuals all over the world throughout most of the twentieth century are a testament to this. As has now been shown, particularly by the pioneering work of political scientists like Zeev Sternhell (1995), the common element of most of the major revolutionary doctrines of the this century was hostility to liberal individualism and to capitalist markets.

In short, despite the successes of a liberal approach to development, its future acceptance is no more guaranteed now than at the start of the twentieth century, when all these lessons were already available. Francis Fukuyama's prediction that now, finally, we have all learned the lessons of the twentieth century and seen that only liberal capitalism leads to successful modernization is unlikely to be correct (Fukuyama, 1992). The resistance to change among theorists, ideologues, and among large portions of populations everywhere has not been eliminated, though some of the most egregiously harmful alternatives to liberal capitalist modernization have been disgraced. If it were only a matter of Marxism, or fascist corporatism, it would be possible to say that these have been shown to be failures, so they will not be repeated. But anti-liberal nationalism, especially in the form of resentment against the rich and powerful nations of the West, has in no sense disappeared. It will find new theories, neo-Marxist, fascist, religious, or who knows what, to serve as the base of movements and parties determined to resist the Western form of modernization.

WORLD-SYSTEM THEORY AS A METHOD OF DIAGNOSING THE CONDITION OF THE WORLD CAPITALIST ECONOMY

We must all accept the idea that neither liberal capitalism nor its opponents will go away, and that modernizing progress will continue along with economic cycles and uneven development. What, then, is the best means of analyzing the ideological, ethnic, national, and class conflicts that will continue to occur in response to continuing modernization? Here, very obviously, the approach developed by world-system analysts offers what none other can provide.

Whereas few contemporary economists are interested in, or even believe in the existence of long-term cycles, world-system theorists have continued to believe that a historically grounded study of capitalist development must take such recurring and regular occurrences into account.[14] It is more than a little ironic that the only noted recent economic historian to have taken long cycles seriously is Walt Rostow. Rostow, however, is despised by world-system theorists because he is seen as the ultimate defender of modernization theory, and few economists take him very seriously.

Unfortunately, much of what passes as cyclical theory among those interested in world-system theory ignores recent developments in economic theory that lend themselves precisely to the kind of long-term, comparative analysis required. The "new institutionalism" that stresses the imperfection of markets, the historical path dependence of economic development patterns, and the importance of political cultures is ideally suited to the blend of economics, sociology, and history that world-system theory espouses (Hodgson, 1994; Williamson, 1994). The related growth of evolutionary economics has brought back classical, holistic theorists we have long admired, but who were ignored by economists for many decades—namely, Thorstein Veblen, Joseph Schumpeter, and even Karl Marx (Hodgson, 1996).

For those who have been studying the political economy of the world system for many years, the idea that "globalization" is something new must seem bizarre. On the contrary, of all the methodological approaches to the study of change in the social sciences, ours is one of the few that has consistently seen social change as a "global" phenomenon for many centuries, at least since the spread of capitalism. But here again, to contribute to the discussion about globalization in a useful way, we must be prepared to abandon certain ideological preconceptions. Globalization has been going on for a long time, and as this chapter has tried to suggest, there is no discernible evidence that the process leads inevitably to the collapse of liberal, capitalist systems. Therefore, objectivity requires that we pay much greater attention to the nature and results of technological progress. One need not be as inveterately optimistic about the future of capitalist progress as the late Julian Simon (1996) to recognize that there is something valid about his main point: In the modern age our capacity for innovation has saved the world capitalist system from the problems created by industrialization, rapid population growth, and uneven development. We should at least take such arguments seriously.

Finally, if some economists, for example, Douglass North, are willing to talk about "culture" and "norms," we might reconsider world-system theory's virtual neglect of sociology's rich Weberian tradition. Western ascendancy and the industrial revolution did not take place just because or even primarily because a few Western powers were better and more ruthless thieves, as Janet Abu-Lughod once proposed (Abu-Lughod, 1989). Rather, there was a profound transformation in the Western system of thought that resulted in an explosion of knowledge and technology (Shapin, 1996). For better or for worse, we have to understand how that happened, and why, even today, this continues to confer a distinct advantage on Western societies and those few non-Western societies that have most self-consciously tried to imitate them. Without this attempt to understand the essence of modern, Western thought, world-system theory risks becoming little more than a convenient vehicle for raging against modernization and wishing it away.

NOTES

1. An old, but still relevant, book about the strains of modernization is Eisenstadt's (1966).

2. For a good discussion of the history of liberalism, see Manent (1995); for a history of its critics, see Holmes (1993); and for a popular celebration of its recent success, see Fukuyama (1992).

3. For some recent analyses of nationalism, see Hobsbawm (1990); Ernest Gellner, (1983); and the more controversial analysis of Liah Greenfeld (1992).

4. In a survey of the world's economy, Le Monde, France's most prestigious newspaper, emphasizes this astonishing reversal of opinion between the early and mid-1990s, as the Europeans and Japanese realized that far from becoming obsolete, American industry had become the leader in high-technology goods, as well as maintaining its dominance in services (Izraelewicz, 1996: 13). As for Eastern Europe, Poland in 1995 registered economic growth of 6 percent. This success continued into the late 1990s. In fact, by and large the poorest countries in Eastern Europe remain those that have remained the most socialist. This is even more noticeable in the former USSR, where the Baltic Republics have taken important steps to undo socialism, whereas most of the Central Asian Republics and Belarus have done the least to reduce the role of the state and continue to suffer from catastrophic economic declines (Gherardi, 1996: 25; Le Monde, 1996: 36–56).

5. See Joseph L. Love's definitive new book on this subject (1996).

6. Rostow (1980) posits a set of similar cycles. For details on this particular version, see Chirot (1986: 61–63, 223–26, 293–94).

7. It is astonishing, to say the least, that Marx's predictions, based as they were on the very first industrial cycle, continue to be trotted out to predict the imminent collapse of capitalism every time a new cyclical downturn occurs. Nevertheless, this is what happened and what accounts for some of the enormous popularity of Marxist theories in the social sciences in the 1970s during the waning stages of the fourth industrial age.

8. See the articles by Robert Brenner, Peter Gunst, Jacek Kochanowicz, Fikret Adanir, and John Lampe in Chirot, ed. (1989).

9. In *Modern Tyrants* (Chirot, 1996), I discuss the cases of Argentina and Burma in detail in Chapters 8 and 9, emphasizing the disastrous results of policies that were meant to keep these countries free of "foreign" interference and markets. The case of India is more complicated, but there is little question that a recent opening that is starting to produce significant economic growth is under intense attack by nationalists incapable of understanding the harm they would inflict on their own population, particularly the poor, if they succeeded in reimposing closure on the Indian economy. See *Le Monde* (1996: 115). On Mussolini's Italy, see Clough (1964).

10. Describing what should be black Africa's richest country, *Le Monde*'s Bilan du Monde (1996, 83), says that Nigeria is beset by "fleeing capital" and "a continuing decline into total torpor." That is not because of socialism but because under military rule Nigeria came to be ruled by what was regularly called the world's most corrupt government. Despite the recent rebounding of some African economies that have opened themselves to the outside and renounced socialist planning, such as Ghana and Tanzania, others beset by immense corruption are getting worse. Perhaps even more notorious than Nigeria was Zaire under Mobutu, also a territory of immense potential wealth. But there the economy disintegrated to such an extent that it ceased to be discussed in the world press. See Young and Turner (1985) for the sad story of how this came about.

11. For some of the background and delusions about how to fix Southern Italy's problems, see Mountjoy (1973). Southern Italy has been the only region in the European Community that has fallen further behind the developed parts of Europe in recent years. See Apicella (1996, 119–27). The public authorities in the south are so corrupt and ineffective that, as A. Jobert (1995) found, money spent on education and training has no positive effect on development. Yet, the rest of Italy has undergone an economic miracle since the late 1940s that is almost as impressive as what has happened in East Asia since the 1950s. Inept and corrupt government has been, in a sense, overcome by Italy's participation in the Common Market, and by a lot of semi-undercover business activity that simply bypasses the government.

12. This topic has now been explored by hundreds of studies. My position on the reasons for the collapse of communism is found in Chirot (1991).

13. Vogel (1992: 83–84). This is not to deny the virtues of having a meritocratic bureaucratic ideal, a sense that the family must be nurtured and preserved, or that every individual owes his or her duty to a larger community, all stressed by many of the admirers of "neo-Confucianism," including Vogel, pp. 92–103. On the other hand, the high bureaucratic elite's ethos despised commerce and industry; so as long as it ruled, economic progress was retarded.

14. Even an economic historian such as Thomas Rawski (1996, 24) writes, "There is no general theory of economic cycles." He explains that technological changes and institutional changes do produce cyclical patterns that are empirically observable for short periods of time, but then further changes create entirely new types of cycles. Thus, for example, the cycles observed by Simon Kuznets in the American economy between 1840 and 1914 "cannot help us understand recent changes."

6

Mr. X? Doctrine X? A Modest Proposal for Thinking about the New Geopolitics

Bruce Cumings

"Where is Mr. X now that we need him again?" might be the simplest way to convey the dilemmas of American power in the 1990s, with the Soviet Union gone, the Cold War to all appearances over, and a new but also unprecedented world order in motion. That American power towers over that of any competitor is not in question: there is near unanimity, whether broadcast openly in Moscow or *sotto voce* in Washington, that we live in a unipolar world. That American power is great, indeed much greater in 1999 than most would have predicted in 1989 amid a widespread discourse of American decline, is unquestionable. But of what does that power consist? Is it a preponderant military power? Yes. Is it geopolitical power? Yes, both in the continental base of American hegemony, and in the archipelago of military bases that it maintains around the world. Is it an economic power less dominant than it once was, but still more formidable than any other? Yes. Is it a power that comes out of the barrel of attractive ideas? Yes, and even if that set of ideas has not changed much in the post-Cold War era, it now holds sway amid a vacuum of serious alternatives. Is it a deeper, structural form of power that shapes and constrains its constituent parts and militates against the emergence of any conceivable rival? Perhaps, but here we encounter a dilemma: for if we answer in the affirmative, then the answers to our first three questions might appear to be mere corollaries of our last. Curiously, it is this last question that rarely intrudes into post-Cold War debates. In this chapter I want to argue that one way of thinking about the world does help us to grasp both the meaning of the end of the Cold War and the course of global politics since 1989: but instead of *Mr. X*, let me call it *Doctrine X*.

Three views have dominated mainstream Western discussions about global

politics in the 1990s, which we can summarize with three names: Francis Fukuyama, John Mearsheimer, and Samuel Huntington. Each of them drew on a
broader discourse through which Americans have historically defined their
global purpose: realism and idealism. Mearsheimer (1992) was the frank realist,
arguing that we will learn to love the Cold War when we experience the instability of power politics and national rivalries long held in check by the structure
of bipolar confrontation. The so-called "long peace" would soon give way to
sharp rivalry among the big powers. Fukuyama (1992) was the idealist, if one
not fully in the American mold, drawing as he did on an obscure strain of
Hegelian theory identified with the Hungarian philosopher Alexandre Kojève.
But he arrived at his general theme through a critique of realism and that theme
could not have been more American: not only was liberal democracy triumphant
over communism, but it was the best (or "most just") system. This stunning
success, however, would perhaps have a more melancholy result: the end of the
contested history that had marked the modern world, as liberalism dissolved all
its opponents. Huntington (1996a) is even less clearly an American idealist, but
his "clash of civilizations" rested on the assumption that several distinct bodies
of inherited ideas and practices existed in our world, and that they either already
had or soon would constitute themselves in opposition to each other; as they
did so, the new axis of global politics would spring forth. The United States
should prepare for this by coming to understand that there was, after all, one
superior form of civilization (the Western), one that could only be sustained by
a return to Atlanticism in American foreign policy.

For many people the war in Bosnia seemed to confirm the wisdom of
Huntington and Mearsheimer, and for others the global transition to representative democratic forms in the past decade confirmed Fukuyama. Through all
this, little if anything was said about the continuing salience of Cold War structures of power: 1989 seemed to be year zero. The most formidable of these
arguments was to be found in *The End of History and the Last Man*, and I will
take stock of Fukuyama's argument a decade after it first appeared, before re-
turning to the question of whether the end of the Cold War has in fact been so
determinative of the world we live in.

The end of the Cold War also, of course, prompted a spate of melodramatic
literature seeking to give meaning to this evidently cataclysmic event, a genre
that we might label "the end of the Cold War and me." The dramatic events of
1989 encouraged a host of people to say "I told you so," rushing into print with
musty prognostications about the bankruptcy of communism written back in
1955, or various triumphalist claims about the West's future. This tendency was
perhaps most pronounced in John Lukacs' fatuously self-important 1993 book
entitled *The End of the Twentieth Century and the End of the Modern Age*, but
he was by no means alone. In this genre *The End of History* was certainly
different: Fukuyama did view the end of the Cold War as a millennial transition,
but few would have imagined doing so through a reprise of the thought of Georg
W. F. Hegel—and perhaps least of all the great philosopher himself, who would

roll in his grave to see his dialectic grinding to a halt in the valhalla of George Bush and Bill Clinton's philistine United States. Hegel gave us history with a purpose, with a telos, with a capital H, an unfolding with a beginning, a middle, and an end: behold, all the past as pre-history, as mere prelude to the manifest world-historical spirit of the present age. Fukuyama's argument had an unquestionable ingenuity, taking the thinker perhaps most alien to the pragmatic and unphilosophical American soul, Hegel, and using his thought to proclaim something quintessentially American: that the pot of gold at the end of History's rainbow is free market liberalism. History just happened to culminate in the reigning orthodoxy of our era, the neo-liberalism of Thatcher and Reagan.

In the book Fukuyama adopted the perspective of a particular Hegel scholar whom he had heard about years before in one of Allan Bloom's classes at the University of Chicago. Alexandre Kojève is hardly a household word in America, but he has been taught for decades at Chicago, mainly within the confines of the Philosophy Department or the Committee on Social Thought where Bloom taught for many years. Kojève established his reputation in France during the 1930s by leading many French philosophers (who naturally had looked to Rousseau and Baudelaire) to understand that Hegel was in many ways both the culmination of traditional philosophy and the first great philosopher of the modern age. Nearly as important as Hegel to Fukuyama's argument was another German philosopher: Friedrich Nietzsche, who, the author says, gave us "the last man" as the likely culmination of Western liberalism, and counterposed to that figure the type he preferred, the *Übermensch*, a difficult term often (mis-) translated as "Superman." According to Fukuyama's rendering, "the last man" is a comfortable slave, with physical security and material plenty, a person who believes in nothing (or everything), with a sunny disposition and a polite willingness to listen to all views that masks an inner emptiness; to the extent that "the last man" has any culture at all, he is a cultural relativist. The *Übermensch* is the opposite: a "man with a chest," whose will to power triumphs over the herdlike conformity of modern democracies: "Nietzsche believed that no true human excellence, greatness, or nobility was possible except in aristocratic societies" (Fukuyama, 1992: 304).

According to Fukuyama, Nietzsche had radicalized Hegel's argument that people are motivated by *thymos*, a striving for recognition that Hegel regarded as the most basic human need, and which can be compared to Rousseau's *amour-propre*, Alexander Hamilton's "love of fame," James Madison's ambition, and Nietzsche's conception of man as the "beast with red cheeks" (ibid.: 162). Believers in liberal democracy might follow the others, but they can't follow Nietzsche "very far down the road" because his *megalothymia* made him "an open opponent of democracy and of the rationality on which it rested." (Indeed, Fukuyama sees Nietzsche as a precursor of Nazism.) Kojève, on the other hand, is acceptable because even if he agreed with Nietzsche that Western man was going to hell in a handbasket, unlike Nietzsche he "did not rage at the return to animality at the end of history," but merely quit teaching and took a job in a bureaucracy "meant to supervise construction of the final home for the last man." The reader might expect this to be the architectural firm responsible for *Animal Farm*, but it was in fact the European Commission (ibid.: 311).

Fukuyama's theory does not go beyond this level of abstraction, however much he may repeat it throughout the book, but he does seek to relate the march of History, the need for *thymos*, and the perils of *megalothymia* to the current age. The good guys are "the most free and therefore the most human of beings," people like "the revolutionaries who battled with Ceausescu's *Securitate* in Romania, the brave Chinese students who stood up to tanks in Tinananmen Square, the Lithuanians who fought Moscow for their national independence, [and] the Russians who defended their parliament and president" (ibid.: 312). The bad guys are of course communists and fascists, but also "cultural relativists" and those who "struggle for the sake of struggle," like the protesting French students of 1968 "who had no 'rational' reason to rebel, for they were for the most part pampered offspring of one of the freest and most prosperous societies on earth" (330). Fukuyama sprinkles criticisms of American liberalism through his text, especially the inability to come to agreement on moral issues, the failures of our leaders (but usually just the ones from the Democratic Party), and the perils of community in a time of atomized individualism. But he still argues that "a contemporary liberal democracy like the United States permits considerable scope for those who desire to be recognized as greater than others" (*thymos* again), and "the first and foremost of these outlets in a liberal society is entrepreneurship" (315). He ends the book with his hope that the unfolding events of the past few decades mean that "the idea of a universal and directional history leading up to liberal democracy may become more plausible to people, and that the relativist impasse of modern thought will in a sense solve itself"; mankind will come to seem like "a long wagon train" that finally reaches the end of its journey, which is of course free-market liberalism (338–39).

It is not just the average American who would need a scorecard to follow the tortured logic of Fukuyama's argument, but also philosophers knee-deep in Hegel and Nietzsche. Can it be that the antithesis of "the last man" is Ronald Reagan, a person whom Washington insider and fixer Clark Clifford once called "an amiable dunce"? Is the thymotic entrepreneur-cum-monopolist Bill Gates the ideal American? Can Daniel Cohn-Bendit of Paris '68, whose red hair once added to his "Red" reputation, really be the "beast with red cheeks"? And did the Monica Lewinsky scandal mean that Bill Clinton is the real "last man"? (He does have red cheeks.)

An endless list of similar puns crowd the mind, but these are easy points to make. Futhermore, in regard to our "relativist impasse," Fukuyama is unquestionably right. The moral and ethical debates of our time, as Alasdaire McIntyre has argued, proffer an unresolvable choice between politicized alternatives: pro-life versus pro-choice, affirmative action versus white rights to equal access, the impeachability of low crimes-cum-hijinks as opposed to the rule of law and the injunction to tell the truth (or at least not to lie under oath), whether our kids should be protected from smut on the Internet, or whether smut is protected under the strictures of "free speech." It is not the debates that are characteristic, so much as the inability to form a principled moral position that would resolve them—and even to see that very thing as a form of oppression. To have a strong, self-confident point of view is almost to appear as a totalitarian. The more common response is to settle down amid an uncomfortable anarchy of view-points, dismissing each as the incommensurable product of our visceral feelings rather than our rational thought, yielding the common practice of being con-tented with one's own feelings, conceived (by ourselves) as mere prejudices—but pleasant and even precious nonetheless, because they are *my* prejudices. But Fukuyama merely highlights these dilemmas, without the slightest indication how we might go about resolving them, short of becoming Hegelians.

Fukuyama's book delineates much of what passes for debate in American intellectual life. Like many celebrants of liberalism and "the West" (e.g., his mentor Allan Bloom), Fukuyama substitutes for actually existing liberalism an ideal version, drawn from the fine words and high-minded phrases of iconic figures like John Locke, John Stuart Mill, and Alexis de Tocqueville—and even then, with a highly selective reading. In the leading intellectual journals these days it often seems sufficient to settle an argument just to quote Locke or Tocqueville or Jefferson, or to derisively dismiss a "modern" like Marx or a "postmodern" like Jacques Derrida. Fukuyama is now sufficiently centrist or mainstream to get called upon by *Foreign Affairs* or *The New York Times* for commentary, just as most mainstream publications accepted without comment his treatment of Hegel and Nietzsche, whereas anything that can be deemed "postmodern" is continuously subjected to ridicule and calumny—especially in the flagship intellectual magazine, *The New York Review of Books*. What would a critique look like that took Fukuyama to task on his own terms? It would begin with his treatment of Hegel and Nietzsche, whose thought is caricatured almost beyond recognition in this book.

Fukuyama is wrong to assume a deep difference between Hegel and Nietzsche over the nature of modernity. It is true that no one was more critical than Nietzsche of Hegel's abstracted notions of "the idea" or "the spirit," but as Keith Ansell-Pearson has shown, he shared with Hegel an aversion to the anomie of modern society, with its narrow, economistic notions of individualism, and both thinkers hoped to restore an ethical basis to citizenship, or to the idea of being human. The major agenda of modernity, in Hegel's view, was to found a new form of ethical life (*Sittlichkeit*), in the face of the war of all against all brought forth by modernity. Likewise Nietzsche offers his *Übermensch* as the way to overcome the quiet nihilism of "the last man," a person without passion or commitment pursuing an empty relativism; Nietzsche's great interpreter and translator in the United States, Walter Kaufmann, saw in the term "über" a meaning of going across, or over, or beyond, the idea being that man is a bridge and not an end-point, a bridge to one's best self, with self-overcoming as the law of life itself. For Kaufmann, therefore, the *Übermensch* connotes "a notion of noble human agency," the devotion of one's life to great deeds, to going beyond the conforming and confining morality of the herd (Ansell-Pearson, 1994: 89, 105–7)—something not far from Allan Bloom's teaching in *The Closing of the American Mind*. Such a person lives, however, without the comfort of God or religion, and must be the law-giver for himself—or as Nietzsche put it in *Beyond Good and Evil*, an individual who is "obliged to give himself laws and to develop his own arts and wiles for self-preservation, self-enhancement, self-redemption" (211).

The name "Michel Foucault" is enough to make some people terminate a discussion, and that name does not appear in Fukuyama's book—in spite of Foucault's famously saying in 1967, "All philosophical reflection today is a dialogue with Hegel" (Eribon, 1991: 89). But if there is one person who was clearly Nietzsche's disciple in our time, it was Foucault; for him, Nietzsche was the first philosopher to think about power outside the confines of political theory. Foucault's absence is doubly interesting because Kojève's analysis of Hegel was among the greatest influences on Foucault's thought, at a time when concerns about "the end of History" gripped a generation of young French intellectuals, and, moreover, at a time that made it all seem plausible: 1945. The defeat of fascism, the collapse of European empires, and the substitution of American for British global leadership appeared to signal the end of the pre-history of the modern: but then the modern took two forms, liberal America and the socialist Soviet Union, each providing a stark alternative to the other, and thus an occasion for philosophers like Jean-Paul Sartre, Maurice Merleau-Ponty, and Raymond Aron to mount the deepest inquiry into the meaning of the bipolar rivalry that came to dominate the postwar world (Eribon, 1991: 19–20). To this debate Foucault eventually provided a radical alternative, a highly sophisticated body of thought that was nonetheless consonant with the global emergence of a "new Left": the United States and the USSR were two sides of the same modern coin; for each their pretensions to new forms of freedom were less important than their joint acceptance of the modern project to discipline, mold, and punish their citizens. Drawing on Jeremy Bentham's Panopticon as a master metaphor, Foucault's lasting contribution was to redefine power for our (modern or postmodern) time by looking not at its central fount (e.g., sovereign state power) but at its distant sources, in the rivulets and eddies where power affects everyone— "those points where it becomes capillary," in his words (Foucault, 1980: 96). These include the production of effective instruments for the formation and accumulation of knowledge, and thus power—methods of observation, techniques of registration, procedures for investigation and research, apparatuses of control and surveillance, taken to their logical conclusion in the ubiquitous closed-circuit television cameras that monitor so much of daily life in America. Foucault used these insights to draw attention to the abuses of human dignity by various modern systems of power (schools, prisons, mental asylums), thus founding a radical critique of all of modernity, whether here, in Moscow, or in Tokyo.

Fukuyama, on the other hand, develops a tortured logic leading to a deeply conservative argument in favor of the status quo, to a kind of iron cage in which every person is presumptively free and every interest is represented. *The End of History* creates a discourse of power that says in essence, you've never had it so good, so what are you complaining about? Anyone who protests infringements on his or her rights in today's America gets little help from the author, because he thinks Americans have too many "rights" as it is: rights to "recreation, sexual preference, abortion, childhood, and so on." Fukuyama attributes this mad extension of frivolous "rights" and the inability of people to agree on the true nature of human dignity, to the denial of "the possibility of autonomous moral choice," which in his view has been "the entire thrust of modern natural science and philosophy since the time of Kant and Hegel." Once again Nietzsche gets his due load of abuse: "Modern man now sees that there is a continuum from the 'living slime,' as Nietzsche put it, all the way up to himself," thereby ending up in "the justification for man's dominion over nature," an ineluctable logic leading to "the animal rights movement" (Foucault, 1980: 296–97). Fukuyama thus overlays caricatures of Hegel and Nietzsche on an argument about contemporary politics in America, with "philosophy" brought in to buttress, say, "family values" and Gingrich Republicanism, and every calumny laid against the many changes in American democracy since the civil rights movement, the student protests of the 1960s, and the rise of feminism and multiculturalism.

The essence of Nietzsche's teaching about modern life is that we are told we are free individuals, thus to deprive us of our real freedom; we are told that the people rule, so we won't notice how we are ruled; we are told to be moral, just as our leaders squander the moral capital they inherited from exemplary forebears; we are told that we live in the best of all possible worlds, so that we do not think about other possible worlds. Fukuyama encourages us to think that "History" has brought us to a state of grace, to the only conceivable system, whereas Nietzsche teaches that "man should above all learn to live and should employ history only in the service of the life he has learned to live" (1997: 116). He was in many ways the greatest of individualists, asking of human beings that they found their own true freedom, thus to overcome the false freedoms of contemporary society. This central element in Nietzsche's philosophy has resonance with Hegel's desire to find a higher unity in the "spirit" or "idea" that would overcome the discontinuities and fragmentation of modern life. For Nietzsche, however, Hegel's philosophy was the most elaborate justification imaginable for a self-satisfied complacency about the present, as if all history were merely the prelude to the age one happened to inhabit: as he wrote in *Untimely Meditations* (1997: 104), "for Hegel the climax and terminus of the world-process coincided with his own existence in Berlin. Indeed, he ought to have said that everything that came after him was properly to be considered merely as a musical coda to the world-historical rondo or, even more properly, as superfluous." (Elsewhere he was even less reverential toward Hegel: "Heirs of the world-process! Summit and target of the world-process! Meaning and

solution of all riddles of evolution come to light in modern man, the ripest fruit
of the tree of knowledge! . . . Overproud European of the nineteenth century,
you are raving!" [1997: 107–8])

If Fukuyama's philosophical learning is entirely one-sided, his broader argument cannot be dismissed by pointing out that history did not end in 1989—
for example, in the recrudescence of non-liberal politics in the 1990s, as in
Balkan collisions, Islamic fundamentalism, or skin-head fascism in Germany.
These he would see as atavisms that make his point that there is no longer a
significant alternative to liberalism that can excite men's minds or organize
masses of people; there is no longer any force that offers a top-to-bottom alternative to the liberal organization of modern life. In that he is right, if for the
wrong reasons; it is not the absence of the Soviet alternative, but the absence
or diminution of a variety of humane palliatives to an untrammeled capitalism
that marks our time. Today there is no serious alternative to neo-liberal orthodoxy, anywhere. Beginning around 1980 and pioneered by Margaret Thatcher
and Ronald Reagan, its demands for unfettered markets, massive deregulation,
and a pox on the house of labor carried before it not just the Western communist
states but deeply threatened the entire postwar domestic compact by which peoples the world over evolved some form of social market or safety net to protect
large sectors of the population against the worst effects of the capitalist business
cycle. Whether it is Germany's social market, Japan's egalitarian lifetime employment, France's admirable health care, vacation, and retirement system, the
American New Deal, or the manifold economic gains of the "Asian tigers," the
ruthless efficiencies of neo-liberalism have placed their political economies under the global jurisdiction of multinational corporations and their administrative
allies, like the International Monetary Fund.

What is the quality of life in this neo-liberal heaven, for the mass of humanity? The 1998 *Human Development Report* compiled by the United Nations
found that 80 percent of the world's people live in Third World countries, but
they have just 22 percent of the world's wealth. The lowest fifth of the nations
held 2.3 percent of the world's riches thirty years ago; today they possess exactly
1.4 percent. In more concrete terms, the assets of the three richest people in the
world exceed the combined GDP of the forty-eight least developed countries;
some 358 global billionaires have wealth equal to the combined incomes of the
world's 2.3 billion poor people, that is, nearly half of the global population; the
richest fifth of the world's people consume 86 percent of all goods and services,
45 percent of all meat and fish, 74 percent of all telephone traffic, and 87 percent
of all vehicles. Of some 4.4 billion people in the Third World (still connoted
as "developing countries" by the UN, even though most of them have not been
developing), three-fifths lack access to safe sewers, two-thirds lack toilets, one-
third have no access to clean water, and a fifth lack any kind of modern health
care. About one-quarter of Third World peoples are illiterate and, of these, two-
thirds are women. This report estimates that it would cost $13 billion to provide
basic health and nutrition to everyone in the world and $6 billion to give every

human being a basic education; meanwhile, Americans spend $17 billion annually on pet food and $8 billion on cosmetics.[1] It would be unfair to use such information in criticism of *The End of History*, however, if only because Fukuyama evinced not the slightest interest in the plight of Third World peoples; he was entirely concerned with the affairs of the First World.

THE END OF HISTORY OR THE CRISIS OF LIBERALISM?

It is a scandal that the end of the Cold War should have given us a book that flatters us to such unseemly degree, that plays up to the famed complacency and optimistic spirit of Americans, couched in the thoughts of a nineteenth-century German philosopher of legendary stuffed-shirt pretensions whom most college-educated Americans can be counted on never to have comprehended even if they chanced to read him, a philosopher whose relation to political power was also celebratory and complacent but about whom our author is gullibly idolatrous, an author who likewise moves seamlessly between political power (the State Department, the RAND Corporation) and ersatz punditry—and that this same book would not just become a bestseller, but be applauded by conservative and liberal alike, providing a vocabulary and a grammar to understand the 1990s. The megalomaniacal (or *megalothymotic*?) attempt to claim for the American defeat of Soviet communism an "end of History," a conclusion to the struggles of the modern world, flatters us and fools us into thinking that we triumphed over a worthy adversary, rather than a defensive and brittle movement that aspired to essentially the same things as "the last man" of contemporary American couch-potato-dom. Both World War II and the Cold War were contests of unequals, not in the sense that the United States towered over its antagonists—Germany, Japan, the USSR—in the sinews of national power (even though it did), but in the incommensurability of the enemy: to pit Hitler against Roosevelt, Truman against Stalin, or Brezhnev against Reagan and then tell us we must choose "freedom" is to completely trivialize the meaning of freedom; assuming the freedom to choose, who could possibly choose otherwise? In this sense, however, we have indeed moved into a new realm of freedom, because if we fail now there will be no Hitler or Stalin, no alien "ism," to blame it on. History is now up to us; it is no longer a matter of vanquishing monsters and demons: we are alone with ourselves and our fate.

To return to the question posed at the beginning, is there anything new about our world apart from the absence of the Soviet Union and the Cold War? The answer, in general, is no. Our contemporary world is an anticipated consequence, the liberal capitalist world order that was the ultimate goal of American planners in the 1940s. When the Other disappeared, the global structure they created continued in place and, in the 1990s, achieved the full florescence that its makers had imagined in the 1940s. That is, the "New World Order" that George Bush and many others cast about for after 1989 was both the same old order, and the ongoing fulfillment of it (to write like a Hegelian). The stunning events from

1989 to 1991 helped to unearth this obscured system, and the hegemonic role
that Roosevelt grasped for in 1941 and that Truman and Acheson consummated
in 1950: a hegemony that substituted for Great Britain's role as leader of last
resort in the world system, a hegemony never explained to the American people
but instead rationalized by an enemy made the more fearsome by being remote
and encapsulated, whether abroad or at home—an enemy of which we were
abruptly deprived by Gorbachev, thus terminating the countersystem that justified it all, and finally making conspicuous the other name of the Cold War
game: world economy. And as we come to understand that, we come to
understand the logic of the security structure formed in the early Cold War
period, one ostensibly directed against communism, but that also had the sur-
reptitious goal of containing our allies (a.k.a. our just-defeated enemies), Japan
and Germany. The second and third largest economies in the world, they are
still host to tens of thousands of American troops and to a raw material and
defense dependency that began in the 1940s and that shows no signs of ending.
It is that very structure that has held the peace since 1989, and that makes
realpolitik impossible for leaders in Tokyo and Berlin (Cumings, 1991).

Unified Germany does not dominate Europe, Japan has not gone nuclear,
China discovered the market, France has a world-historical predicament of national identity, and the American Century continues apace. This, in brief, is the
answer to why Fukuyama, Mearsheimer, and Huntington all got it wrong: *realpolitik* does not govern the contemporary actions of the big powers, local clashes
of older civilizations mask the burgeoning triumph of modern civilization (to
which they are also—and ineffectively—reactive), and the triumph of the liberal
program does not mean "the end of history" because modern liberalism is itself
a heterogeneous, contested and deeply unfinished business.

The Cold War order that came into being in the five years after World War
II was not a function of *realpolitik* strategies, geopolitical advantage (alone), the
triumph of American liberalism, or the aggression of the Soviet Union and its
allies. It took shape through a positive policy of industrial growth, designed to
restart the world economy in the 1940s, and in reaction to the anti-colonial
revolutions that swept the world for the three decades from 1945 to 1975. The
United States reacted to these forces by fighting two major hot wars in Korea
and Vietnam, by supporting some anti-colonial movements and opposing others,
by containing Soviet power, by establishing anti-communist points of strength
around the world, and by establishing distinct outer limits on its allies (especially
the just-defeated states of Germany and Japan), the transgression of which was
rare or even inconceivable, provoking immediate crisis—the orientation of Berlin or Tokyo toward the Soviet bloc, for example. The typical experience of this
hegemony for those included within it, however, was a mundane and mostly
unremarked daily life of subtle constraint, in which the United States kept allied
states on defense, resource, and, for many years, technological and financial
dependencies.

The hegemonic project of the 1940s was a complex and problematic episode in the history of a modern practice of liberalism that had defined as liberal an England that had a sharply inegalitarian class society, a highly restricted franchise (even after the reform act of 1867, only 30 percent of the adult population could vote), and an empire—one that had included not just a host of disenfranchised colonial populations, but through its trading relations, cotton production by millions of slaves and sharecroppers in the American South. The "free world" would include a United States that in 1945 was a democracy for the adult white population and an apartheid-like southern autocracy for the black population and other peoples of color. And during the Cold War, the liberal world order led by the United States included Trujillo's Dominican Republic, Tito's Yugoslavia, Suharto's Indonesia, Park Chung Hee's South Korea, and Mobutu's Zaire.

In other words, this was an order that could not be categorized simply as market driven or democratically governed. But there is still something distinct about what Robert Latham calls liberal modernity: it cannot be reduced to a mere capitalist modernity, a sly cloak for empire, or a libertarian empyrean where firms interact in the market and free individuals construct a civil society. Both states and markets existed long before capitalism and liberalism; liberalism may have "transformed states and markets in distinct and decisive ways," Latham writes, but to stop with that (say, representative democracy as a liberal political form) would ignore the international dimension of liberal modernity. If for Karl Polanyi the self-regulating market had an inherent tendency to transcend national boundaries, for Latham the same is true about the emergence and ordering logic of liberalism. One logic is indeed that of the market: liberal modernity is closely associated with open international exchange. But there is also the logic of individual rights, representative government, and collective self-determination. Then there is the historical recognition that so much of this was brand spanking new: most of those practices associated with liberalism—free trade, basic civil and political rights, universal suffrage, and national self-determination—can only be dated from the mid-nineteenth century as doctrine and (limited) practice, and only achieved global dominion after 1945. That states could be liberal but not democratic was a commonplace before that time. This is why Latham rightly emphasizes the "historicity, contingency, and mutability" of liberal modernism, as well as its heterogeneity: a dictatorship like Trujillo s was obviously not liberal, but its partial incorporation into the American-organized world order (connoted as the "free world") was a commonplace aspect of a plural and diverse order that, as a whole, remained a central part of liberal modernity. The partial inclusion of a tyrant like Trujillo reflected an essential element of liberal hegemony: the demarcation of boundaries, of limits to the realm, most often expressed negatively. The best thing one could say about Trujillo was that he was not a communist, and Washington would only support his overthrow if it were assured that the Dominican Republic would not go communist as a result.[2]

This is a potent form of hegemony, and it has a message: in the 1940s it crushed one form of statist empire and in the 1980s, another. Today it is eroding if not erasing the last formidable alternative system, the Japan-Korea model of state-directed neo-mercantilism (one undermined and made vulnerable by its inclusion in the postwar regional order). What is the message? The capitalist market, the open door, pluralist democracy, and self-determination. If this last element was often honored in the breach by Washington, it nonetheless has been a potent political and cultural ideal in the American arsenal since Woodrow Wilson first articulated his famous "Fourteen Points." Today this heterogenous mix of Wilson and Trujillo, Roosevelt and Batista, Bill Clinton and Jesse Helms, seems to have no rival on the horizon that could possibly hope to take its measure.

But just at this point of manifest victory and destiny—say, as the long boom that began in 1992 crested with modest worries a year ago about whether the stock market would gain another 20 percent in 1998—we were thrown unexpectedly back to the origins of our time, to a world economy ceasing to function. It began again surreptitiously, padding in on cat's feet with the run on the Thai *baht* in the early summer of 1997, then extending to South Korea and Indonesia, Russia and Latin America, with the insolvency of the world's second-largest economy shadowing curiously inert engines of growth. In September 1998 Bill Clinton called this the worst economic crisis in fifty years, and George Soros intoned that the world economy is "coming apart at the seams."[3] The global financial crisis has created a watershed in contemporary history where questions long buried by the demise of Western communism and a militant left in the democratic countries amid an appallingly self-congratulatory liberal triumphalism now come sharply to the fore. A systematic failure of capitalism struck precisely those economies long held up as models of industrial efficiency—the Asian "tigers"—and no one is quite sure what to do about it, or where it will end. Standing behind the travail of the smaller afflicted countries is perhaps a more stunning phenomenon: the shaky financial condition and political immobilism of the world's second largest economy, Japan, which has more than $1 trillion in bad loans and (for a country long praised for its efficient "administrative guidance"), a truly amazing crisis of governance. A sober and influential American economist wrote recently that this turmoil "produced financial contagion on a scale unprecedented since the collapse of the Creditanstalt in 1931," and he could not be sure that the ministrations of the International Monetary Fund (IMF) had halted its progress.[4] Nothing to date has come close to this crisis as a defining moment that tells us what the post-Cold War world will really look like and the problems it will present. The global financial crisis poses a host of questions unvoiced since the 1930s: What if investors panic? What if markets don't work? What if military and political power is beside the point?

In the first year of the crisis, roughly from July 1997 through July 1998, the United States used it to demand reforms in allied economies that had long been ignored during the Cold War. But when Acheson's second-best world, the world of blocs, of iron and bamboo curtains, unexpectedly disappeared, so did American indulgence for the neo-mercantilism of its East Asian allies, which was always a function of the Cold War struggle with their opposites. Since 1993 the "Clinton Doctrine" has been one of aggressive foreign economic policy designed to promote exports, to open targeted economies to American goods and investment (especially in service industries that now dominate the U. S. economy—accounting for 85 percent of GDP—and in which it has a barely challenged global lead), while maintaining the Cold War positions that give Washington a diffuse leverage over its allies like Japan and Germany and that pose a subtle but distinct threat to potential adversaries like China. All this goes on under the neoliberal legitimation of Smithean free markets and Lockean democracy and civil society.

Just as one would predict of a mature hegemonic power, the United States now prefers the virtues of a multilateral economism to the vices of direct coercion and intervention, and thus the IMF and the World Bank have vastly enhanced their utility in Washington's eye, and even the abandoned Bretton Woods mechanism—an international trade organization—has materialized in the form of the World Trade Organization (WTO). As China waxed and Japan waned on American horizons in the 1990s,[5] perhaps the breadth of American hegemony can be appreciated in China's beleaguered efforts to polish its application to the WTO, while Washington continues to demand more reform before approving Beijing's entry. A central preoccupation of American policy is to shape and channel China's position in the world market, so as to block the emergence of "another Japan," and the deep meaning and intent of the American and IMF response to the Asian liquidity crisis is to close the historical chapter in which the sheltered "developmental states" have prospered.

Japan, which pioneered the "developmental state," seemed just a few years ago to be the likely regional hegemon of the Pacific and perhaps the dominant force in the twenty-first century—quickly labeled a "Pacific Century." It had a dominant economic position in Southeast Asia and soon might organize China's entry into the world economy. But that did not happen, and the reason it did not happen lies in the history and practice of American hegemony: South Korea and Japan were sheltered economies, indulged in their neo-mercantilism and posted as engines of economic growth, because of the great value that had in the global struggle with communism. Now that this struggle is over, however, the issue of their "fit" with a new era of free markets and neoliberalism comes to the fore—to the surprise and shock of Koreans, and the consternation of the paralytic Japanese elite. The deep meaning of the Asian crisis therefore lies in the American attempt to ring down the curtain on "late" development of the Japan/Korea type, and the likelihood that they will be successful—because the strong, nationalistic neo-mercantilism of Japan and South Korea was propagated in the soft soil of semi-sovereignty, and because the Americans have paradoxically had willing accomplices in Northeast Asian peoples who have sought to reform or nullify this same model themselves. The central experience of Northeast Asia in the postwar period, in short, has not been a realm of independence where autonomy and equality reigned, but an alternative form of political economy enmeshed in a hegemonic web.

Washington's enduring regional configuration is suddenly shaky, however. The Asian crisis rippled through the region as the world market has begun to approximate the globe itself, with the recent addition of hundreds of millions of people in China and former Soviet bloc territories. The collapse of the Russian economy in August 1998 and the loss of billions of dollars of Western and IMF loans put a big hole in the world economy, and as this is written Brazil is teetering on the edge of collapse. Capital has entangled "all peoples in the net of the world market," in Marx's words, accounting both for the current economic boom in the core and the widespread sense that the dynamics of the whole are unstable. Americans now envision "Communist" China being an anchor of stability in East Asia, something that led President Clinton to dramatically cozy up to Beijing during his visit in June 1998, and to praise it for keeping its currency stable. Because the Chinese *renminbi* is nonconvertible, hedge fund speculators couldn't traffic in it, and because China (like Taiwan and Hong Kong) has maintained large foreign currency reserves, it has continued to grow (8 percent in 1999, a projected 7 percent in 2000). Meanwhile, the capitalization of the American equity market is now approaching 140 percent of GDP (compared to 82 percent in 1929), and the mutual fund industry has assets higher than all the banks ($5 trillion). Right now the global crisis is keeping American monetary policy expansionary, but a stock market crash is easily imaginable in the next couple of years (Hale, 1998: 13).

The pointman for the new ecumenical gospel, the IMF, attempts to impose hegemonic rules on everyone, "creating a level playing field" in conditions of structural inequality and hierarchy that tilt the game toward the United States and the advanced industrial countries; meanwhile, "free market" advocates castigate the IMF's secrecy, and even the global managers themselves wonder if a world in which trillions of dollars slosh around uncontrolled might be the source of financial chaos. This calls forth a demand for global regulation, for international macro-economic policies to stabilize the whole. Here is the essence of the conundrum that not just ordinary people, but the global bosses themselves cannot predict: can this brave new world in which capital spins out its telos in an historically unprecedented vacuum of alternatives be controlled or not?

And here we come, finally, to Doctrine X: Karl Polanyi's formula for understanding the deep meaning of the collapse of the world economy and the onset of global war in the 1930s (in *The Great Transformation*), and Immanuel Wallerstein's systematization of Polanyi's circulationist theory of market capitalism and a host of other insights from Polanyi, in his world-system theory. Nothing I have said so far is inconsistent with the analyses of either Polanyi or Wallerstein, and thus, Daniel Chirot's never-ending polemic against Doctrine X notwithstanding, it provides the most satisfying theory for figuring out what makes our world go round as we greet the twenty-first century. Chirot writes in this volume that "at its core," this perspective is "an argument about how the few core societies in the world enrich themselves by exploiting the majority in the periphery." I would say that this perspective is a theory about how the hegemonic power (that core power that designates itself as first among equals) helps to arrange a world order, or even a world society, by using its manifold, across-the-board superiority in a period of unusual dominance (England, 1815–1850, the United States, 1941–1970), to (in order of importance):

1. Write the rules of the game of the world economy.

2. Encourage global stability over long periods of time, by both promoting and satisfying a global middle class and a group of "middle class" rising powers (connoted as the "semi-periphery"), providing upward mobility to each and thereby keeping the system from polarizing into extremes.

3. Provide a discourse of involvement that appears to be universal, seeking to encompass all of humanity in ideals of liberty, equality, democracy, and self-determination; these ideals also possess a reverse dynamic, bringing pressure to bear inside the core to live up to those ideals (i.e., Washington's human rights programs since the 1970s are inexplicable apart from the civil rights movement and other struggles of the 1960s).

4. Maintain a shrewd *realpolitik* that keeps military bases near enemy territory and on allied territory, pragmatically making do with the material at hand (Trujillo again) while pushing that material in a liberal direction.

There is much more to be said, but an approach like this can make much more sense of the world we live in than can Fukuyama, Mearsheimer, or Huntington. This does not mean that Immanuel Wallerstein is Mr. X, but it does mean that he and Polanyi have understood the dynamics of global capitalism better than most of their peers, which is to say that they understand them almost as well as a Dean Acheson or a Robert Rubin. Lest you think this is facetious, listen to the thoughts of Dean Acheson, who expressed it concisely in a speech delivered shortly after Germany invaded Poland, entitled "An American Attitude Toward Foreign Affairs," a text truly pregnant with ideas that built the American Century.

As Acheson later put it in reflecting back on this speech, he had really sought at the time to "begin work on a new postwar world system."[6] "Our vital interests," Acheson said in this speech delivered at Yale, "do not permit us to be indifferent to the outcome" of the wars in Europe and Asia; nor was it possible for Americans to remain isolated from them—unless they wished a kind of eternal "internment on this continent" (only an Anglophile like Acheson would liken North America to a concentration camp). He located the causes of the war and the global depression that preceded it in "the failure of some mechanisms of the Nineteenth Century world economy" that had led to "this break-up of the world into exclusive areas for armed exploitation administered along oriental [sic] lines." In its time, "the economic and political system of the Nineteenth Century . . . produced an amazing increase in the production of wealth," but for many years it had been in an "obvious process of decline." Reconstruction of the foundations of peace would require new mechanisms: ways to make capital available for industrial production, the removal of tariffs, "a broader market for goods made under decent standards," "a stable international monetary system," and the removal of "exclusive or preferential trade arrangements." The world economy was his main emphasis, but in good Achesonian realpolitik fashion he also called for the immediate creation of "a navy and air force adequate to secure us in both oceans simultaneously and with striking power sufficient to reach to the other side of each of them." Dean Acheson later had the opportunity to implement these ideas, first at Bretton Woods, then with the Marshall Plan and the Truman Doctrine, and finally with NSC-68; he is the person who comes closest to being the singular architect of American strategy from 1944 to 1953.

But to return to our time, where will the world go from here? Perhaps the contemporary global crisis will prove to be just another *rondo* in Fukuyama's movement, toward the universality of liberal modernist norms and practices—after all, a major feature of American remedies for the crisis has been to call for an end to Japanese and Korean neo-mercantilism, and to continue the structural reform of the Russian and Brazilian economies. But it may also foretell a new chapter in world history, as the market approaches its full global reach, unfolding in a vacuum of alternatives and therefore testing, perhaps really for the first time, whether the self-regulating market can be the basis for global order—the recipe for a truly long peace, or for a truly unprecedented disaster. It is, in short, a crisis of liberalism, and it will tell us whether the unfolding development of liberal modernism has a proper claim to universality, or whether it remains merely the partial and limited world view of its original author, the modern middle class—and therefore unavailing to the continuing plight of the world's majority peoples.

NOTES

1. United Nations, *Human Development Report 1998*, as cited in "The News of the Week in Review" in *The New York Times*, 27 September 1998.

2. For elaboration see Cumings (2000), where I treat Robert Latham's argument (1997).

3. Quoted in *The Wall Street Journal*, 15 September 1998.

4. David Hale (1998: 1). I am indebted to Mr. Hale for sending me this paper.

5. An important nationwide poll of American attitudes on foreign affairs found in 1995 that while the mass of Americans (62 percent) continued to worry about economic competition from Japan, far fewer among the American elite (21 percent) still did so. Five years earlier the figures for both groups were 60 percent for the public, 63 percent for the "leaders." See Reilly (1995: 25).

6. Dean Acheson, "An American Attitude Toward Foreign Affairs," 28 November 1939, in Acheson (1965: 267–75); see also Acheson's reflections on the speech (ibid., 216–17). I am indebted to Heajeong Lee for bringing this text to my attention.

7

Radicalism, Resistance, and Cultural Lags: A Commentary on Benjamin Barber's *Jihad vs. McWorld*

Bernard Beck, Scott L. Greer, and Charles C. Ragin

In 1997, McDonald's ran a series of advertisements in the London Underground. Each had the phrase "A taste of home" in one of a dozen languages and a picture of an identical McDonald's meal: "Sabor Casero." "Un goût de chez vous." Should one eat such a meal, seeking familiarity in the foreignness of London, one could not then throw away the wrappers. The wastebaskets in the Underground system had been removed so that they could not hide bombs.

A reflective individual riding the Underground certainly might agree with Benjamin Barber that democracy does not really have the initiative. Barber bases his *Jihad vs. McWorld* (1995) on the observation that the most dynamic forces today are not states, or democratic communities, but two other forces that are both newer and much more malign. The first, "McWorld" is his name for the giant, unaccountable, Philistine, and faceless transnational corporations that are placing fast food restaurants on every city corner and attempting to control the contours of culture in their quest for growth and profit. Diminishing local difference and replacing it with plastic, vaguely American homogeneity, these corporations are internal dictatorships that are only barely subject to states or accountable to anybody. The second, "Jihad," is the angry and unreasoning response of the people who cannot be defined by their consumerism: the excluded, or those who are so starved of meaning that they join the most exclusivist and fanatic organizations to defend and purify their local culture. Jihad is the wave of violent assertions of local purity and exclusiveness that began with a trickle in the Basque Country or the West Bank and now propels new and increasingly violent struggles for recognition from any part of the world into the newspapers: American militias, Western European neo-fascists, Russian re-cidivists, Israeli settlers, Colombian narco-guerrillas.

With its echoes of 1960s critiques of consumerist mass society, and its intellectual roots sunk in a literature of cultural alienation that stretches through-out modernity from Romanticism to Riesman and Marcuse, Barber's description of McWorld echoes the disquiet anybody feels when they find that the oldest building in Heidelburg or a prime spot on the Boulevard Saint-Michel in Paris contain McDonald's outlets with counters and booths that look just like the ones back home in Muncie, or Tokyo. With its summary of the seemingly idiosyn-cratic groups that haunt modern politics or drive intimidating airport security measures, the concept of Jihad holds its appeal as a way to understand the inexplicable fanaticism of terrorists and rebels around the world. Both appear as valid ways to link what otherwise seem to be an almost random assortment of disturbing facts, from attacks by obscure "national liberation" warriors to the homogenous appearance of the world's teenagers.

Barber's further analytic innovation is to link the two forces. McWorld, dis-appointingly for those who see Western consumer culture as the ultimate cultural solvent, will call forth Jihad's radical local resistance as it displaces cultures and replaces them with a hedonic but ultimately vapid and intolerable consumerism. Thus does Jihad and its total denial of individualism or internationalism in the name of cultural purity feed off of the growth of transnational corporations employed in "content provision," or culture. A scholar who has published on Hegel, Barber adroitly links the two to argue that they exist only because of each other: those who argue that Western liberal capitalism excises "age-old ethnic rivalries" or "ancient demons" are in for an unpleasant surprise. He then draws the conclusion: in a world defined by the struggles of these two twinned forces, there is no place for democracy. The liberal democracy of the twentieth century, let alone more democratic forms of governance, is simply irrelevant to McWorld. Neither democracy's size, nor its preoccupations, nor its very under-standing of citizenship, dignity, and personhood have a place in a world where people are, simply, consumers. But the small communities of Jihad are no more willing to take democratic forms: as cries of rage they are hardly interested in moderation and rational citizenship, while as assertions of an identity in the face of homogenization they cannot tolerate the internal debate that makes a democ-racy. When Jihad and MacWorld are advancing, democracy must be retreating.

But is democracy retreating? For that matter, do Jihad and McWorld exist? Barber's thesis does fly in the face of some well-established social science, but its interest lies more in the issues that it brings to light. Something is causing cultural homogenization, and transnational corporations must have some effects; and on the other hand, the existence of radical localism and its increasingly bloody political effectiveness is difficult to dispute. After noting some of the points at which established research questions Barber's claims, this chapter will use Barber's descriptive concepts of radicalism, resistance, and laggardliness to rethink his categories.

Social scientists have had little difficulty ignoring Barber's work. *Jihad vs. McWorld* pays no attention to some of the most robust theories of democracy and the state. The clearest reason lies in one of the best-established facts about modern politics: the same rich advanced industrial states that are the heartlands of McWorld are also the longest and best-established democracies (Ruesche-meyer, Stephens, and Stephens, 1992). It is these states that show a clear relationship between prosperity and pluralist democracy (Przeworski and Limongi, 1997). In short, the data imply that liberal thinkers might have a point when they suggest that affluence and democracy are mutually constitutive. Certainly, the simultaneous advance of democracy and markets in the last two decades implies that liberal democracy and McWorld are not absolute opposites.

It is not, of course, difficult to critique the quality of democracy and the reach of the contemporary state: it excludes many and might be unable to act on their behalf even if it tried. And its democratic qualities might be seriously deteriorating. But, as Barber's baffling list of events, actors, institutions, and habits that constitute McWorld's threat to democracy implies (Barber, 1995, Chapters 2–9), the link between liberal democracy and liberal market economies is too complex to summarize only with the idea of "McWorld."

As for the nation-state, while there is no shortage of respectable current work lamenting or cheering its decline and fall (Garrett, 1998, Chapter 1), several intellectual traditions are well equipped to argue that the state system and the international capitalist economy grew up together and depend on each other. In world-system theory, Wallerstein (1979) has pointed out that the political fragmentation afforded by multiple independent states was what allowed capital and capitalists to escape political control and create the first transnational world economy. A polity the size of the world economy could control the disruptive effects of market society and thereby strangle McWorld, along with much economic growth and much misery, in its crib. The Western state and the state system, on the other hand, provided stable markets, a useful legal framework, and an exit option to capital. It thereby created the opportunity for the first market society to develop. This process is nothing new, of course; the Western, capitalist, world economy that drives talk of "globalization" today began in the sixteenth century.

Although these arguments have caused intellectuals of many stripes, from world-system to neoliberal and postmodern, to ignore, or occasionally mock, Barber's book, there is still significant value in using the phenomena that interest him and his analytical categories to raise new questions about the interplay of the local and the global. Barber interprets the phenomena of McWorld and the phenomena or Jihad as two dialectically opposed forces, a classic case of opposites that constitute each other and the whole. It is more valuable, however, to regard them both as part of a much longer and more complex historical process, one in which capitalists, states, intellectuals, and the middle classes all play their roles and which is too complex to be captured with only two analytic labels. To illuminate these historical forces and redeem the observations of Barber, this chapter advances a series of questions. What is radicalism? What is resistance? Who are the laggards? And which way is forward? The answers to these questions lead to a sketch of a future that differs from Barber's, but engages with the disquieting sense of cultural alienation and fear of fanatics that he observed.

WHAT IS RADICALISM?

One person's freedom fighter is the next person's terrorist. One person's social reformer is the next person's reactionary. Radicalism is relative. Like most things we are interested in, radicalism is socially constructed. It is important to go beyond this commonplace sociological observation, however, and explore how and under what conditions radicalism is constructed.

The meaning of radicalism matters for Barber's argument because, in effect, he posits that McWorld is radical. We are all prepared to accept the idea that the proponents of Jihad are radicals because they appear radically anti-modern in their use of traditional cultural forms linked to specific locales. But Barber, in effect, points out that a second radicalism haunts the globe today—McWorld. He makes McWorld seem radical by arguing that it is anti-democratic and then pairing it with a radicalism that is conventionally demonized—Jihad. Barber can label these two forces radical because they threaten institutions "we" (his readers) hold dear—democracy and its primary guardian, the nation-state. Barber, confusing radicalism with radical change, argues that both oppose these institutions with claims that are incommensurable and indigestible.

Radicalism, the label, is simply a way to tag the things one finds unpalatable. In many countries, having mass media owned by religious groups would be unpalatable. These radicals, it would be reasoned, sow seeds of conflict between religious groups and threaten the foundation of a carefully negotiated secular state. In other contexts, those advocating laissez-faire, market-driven economies would be seen as unpalatable radicals. These ideas could threaten a carefully constructed social contract.

How does any practice or movement come to be called "radical"? Who calls it so? At different times and in different circles, radical may be a compliment or an epithet. In Barber's lexicon, radical is negative, suggesting change that undermines fundamental, vulnerable institutions. The fragility and unlikelihood of democracy as established in nation-states is the conservative spirit of this approach. In action, however, radicalism is like chemotherapy. You don't pay the high price if you have other resources or other choices. From this perspective, the radical tag does not stick well to McWorld. The reputation for radicalism of the inexorable globalizing commodity market is not particularly central to its spread. The radicalism of sacred localism, though, is often seen as radical both by respectables and by the faithful.

Radicalism may be an attractive advertisement, capable of mobilizing masses and previously unorganized and unmobilized forces, but it is an expensive and risky strategy, because it scares and repels some respectable and resourceful forces. Although some enterprises may court support in the guise of a radical movement, some are so challenged that they are powerless to avoid the discrediting label of radical. The radicalism of fanatical sects is a tool that carries real costs and is taken seriously by many important audiences, while the "radicalism" of cosmopolitan rationality is often shared as a titillating metaphor by its agents in the first-class lounges of international airports. The fanatics cannot avoid the imputation of radicalism, a concomitant of attempts to swim against globalizing tides, while the cosmopolitans often relax in the knowledge that they need not announce their radicalism, nor need they sit still for the imputation.

Radicalism, therefore, is the label that must be borne by the less resourceful who are dependent on mass conversion. For them, radicalism is a character trait demanded of the faithful. Mother Courage says in the Brecht play that if the generals are unwise, then the soldiers must be brave. Likewise, when social change is not imminent, then change agents must be radical.

WHAT IS RESISTANCE?

McWorld will not prevail over Jihad, nor will Jihad prevail over McWorld. This is not a life-and-death struggle, but simply the order of things. Every system of power generates its own forces of resistance. As Foucault argued, where there is power, there is resistance—and the nature of the resistance against a structure of power is partially constitutive of the power structure itself.

Jihad, as radical localism, is a form of resistance that is partly a response to and partly constitutive of emerging globalism. It was not coincidental that Mexican peasants in Chiapas launched their offensive against the Mexican state on the very day that NAFTA took effect. Today, even the most peripheral social and political actors manipulate international media to press their demands against nation-states and transnational corporations. To be effective, local resistance must be globally framed. It must challenge not only the state, but also transnational actors. It must catch the eye of not only the local political authorities, but also CNN and the BBC.

Resistance, like radicalism, is thus relative. Resistance to social change is the continuation of social change by other means, and it accelerates change rather than slowing it. To choose another metaphor, resistance is a strategy for commandeering a seat on the exchange. Globalizing under the pressure of an international market system leaves most of humanity without any effective access to the trading pits. Resistance quite often wears the colors of implacable opposition in the process of demanding admission. It is a sign of the scarcity of official tickets of admission. The irrationality and fanaticism of this resistance is a necessary feature of an attempt to achieve participation without a license; it is in that sense highly rational, a refusal of "reasonable" rules that guarantee exclusion.

Resistance as a means to admission, which is at the core of most radical localism, is very different from a resistance that is more clearly radical. Consider the contrast between Jihad and the Unabomber. The Unabomber has recently found alternative means of access to publication, taking on the mantle of radicalism, announcing a project of resistance, based on the thesis that forward is altogether the wrong direction, when seen in terms of the possibilities for individuals to experience powerful action. His example shows the coincidence of Jihad and McWorld: both are clearly examples of mass action, dependent on the mobilization of collective forces and modern technologies.

The terminology of individual empowerment, self-esteem, actualization, and so forth, is recognizably descended in tone and spirit from the ideologies of civic virtue of the middle class, the union of democracy with individualistic spirituality. The Unabomber proposes a truly radical direction, not merely the anarchist smashing of the state and its rational culture, but the shrinking of the social world and the sacrificing of its tools and habits. Against that background, both Jihad and McWorld are virtual twins: they are simply the haves and the have-nots. The nation-state and its virtues are thus unlikely to be preserved except in their company, however noxious it may now appear to some.

WHO ARE THE LAGGARDS?

There is great temptation to make the contrast: McWorld (global, inevitable) versus Jihad (local, residual) and to see Jihad as anti-modern and reactive. If we look longitudinally, McWorld is the latest stage in a historical process that can safely be measured at 500 years. The conventional wisdom about social change is that McWorld is the ineluctable destination of history under European expansion. In fact, Europe is its incarnation. Jihad, on the other hand, is the big surprise of the last two decades; it was not supposed to be possible any more, according to futurists. McWorld is the direction of technological innovation and Jihad is the intense resistance of laggards.

Radical localism today, however, is anything but a primordial lag. Very often these "traditional" identities are carefully crafted and then exhibited on the world stage with great fanfare. If these identities were not consciously created, manipulated, and presented, they would escape the attention of global media. A commonplace sociological observation is that the larger and more powerful the core, the more powerful any successful opposition to the core must be, especially when it originates in the periphery. Typically, the accumulation of such power involves joining people together who before viewed each other as "different."

The Islamic Brotherhood, for example, brings together people in urban areas of Moslem countries around the largest social identity available to them—their religion. Their calling card is their provision of modern social services that the state has proven incapable of delivering. Fifty years ago—before massive urbanization in Third World countries—to join all these people together through religion would have been much more difficult. They would have viewed each other as being "too different." After all, they would have been from different villages, different geographic regions, and so on. Again, Jihad is not a primordial rejection of McWorld; it is the resistance of locals who are fully attuned to the new global order and who use up-to-date organizational strategies, technologies, and tactics.

Thus, mobilization around large-scale identities, even if they are relatively limited in scope (e.g., "Bosnian Serbs"), is as modern as the consumption of highly standardized global products. In fact, it could be argued that such mobilization involves the creation of a standardized product in the form of a relatively large-scale identity that is marketable in the social arena (Anderson, 1991). Groups representing these newly mobilized identities use media, political, and military strategies to enhance their visibility on the world stage. They bypass the nation-state in their attempts to gain leverage against the nation-state and against global forces.

If the radical locals are not the laggards, maybe it's those who advocate the nation-state and democratic institutions who are the laggards. In this perspective, these institutions are archaic forms that have outlived their usefulness. The world today offers two choices—the secure localism of Jihad and the vapid consumerism of McWorld. Nation-states are losing not only their sovereignty, but also their limited ability to offer solutions to the problems faced by the various subnations within their boundaries. As a primary mediator of the global economy, the nation-state fails as a site of resistance to McWorld. In fact, when there are globally induced crises like the debt crises of the 1980s, the state must struggle to maintain any semblance of legitimacy while the radical locals shine by comparison. But nation-states also fail as effective promoters of McWorld. For the most part, nation-states appear as nuisances to transnational corporations. They seem incapable even of keeping order among their subnations.

And what about the proponents of McWorld? It also could be argued that they are the cultural laggards. As is well known to anyone who has studied its history, capitalism, both global and national, promotes standardization and thus uniformity. But it also promotes difference. When consumers consume, they purchase identities. The identity-spawning nature of consumption is the key to understanding how modern (and postmodern) advertising works. Consumers reason: I am this kind of person (e.g., environmentally conscious), so I should purchase this kind of laundry detergent ("green"). Business enterprises today thrive on creating difference where none may have existed before. In effect, they create markets; they do not simply "identify" them. An examination of the recent history of Western capitalism (especially since the expansion of mass media in the middle part of this century) shows that its strength derives from its ability to exploit difference and to commodify identities, not its proclivity for standardization. Whether or not there are identities that are resistant to commodification (e.g., some Jihad-based identities) is an empirical question. The experience of the 1960s in this country and the more recent commodification of a variety of "New Age" religions suggest that such identities may be extremely rare.

What is McWorld? In Barber's view it is standardized production of standardized commodities, as devoid as possible of cultural content so that they are palatable to a world market. If this is McWorld, it is a cultural laggard. Modern (and postmodern) capitalism is centrally involved in the creation and exploitation of difference and identity. This feature, in fact, may be its greatest strength. To the extent that McWorld involves forced standardization, it is doomed to be superseded by a global capitalism that creates, exaggerates, and exploits difference.

WHICH WAY IS FORWARD?

The question: "Which way is forward?" can always be usefully approached through the question: "Who is driving?" or "Who is minding the store?" or, even more precisely, "Who are the proprietors of the movement in a particular direction?"

Preserving and strengthening the republic—Barber's central concern—continues to be the project of a particular segment of society: its middle-class, cultural elite. The proprietors of either Jihad or McWorld are less committed, perhaps grudging participants in the national contract. The middle-class perspective in the nation-state is based on ideologies that promote distinctive virtues:

- Order: people should be protected against the impulsive conduct of the mob or the plutocrat.
- Justice: disputes should be settled on the basis of rules, not power.
- Opportunity: enterprises and programs should be allowed to operate unmolested.
- Responsibility: everyone should be obligated to respect middle-class public goals.
- Freedom: no one should take advantage of middle-class weaknesses.
- Expression: negotiations about legitimacy should be respected by all.
- Learning: middle-class resources and advantages should be respected and valued, so the middle classes are respected and valued.
- Culture: ideologies and sentiments extolling middle-class excellence should be protected and fostered.
- Morality: conduct that cannot be compelled must be valued.
- Citizenship: the weak, the few, the obscure, the modestly endowed can take part in politics.

Respect for these virtues allows the middle class to achieve a powerful role in national society via legitimacy with other classes. The legitimacy of these working principles is a foundation for power that must operate in a world in which others have power through concentrated wealth, technical resources, the solidarity of large numbers, or the passionate energy of the committed.

The middle class is most concerned with the legitimacy of distinctively "civic" virtues because it depends on the forbearance of others. The middle class can enjoy benefits of social life if they are not excluded by the greed of those with more resources (e.g., college access to the "meritorious" children of the middle class) or expropriated by the resentment of those with less (e.g., quiet enjoyment of public parks and transportation). While the lower classes sometimes benefit from competitive access to opportunities and the upper classes sometimes benefit from the prevalence of civility, the middle class is the main beneficiary.

For these reasons, the nation-state is especially valuable to the middle class. The customary usages and sentimental supports for synthetic communalism that the democratic state embodies are the major protection for middle-class prosperity (in the widest, not merely financial, meaning of that word). The middle class is most vulnerable to the war of all against all, so it needs the sovereign most. Therefore, it is most devoted to the Hobbesian ideology that explains why everyone should prefer to live under Leviathan. When the nation-state is not the primary reference point for "society," the rules of "society" are more negotiable, negotiable in ways that leave the middle class disadvantaged.

Both Jihad and McWorld undermine or at least by-pass the guardian of the middle class—the nation-state. If, as Barber implies, these two forces are locked in a terminal struggle—each growing more powerful as it counteracts the other—then the democratic nation-state is truly threatened. However, the proprietors of the democratic nation-state—the middle class—are also central to the advancement of both McWorld and Jihad.

The core idea driving McWorld is an image of a world of consumers—mostly mass-market, middle-class consumers. Mass consumption is as much a middle-class project as is the nation-state. The success of McWorld implies an expansion of the world's middle class and a deepening of the global process of commodification. If indeed, as we have argued, the middle class is most dependent on the nation-state, the expansion of McWorld will entail a growing demand for the kind of "protection" that the nation-state offers. Today, the nation-state is the one institution that enshrines and protects middle-class values.

Jihad is also dependent on the middle class. Although the literature on subnationalism (the key example of Barber's idea of Jihad) is chaotic and inconsistent, one idea that has gained much empirical support is that the primary social basis of subnationalism is the middle-class intelligentsia (Anderson, 1991; Gellner, 1983; Hroch, 1985; Ragin, 1986). As already noted, the cultural differences that inspire subnationalisms often require careful crafting and marketing. These are middle-class skills, especially those of the middle-class intelligentsia. Furthermore, the primary beneficiaries of the subnational project are often "local dominant strata," especially the local promoters and guardians of place-based culture (Ragin, 1980, 1986). These range from government bureaucrats and school teachers to shopkeepers and cultural entrepreneurs. The proliferation of mini-states implied in Jihad also involves a proliferation of government jobs and cultural institutions. Jihad is thus based in part on the middle

class, and, if successful, expands the size and influence of many different segments of the middle class.

Add to this mix a heavy dose of postmodern capitalism—an economic system
that thrives on difference—and you have a potent social cocktail. This view
rejects the idea that there is a fundamental antimony between McWorld and
Jihad—an argument that is central to Barber's theses. Instead of a world torn
apart by the conflict between McWorld and Jihad, we have cultural and political
cacophony, with the forces of "difference" (which often include both McWorld
and Jihad) sometimes reinforcing, sometimes contradicting the forces of middle-
class order and civility (as represented in the project of the democratic nation-
state). This global socio-cultural soup includes:

- A globalized capitalism that attempts to exploit difference, including differences generated by Jihad.
- Continued expansion of the world's consuming classes and a deepening of commodification.
- A continuing Jihad of radical localism, enlarging in it a. a middle class of state-
  needing citizens.
- Continued expansion of the middle class, including many who are devoted to place-
  based cultures that they can control or monopolize.
- Increased demands for the protection by the nation-state of middle-class values, as
  various forces expand the size of the middle class and increase its sense of vulnerability.
- Increasingly serious legitimation problems for the nation-state, as it appears more and
  more impotent in the face of economic globalism and radical localism.

Both Jihad and McWorld offer dubious temptations to the middle class in the
short run. In the long run, however, these two forces strengthen the middle class
that constitutes them in complementary and contradictory ways, and the demand
for effective nation-states multiplies at the very historical moment that they
struggle to maintain their authority and legitimacy.

8

Formations of Globality and Radical Politics

Arif Dirlik

The following discussion undertakes two tasks. The first is to outline a number of influential representations of globality, mark their distinctions, and point to the ways in which they complement and contradict one another. On the basis of what these representations have to say about the condition of globality, secondly, I draw certain conclusions concerning the possibilities for radical politics under contemporary circumstances. I am most concerned here with the reconfiguration in recent years of global relations, why these changes have rendered irrelevant earlier forms of radicalism, associated mostly with socialism, and why the largely invisible radical activities of the present take the forms that they have taken.

My point of departure is globalization, which over the last decade has replaced modernization as a paradigm of change and a social imaginary. Globalization has an obvious appeal to a political left that has been committed all along to internationalism, equality, and closer ties between peoples. The euphoria over globalization, however, has served to disguise the very real social and economic inequalities that are not merely leftovers from the past, but are products of the new developments. There is some question as to whether globalization represents the end or the fulfillment of a Eurocentric modernization.

Globalization as a discourse would seem to be increasingly pervasive, but it is propagated most enthusiastically from the older centers of power, most notably the United States, fueling suspicion of the hegemonic aspirations that inform it. Economic and political power may be more decentered than earlier, but globalization is incomprehensible without reference to the global victory of capitalism, and pressures toward the globalization of "markets and democracy" are at the core of globalization as they once were of modernization. Cultural conflicts are played out even more evidently than before on an ideological and institutional terrain that is a product of Eurocentric modernization. Finally, unlike in an earlier period of socialism and Third World alternatives, challenges to Eurocentrism come mostly from those who have been empowered by their very success in making capitalist modernity their own, whose challenges are voiced in the language of that modernity, and whose vision of alternatives is inescapably refracted through the lens of their incorporation into a capitalist world economy. Despite all the new kinds of challenges to which it has given rise, globalization may well represent the universalization of developmentalism in its capitalist guise (as its socialist counterpart is no longer an issue).

It is not clear, in other words, whether globalization is the final chapter in the history of capitalist modernity as globalized by European power, or the beginning of something else that is yet to appear with any kind of concreteness. The emancipatory promise of globalization is just that, a promise that is perpetually deferred to the future, while globalization itself creates new forms of economic and political exploitation and marginalization. Some problems thrown up by globalization, especially environmental ones, are conceded by its very engineers. Others are represented merely as legacies of the past that will be eliminated as globalization fulfills its promise. Ideologues of globalization may promise plenty for all, but as a number of studies have revealed, the actual forecast of what globalization promises is much more pessimistic: the marginalization of the majority of the world's population, including many in the core societies. Economic marginalization also implies political marginalization as, in the midst of spreading democracy, the most important decisions concerning human life are progressively removed beyond the reach of electorates. The world may be reconfigured, but the reconfiguration takes place under the regime of capitalism that continues to reproduce under new circumstances, and in new forms, with the inequalities built into its structuring of the world.[1]

This is what makes a radical critique as relevant today as it has ever been, perhaps more so. Such critique, if it is to be meaningful, must be informed by a recognition of changed circumstances, rather than a nostalgic attachment to its historical legacy. It is important, therefore, to begin with a few words about what may or may not be new about globalization as a contemporary phenomenon.

GLOBALIZATION OLD AND NEW

There is a paradox in arguments for globalization. Its proponents represent it at once as a novel phenomenon of the contemporary world *and* as a process that has characterized the human condition since its origins. The latter on occasion takes trivial forms that are not easily distinguishable from earlier diffusionist arguments. It is hardly big news that human beings have been on the move since their origins somewhere in East Africa more than two million years ago. Nor is it a major breakthrough in views of the past that there have been all along interactions among societies, some of them quite consequential. That we should analyze the histories of societies in terms of these relationships rather than in their isolation is an important epistemological argument, but that too has been around for quite some time, perhaps going back to Herodotus and Sima Qian but most conspicuously to Enlightenment views of history. What may be novel about the present, at least in the United States, is the projection of a contemporary consciousness of globality onto the entire past, therefore erasing important historical differences between different forms and dimensions of globality not only in material interactions among societies but perhaps more important in the consciousness of globality. It also erases critical consciousness of its own conditions of emergence.

The confounding of these differences also obviates the need to account for the relationship of contemporary globalization and its material/mental consequences to its historical precedents, including its immediate historical precedents. Is it possible that consciousness of globalization ebbs and flows in response to historical circumstances, but that the ebbs and flows carry different meanings at different times, and for different peoples occupying different locations in global arrangements of power? If so, what is the relationship between power and ideologies of globalization? On the other hand, if there is a secular trend to globalization, where in the past do we locate it?

The preferred answer to the last question is the origins of capitalism, because it is with the emergence of capitalism that it is possible to detect a continuing trend toward the globalization not only of economic activity, but of politics and culture as well. To privilege capitalism in the dynamics of globalization is not to imply that capitalist globalization itself has no history. As I will suggest, the "ebbs and flows" either of globalization or consciousness of it did not disappear with the emergence of capitalism. But aside from culminating in the eighteenth century in the mapping of the world as we know it today, capitalism provided not only a sustained motive force for globalization, but served also as the vehicle for the unification of the world under a new European hegemony. If the origins of capitalism lay in its prehistory in earlier modes of production, that neither negates the unprecedented historical role capitalism was to play in unifying the world, nor does it render the whole of human history rather than the structures of capitalism as the historical context for contemporary globalization. What Karl Marx and Friedrich Engels wrote in the middle of the nineteenth century might have seemed fantastic in their day, but it is an eerily apt description of ours:

The discovery of America, the rounding of the Cape, opened up fresh ground for the rising bourgeoisie. The East-Indian and Chinese markets, the colonisation of America, trade with the colonies, and increase in the means of exchange and in commodities generally, gave to commerce, to navigation, to industry, an impulse never before known. ... Modern industry has established the world market, for which the discovery of America paved the way. ... The bourgeoisie has through its exploitation of the world given a cosmopolitan character to production and consumption in every country. . . . All old-established national industries have been destroyed or are daily being destroyed. They are dislodged by new industries, whose introduction becomes a life and death question for all civilised nations, by industries that no longer work up indigeneous raw material, but raw material drawn from the remotest zones; industries whose products are consumed, not only at home, but in every quarter of the globe. In place of the old wants, satisfied by the productions of the country, we find new wants, requiring for their satisfaction the products of distant lands and climes. In place of the old local and national seclusion and self-sufficiency, we have intercourse in every direction, universal inter-dependence of nations. And as in material, so also in intellectual production. The intellectual creations of individual nations become common property. National one-sidedness and narrow-mindedness become more and more impossible, and from the numerous national and local literatures there arises a world-literature. . . . The bourgeoisie, by the rapid improvement of all instruments of production, by the immensely facilitated means of communication, draws all, even the most barbarian, nations into civilisation. . . . It compels all nations, on pain of extinction, to adopt the bourgeois mode of production. . . . In a word, it creates a world after its own image. (Marx and Engels, 1888[1986])

As Giovanni Arrighi has argued recently, capital has been globalizing all along, even before there was a structured and structuring entity that could be recognized as a "capitalist world-system" (Arrighi, 1994). Arrighi in turn draws on the work of Fernand Braudel, which in its analysis of the emergence of a European world-system recognizes the existence of a multiplicity of regional world-systems, with their own interactions, insertion into which enabled the bourgeoisie of Europe first to construct a European world-system, and subsequently to create the economic and political institutions that enabled them to draw all these other world-systems within the orbit of Europe to create a world-system that was global in scope (Braudel, 1979).[2] In the case of both authors, the emphasis is on the role of finance in globalization. Financial expansion required an alliance between a globalizing capital and the territorial state, but also created contradictions between the two because of their conflicting orientations to territorial grounding. The contradiction is important to grasping the changing relationship between capital and the state under the capitalist mode of production; contemporary globalization may represent one more shift in the relationship.

The argument is highly plausible, and so is the definition of capitalism that informs it, which identifies capitalism with the emergence of large enterprises devoted to the accumulation of capital. But it is also questionable for ignoring both production and issues of culture, especially for the period after the eighteenth century. Accumulation may be the goal (and the defining feature) of capital, but production may be essential to comprehending both sources of national power, and the foreshortening of the cycles of accumulation and dispersion that is important to Arrighi's analysis in particular. On the other hand, it is also important to explain why the creation of the nation-state accompanied mechanisms of accumulation at one stage of globalization, while its dissolution or the qualification of its powers would seem to be a feature of contemporary globalization. Such questions require closer attention, I think, to the relationship between accumulation, production, and national markets. It is also important to recognize that national cultures, once they had been created, also have played autonomous roles in influencing, if not shaping, the activities of both states and capital.

Although the capitalist world-system as it emerged in the fifteenth to the seventeenth centuries may provide the historical-structural context for contemporary globalization, it is necessary, however, to comprehend the particular features of the latter to account for the history of capitalism itself, and what I referred to previously as "ebbs and flows" both in its processes, and in the consciousness of globalization. Globalization may be viewed as an irrevocable process, at least from the time when Marx and Engels penned the *Communist Manifesto*. And consciousness of globality would proceed apace, not just among EuroAmericans who through imperialism and colonialism compelled it on increasingly broader constituencies in the world. But the very process of globalization created its own parochialism, including the parochialism of the European bourgeoisie, as Marx and Engels noted in their ironic reference to what the bourgeoisie calls "civilization." If globalization was to become an everinescapable phenomenon, it was through colonialism, nationalism, and socialism that were at once products of globalization and efforts to shape it in some ways, or even to restrain it, as in the case of nationalism and socialism. The immediate predecessor for contemporary conceptualizations of globalization is modernization discourse, grounded in what the (by then predominantly U. S.) bourgeoisie called "civilization," and the alternative to it provided by socialist modernization. While locked in deadly opposition, these two alternatives ironically shared a common commitment to developmentalism, and each sought to draw into its orbit the nations of the postcolonial world, themselves anxious to develop so as to overcome the legacies of colonialism and enhance national autonomy and power. The "three worlds" of modernization discourse, moreover, all conceived of modernization in terms of national units, which disguised the fundamental ways in which both the "three worlds" idea, and the idea of the nation, were premised on prior assumptions and processes of globalization (Dirlik, 1997).

The immediate context for contemporary forms and consciousnesses of globality is the breakdown of this mapping of the world, first with the transformations that rendered increasingly questionable the idea of the "Third World," and subsequently with the abandonment and/or fall of the socialist alternative. Already in the late 1960s and early 1970s important alternatives had emerged that questioned the nation-based, culturalist assumptions of modernization discourse. As a new global situation emerged in the 1980s with transformations within capitalism, most important the decentering of economic power with the appearance of competitors to United States hegemony, the analysis of capitalism itself assumed greater complexity. Finally, as the post-Cold War promise of a "new world order" in the early nineties has given way to evidence of new kinds of disorder, drawing on sources of identity that are as old as, if not older than, modernity, still other analyses of globality have become an urgent necessity.

Contemporary analyses of globality may be divided roughly between those that stress changes in the political economy of capitalism, and those that are primarily culturalist in orientation. Most important among the former in my view are world-system analysis that has its origins in the radical response of the 1960s to modernization discourse, analyses emerging in the eighties that are based on a "new international division of labor," and, most recently, the important contribution of Manuel Castells in his idea of a "network society." Culturalist approaches may be viewed best through the left-liberal proponents of globalization who eschew or are explicitly critical of political economy approaches, and the more conservative culturalism of Samuel Huntington who perceives in culture not a unifying but a divisive force in a renewed fracturing of the world.

THE POLITICAL ECONOMY OF GLOBALIZATION

World-System Analysis

The term "world-system" became current in the early 1970s, primarily in connection with Immanuel Wallerstein's studies of the origins of capitalism. It is necessary, however, to place Wallerstein's own work within the context of the seventies in order to appreciate its impact. World-system analysis was received with enthusiasm above all because of its challenge to modernization discourse, which had dominated the social sciences in the United States and Europe since the end of World War II, and it is not surprising that it found the greatest favor with young radical scholars who had come of scholarly age in the sixties, who were for the most part students of the Third World. Equally influential (intellectually if not institutionally) were the works of Samir Amin, Andre Gunder Frank, and the Latin American "dependency" theorists who proposed alternatives to modernization discourse that shared much in common with the work of Wallerstein in their theoretical assumptions and political conclusions. In all cases, the new approaches to the study of development were informed by the radical movements of the sixties against imperialism. Wallerstein's work was distinguished by his efforts to go beyond contemporary problems of development to offer a systematic account of the rise of capitalism from its origins in Europe to its globalization in the twentieth century (Wallerstein, 1998).

For the last two decades, world-system analysis has offered the foremost alternative to modernization discourse in the explanation of problems of development and underdevelopment. Modernization discourse, as it took shape in the years after World War II, was basically culturalist in the explanations it offered to problems of development, which was evident in the initial phrasing of the problem of development in terms of "modernity" and "tradition." Modern societies were those societies (in Europe and North America, soon to be joined by Japan) that had somehow liberated themselves from the hold of the past to create rational modes of thought and rational institutions; traditional societies were those that remained wedded to the past both culturally and institutionally and were unable, therefore, to break into modernity. In this distinction backward and traditional were nearly synonymous while development was associated very closely with progress toward the norms embodied by EuroAmerican societies. Before the 1980s, modernization proponents rarely spoke of "modernity" with reference to capitalism, but rather represented EuroAmerican modernity as the norm of progress that all societies must follow in order to escape their backwardness. Modernization discourse was Weberian in inspiration in its emphasis on the normative power of values associated with EuroAmerican modernity; what was missing from it was Max Weber's recognition of the fundamental significance of material conditions (necessary but not sufficient) as well as Weber's critique of "rationalization." Modernization discourse took the norms of EuroAmerican modernity as positive values that guaranteed ceaseless human progress. We should note, finally, that modernization discourse, because of its emphasis on cultural values, represented the problem of modernization as a problem internal to societies, a function of their own internal institutional and value structures, without reference to relationships between societies. Hence the impact of Europe and the United States on "traditional" societies appeared as a progressive force, and any impediments to progress derived from the historical inertia of the "backward" societies themselves. It is ironic that for all its emphasis on the burden of the past, modernization discourse was quite unhistorical in ignoring vast differences among "traditional" societies, as well as the shaping of *their* modernities by EuroAmerican capitalism. Similarly, revolutions, understood primarily as communist revolutions, appeared in modernization discourse as some form of inertial resistance to progress that must disappear as modern rationality overtook revolutionary societies.

By the late sixties, even some among modernization theorists, most notably S. N. Eisenstadt and Samuel Huntington, among others, had come to be critical of the teleological assumptions of modernization discourse. But their own efforts to deal with these problems, rather than question the premises of modernization as progress, primarily addressed the question of how to bring under control the disorder created by modernity to salvage the whole process of modernization. Huntington's recognition that revolutions were products not of historical inertia but of the very process of modernization, for instance, was a significant revision of the politics of modernization; his concern, however, was less with what revolutions had to say about modernity than with ways to control their emergence, which was to lead to an affirmation of authoritarian regimes—modernization minus democracy, in other words. What he has had to say about globalization in recent years, which I will discuss below, is in many ways continuous with this earlier position, now shifted to the terrain of civilizations (Huntington, 1968).

The main challenge to modernization discourse was to come from world-system analysis that, informed by a neo-Marxist understanding of capitalism from Third World perspectives, questioned basic assumptions of modernization. To recapitulate briefly what I take to be the fundamental propositions of world-system analysis, that also enunciate its differences from modernization discourse: (a) World-system analysis takes capitalism as the central datum of modernity, and seeks to understand the structuring of the modern world by capitalism as a mode of production. In this, it is clearly Marxist in inspiration. (b) World-system analysis differs from orthodox, Stalinist, Marxism, however, in its insistence that capitalism may not be understood in terms of the internal development of individual nations, but must be understood in terms of spatial relationships that transcend nations and give form to them; hence the term, world-system, which refers not to the whole world (except in its ultimate fulfillment), but to spaces that are more or less self-contained in terms of commodity production and exchange. As a world-system adherent has written, "Rather than taking states as self-evident units of analysis that are then related to each other through trade, investment flows, and labor exchanges, world-system scholars view these units as being constituted and continually reconstituted by the relations between and among them" (Palat, 1993). (c) It follows that world-system analysis introduces space into the analysis of development as a central datum; the relations between different societies are not merely relations in time (say, between advanced and backward, developed and underdeveloped), but also simultaneous relations in space. One consequence of this emphasis on space, to which I will return, is to question the teleology of modernization: that all societies must move in a single temporality of which Europe and North America are the most advanced instances. (d) In the analysis of spatial relations, world-system analysis takes as the most crucial relationship that between "core" and "periphery," which refer respectively to the centers of capital marked by economic and social complexity, relatively autonomous in their economic structure, and the areas that are economically, socially, politically, and culturally dependent on the cores. A third term, "semiperiphery," is used to refer to those areas that do not clearly belong in either one or the other. (e) These premises imply that world-system analysis focuses not on independent and autonomous economic, social, and political units, but on relationships between such units, and how the units themselves are constituted by such relationships. Core-periphery relations are not the premises but the consequences of capitalist development; development and underdevelopment do not describe states that are independent of one another, but are consequences of capitalist relationships. "Underdeveloped" societies are not "underdeveloped" due to some abstract measure, but are underdeveloped by the relations between core and periphery (in Gunder Frank's memorable words, "the development of underdevelopment"), just as the developed owe much of their development to the underdevelopment of others. From this perspective, there are no "modern" and "traditional" societies. All societies that are part of the capitalist world-system are "modern" societies. The difference is that some belong in the capitalist core, others in the capitalist periphery. Second, it is impossible to argue, therefore, that all societies may progress once they have broken with the past; peripheral societies are condemned to underdevelopment by their very peripheral status. This also suggests, finally, that within the capitalist world-system, it is impossible for all societies to advance, since the core-periphery relationship is essential to the structure of capitalism. What may happen, however, is that these relationships may be reconstituted so that cores and peripheries may shift spatially. (f) It is necessary, finally, to note an implication of world-system analysis for socialism. So long as the capitalist mode of production and exchange is the structuring principle of the world-system, socialism is possible only on condition of "de-linking" (the term is Samir Amin's, and the inspiration Maoist), since incorporation into the capitalist world-system by definition precludes the possibility of economic organization directed to the satisfaction of local needs, rather than the demands of capital. This, I may note, was a central issue of Chinese Marxism in the 1920s, inspired by Lenin and Trotsky's analyses of imperialism.

As I noted previously, Fernand Braudel, whose own work was an inspiration for world-system analysis, was to carry world-system analysis further back in time to explain the emergence of a Europe dominated world. According to Braudel, at the beginning of the modern world, there were a number of world-systems, of which the European was only one, and a peripheral one at that. Others were East and Southeast Asia, with China at the core, South Asia with India at the core, the Ottoman Empire, the Russian Empire, Central African kingdoms, and the Indian Empires of the Americas. The history of the modern world is, then, the emergence of capitalism in Europe as Europeans progressively inserted themselves as intermediaries between these more or less self-contained world-systems, and managed in the end to incorporate them into a capitalist world-system emanating from Europe. This is the process through which, by the twentieth century, a global world economy was to come into existence, ultimately with the United States at its core.

I am not concerned here with the merits and the demerits of world-system analysis, which has been criticized from a number of perspectives. These criticisms have not been successful in undermining its explanatory power (Arrighi, 1998a). World-system analysis presupposed globalization before that term acquired popularity, and retains its importance as one representation of global formations. Already by the 1980s, however, changes within capitalism, the emergence of other centers of economic power, particularly in East Asia, and the increasingly visible turn to capitalism in socialist societies were to bring globalization to the forefront of consciousness, and necessitate new analyses that were to produce different representations of globality.

Global Capitalism

Following my earlier usage, I will describe this new phase of capitalism as global capitalism (Dirlik, 1994), although others have described it variously as "the regime of flexible production," "the regime of flexible accumulation," or

"disorganized capitalism." Fundamental to the structure of the new global capitalism is what F. Frobel and others have described as "a new international
division of labor" (Frobel, Heinrichs, and Kreye, 1980); in other words, the
transnationalization of production where, through subcontracting, the process of
production (even of a single commodity) is globalized. Although world-system
analysts have rightly indicated that "commodity chains" (or "integrated production processes") are as old as the history of capitalism, it is undeniable that new
technologies have expanded the spatial extension of production, as well as its
speed, to an unprecedented degree in what David Harvey has described as "time-
space compression" (Harvey, 1989). Nor is it possible to deny the political,
social, and cultural consequences of the new practices. Beginning with East
Asia, the new practices have brought into the processes of production "Third
World" locations, scrambling earlier mappings of the world. As production cuts
across national boundaries, it also calls into question economic sovereignty as
a definition of national integrity. Socially, the new technologies have endowed
capital and production with unprecedented mobility, so that the location of production seems to be in a constant state of flux, seeking for maximum advantage
for capital against labor, as well as the avoidance of social and political interference in the activities of capital (hence, "flexible production"). Combined with
new media practices, its cultural consequences have been equally drastic; as the
new capitalism cuts across political boundaries, so it also does across cultural
ones. Its globalization is accompanied by a localization, as capital moves from
location to location.

For purposes of this discussion, the situation that emerged in the eighties, or
became apparent then, may be summarized as, (a) the decentering of capitalism
with the emergence of new centers, that were themselves the products of globalization of capital, but in turn contributed to the reality and consciousness of
a new globality. East Asia is the most conspicuous, but may not be the only
one. World-system analysts, among others, point to East Asia as a possible new
core in the unfolding of the world-system. The recent crisis in East and Southeast
Asia may be only temporary, the product of a transition. On the other hand, it
has also revealed fundamental structural weaknesses in the new "miracle" economies that have been there all along, but remained unacknowledged so long as
the economies seemed to be flourishing. It is also possible that we are witnessing
the reconfiguration of global relations that is implicit in the description of the
new economic configuration as "a high-tech Hanseatic League"; a network of
"global cities" (in Saskia Sassen's term), in other words, that together form the
core of the global economy (Sassen, 1991). Other observers, such as Kenichi
Ohmae, perceive it more as a network of "regional economies," many silicon
valleys linked together by the "information highway" (Ohmae, 1995). Central
to a core thus envisaged are transnational corporations, which have taken over
from national markets as the loci of economic activity, which provide not just
a passive medium for the transmission of capital, production, and commodities,
but determine the nature of the transmission and its direction. The interesting

thing about a core thus envisaged is that it may be a core without a periphery, because what used to be peripheries increasingly may be marginal to the operations of the core. Hope of survival, not to speak of power, seems to be contingent under the circumstances on the possibility of joining the core. I may note here, if only in passing, that the globalization of capitalism was a crucial reason for the fall of socialist states that insisted on creating their own alternative spaces, for they faced the alternative of joining in, which for the most part they have, or being marginalized. (b) The transnationalization of production is the source at once of unprecedented unity globally, and unprecedented fragmentation that is systemic (hence "disorganized capitalism"). The homogenization of the globe economically, socially, and culturally is such that Marx's comments, premature for his time, finally seem to be on the point of vindication. At the same time, there is a parallel process of fragmentation at work; globally, in the absence of a center to capitalism, and, locally, in the fragmentation of the production process into supra- or subnational regions and localities. As supranational regional organizations manifest this fragmentation at the global level, localities within the same nation competing to place themselves in the pathways of capital represent it at the basic local level. Nations themselves, it is arguable, represented attempts historically to contain fragmentation, but under attack from the outside (transnational organizations) and the inside (subnational economic regions and localities), it is not quite clear how this new fragmentation is to be contained. A global level of governance that the new economic configuration urgently demands further restricts the ability of nation-states to answer to their constituencies. At the same time, fragmentation of state power encourages the resurfacing of dormant conflicts contained earlier by the nation-state. (c) A final important consequence of the transnationalization of capital may be that for the first time in the history of capitalism, the capitalist mode of production appears as an authentically global abstraction, divorced from its historically specific origins in Europe. In other words, the narrative of capitalism is no longer a narrative of the history of Europe; so that for the first time non-European capitalist societies, the very products of European capitalist globalization, make their own claims on the history and culture of capitalist modernity. Apparent cultural homogenization accompanying globalization produces its own cultural fragmentations.

Simultaneous globalization and fragmentation that has characterized the world since the 1980s is visible in many other phenomena, from movements of populations to the emergence of new transnational institutions, challenges to Eurocentrism in the very language that was created by a Eurocentric capitalism, the resurgence of ethnic and religious fundamentalisms in the midst of homogenization of everyday cultural habits, and so on and so on. And at some point, I would hesitate to assign causal priority to some phenomena over others as, all of a sudden, both the products of capitalist modernity and cultural habits long suppressed by capitalism and the nation-state find themselves on the same stage, engaging in cooperation as well as deadly conflict. Challenges to the hegemonies of the past are very much the order of the day, but the challenges themselves would seem to be limited in their horizon by their inability to think beyond their past legacies or present circumstances.

If I may repeat what I suggested at the beginning, globalization as it emerged in the eighties, and has gained strength in the nineties, represents significant departures from the immediate past, but it also contains as some of its vital elements long-standing characteristics of the dynamics of capitalism. World-system analysts are wrong to the extent that they view contemporary globalization as just another cycle in the history of capital waiting for the appearance of a new core before it achieves a structural order once again (Wallerstein, 1996a). But they are also quite right to point out that claims to globalization as a new departure simply ignore all that the present shares with the history of capitalism. In its final fulfillment, capitalist modernity both points in new directions, and reproduces all the contradictions that have marked its history.

Analyses of global capitalism share much in their logic with world-system analysis, but the conclusions to which they point part in significant ways with the latter, most importantly in global configurations of power. Most significant is the status of the nation-state. Although it recast modernization discourse in a new frame by pointing to spatialities beyond the nation, world-system analysis nevertheless continued to take the nation as the unit of analysis when it came to questions of development and emancipation, as with the concept of "de-linking," in which the national unit separated itself from the world-system to seek for alternatives. Contemporary analyses of globalization (as, indeed, the fate of socialist societies that attempted such de-linking) would suggest that this is no longer a viable option. None but the most naive would suggest that the nation-state is already a thing of the past, or that it no longer may have a part to play in countering the effects of globalization, but it is also the case that any reconceptualization of the nation-state must account both for the supranational and the subnational forces that have once again acquired crucial significance in determining the shape of the nation.

Such is also the case with core-periphery relationships that are central to world-system analysis. Such relationships do indeed persist, but it is increasingly difficult to assign them to neatly delineated spatialities of "Third Worlds" or nations. As the core has assumed fluidity, so has the periphery. It is possible presently to find "First Worlds" in "Third World" locations, and "Third Worlds" within the First. Even more so than in the case of the nation-state, this scrambling of cores and peripheries requires new kinds of analyses of problems of development, as well as of political power. It is necessary nevertheless to exercise some caution not to mystify power by equating the scrambling of power with its disappearance. The "disorganizing" of capital does not imply that there are no longer centers to power. The recent crisis in East and Southeast Asia, and the measures adopted for its resolution, are revealing of the power of the capitalist core in shaping global policy. Transnational corporations are not as homeless as they appear on the surface, as their power in some measure depends on state action; it is no accident that the most powerful corporations are those that identify with core states in the world-system. To speak of "Third Worlds" in the First is not to incorporate them into a condition of "Third World-ness" that is the same everywhere. Even the emergence of a transnational capitalist class, or the need for core states to share power with others, is no indication that relations of dependency have therefore been eliminated. Globalization points to the need for accommodating new realities of power. On the other hand, it is also quite evidently more of a concern in the ideologies of core states, particularly the United States, that represents an effort to re-comprehend the world in its totality. Such a vision of totality is not available equally to all who participate in global practices. Neither are all participants in those practices equally concerned to contain global chaos, though they may all feel its effects one way or another.

The Network Society

One possible way of bringing some analytical coherence to the conflicting phenomena of global capitalism has been offered by Manuel Castells in his recent work (Castells, 1997). Castells's metaphor of networks in the description of contemporary capitalism is derived from the central importance he assigns to information technologies, which then serve as a paradigm for the reconfiguration of global relations. The metaphor of "network" offers ways for envisaging the new global capitalism in both its unities and disunities, in its pervasiveness as well as in the huge gaps that are systemic products of the global economy. The metaphor of network shifts attention from surfaces to "highways" that link nodes in the global economy. A network has no boundaries of any permanence, but may expand or contract at a moment's notice, and shift in its internal configurations as its nodes move from one location to another. Marginality to the global economy may mean being outside of the network, as well as in the many surfaces within that are in its many gaps. Marginality does not imply being untouched by the networks, as the inductive effects of network flows affect even those who are not direct participants in its many flows. Finally, the network metaphor offers new ways of accounting for power. It is possible to state that the most powerful nodes in the global economy, for example, Sassen's global cities, may be those locations in which nodes of economic, political, and cultural power coincide. The network militates against neat spatialities, but it also allows for their inclusion in considerations of power; while any location may be included in the network, the most powerful, and controlling, nodes are still located in national spaces of commanding global presence.

Although some of these conclusions may be beyond what Castells intended, they are consistent I think with what he has to say about "the architecture" and "the geometry" of global power. In his words, "there is a basic architecture, inherited from history, that frames the development of the global economy" (1997: 146). As he explains it further,

The architecture of the global economy features an asymmetrically interdependent world, organized around three major economic regions and increasingly polarized along an axis of opposition between productive, information-rich, affluent areas, and impoverished areas, economically devalued and socially excluded. Between the three dominant regions, Europe, North America, and the Asian Pacific, the latter appears to be the most dynamic yet the most vulnerable because of its dependence upon the openness of the markets of the other regions. However, the intertwining of economic processes between the three regions makes them practically inseparable in their fate. Around each region an economic hinterland has been created, with some countries being gradually incorporated into the global economy. (1997: 145–146)

"Within this visible architecture," however, "there are dynamic processes of competition and change that infuse a variable geometry into the global system of economic processes." As he explains this "variable geometry,"

What I call the newest international division of labor is constructed around four different positions in the informational global economy: the producers of high value, based on informational labor; the producers of high volume, based on lower-cost labor; the producers of raw materials, based on natural endowments; and the redundant producers, reduced to devalued labor. . . . The critical matter is that these different positions do not coincide with countries. *They are organized in networks and flows, using the technological infrastructure of the informational economy.* They feature geographic concentrations in some areas of the planet, so that the global economy is not geographically undifferentiated. . . . Yet the newest international division of labor does not take place between countries but between economic agents placed in the four positions I have indicated along a global structure of networks and flows. . . . Because the position in the international division of labor does not depend, fundamentally, on the characteristics of the country but on the characteristics of its labor . . . and of its insertion into the global economy, changes may occur, and indeed do, in a short span. The relentlessly variable geometry that results from such processes of innovation and competition struggles with the historically produced architecture of the world economic order, inducing the creative chaos that characterizes the new economy. (Castells, 1997: 146–47; emphasis in the original)

The power of Castells's analysis lies in its ability to bring together contemporary changes with the legacies of the past, observable concentrations of power with ultimate powerlessness to control the uncertainties of the global economy, globalization with regionalization and the continued relevance of the nation-state, and the persistence of earlier mappings of the globe with its reconfigurations. The world-system all along may have been not so much a stable "system," but a process of systematizations and desystematizations. This may be the condition of the contemporary global economy, with the processes speeded up to a point where order becomes indistinguishable from chaos. The very fulfillment of capitalist modernization issues not in the fulfillment of the promise of modernization discourse, but in its final dissolution.

THE CULTURES OF GLOBALIZATION

One by-product of globalization discourse is the return of culture. Not that culture ever disappeared from discussions of development, but it was driven to the background for a brief while in the preoccupation with political economy, and with the social, that accompanied the repudiation of modernization discourse with its culturalist assumptions. Contemporary preoccupation with culture has more than one source. The emergence of East Asian economies from the late 1970s on once again gave rise to questions of whether or not culture had any- thing to do with development. The scrambling of boundaries with globalization, but especially the increasingly visible motions of populations, not only gave rise to questions of identity, but also empowered the reassertion of suppressed iden- tities; the reemergence of sub- and supranational ethnicity is one of the outstand- ing phenomena that have accompanied globalization. The stress on culture is propagated also not only by the immense power commanded by culture in- dustries (including the media), but perhaps even more fundamentally by the importance of information, a basically cultural force, in production and con- sumption.

In the perspective of political economy, culturalist approaches to globalization appear not just as expressions of this new situation, but also as efforts to bring some order to the untidiness of everyday life. I will look briefly here at two versions of contemporary culturalist paradigms of globality; the one represen- tative of left-liberal approaches that perceives in contemporary cultural forma- tions an unprecedented globalization (as distinct from homogenization) in the human experience of the world, the other representative of, for lack of a better word, a "geopolitical realism" that postulates culture as the defining feature of the new fracturing of the globe by past legacies. I describe both approaches as "culturalist" because they give priority to culture above all other elements; if anything, the left-liberal alternative is more hostile to political economy than the "realist" one.

Globalism

Anthony Giddens has written that "the 'world' in which we now live is in some profound respects . . . quite distinct from that inhabited by human beings in previous periods of history. It is in many ways a single world, having a unitary framework of experience (for instance in respect to basic axes of time and space), yet at the same time one which creates new forms of fragmentation and dispersal" (Giddens, 1991). For Giddens, the media play a "central role" in this world as it is through them that "the influence of distant happenings on proximate events and on intimacies of the self, becomes more and more com- monplace" (Giddens, 1991: 4). Nevertheless, the media do not homogenize the world but only provide a "unitary framework." He writes,

... in a general way, the concept of globalisation is best understood as expressing fundamental aspects of time-space distanciation. Globalisation concerns the intersection of presence and absence, the interlacing of social events and social relations "at distance" with local contextualities. We should grasp the global spread of modernity in terms of an ongoing relation between distanciation and the chronic mutability of local circumstances and local engagements ... globalisation has to be understood as a dialectical phenomenon, in which events at one pole of a distanciated relation often produce divergent or even contrary occurrences at another.... The *dialectic of the local and global* is ... basic. (Giddens, 1991: 21–22; emphasis in the original)

The juxtaposition of the global and the local is common to most writing on globalization in the left-liberal disposition, and represents one of its most important contributions to the debate on globalization that points to new kinds of fragmentation that have accompanied globalization. While the local may on occasion refer to the national, more often than not it points to levels below and within the nation, where the global meets concrete contexts of everyday existence. Similarly, the global in this usage needs to be distinguished from the "international," as it transcends and provides the context for relationships between nations and even regions. The global also shapes the local, we might add, as the local, while by no means just a passive recepient of the global, is most important nevertheless for pointing to the different ways in which the global works over localized configurations. The refusal to entertain the possibility that the local, having been worked over by the global, may in turn shape the global is one of the problems with these analyses.

Giddens's suggestion of a break between the present and the past is shared by most expositions of the left-liberal position on globalization. Roland Robertson, whose enthusiasm for globalization is matched by his extremist culturalism, insists on the necessity of distinguishing globalization even from the forces and the processes of which it is the product:

I argue that systematic comprehension of the macrostructuration of world order is essential to the viability of any form of contemporary theory and that such comprehension must involve *analytical separation of the factors which have facilitated the shift towards a single world—e.g., the spread of capitalism, western imperialism and the development of a global media system—from the general and global agency-structure (and/or culture) theme.* While the empirical relationship between the two sets of issues is of great importance (and, of course, complex), conflation of them leads us into all sorts of difficulties and inhibits our ability to come to terms with *the basic and shifting terms* of the contemporary world order. (Robertson, 1994: 23; emphasis in the longer section is mine)

In the extremeness of its presentist culturalism, Robertson's statement reveals both the virtues and the serious shortcomings of globalization in left-liberal analyses. The assertion of the autonomy of a culture of globality underlines the importance of viewing culture not as a by-product of material conditions, but a constituent of globality. While Robertson has refrained from clarifying his own idea of culture (Forte, 1998: 80), he is nevertheless correct in pointing out the power of "global culture" as a social imaginary that shapes the behavior even of those who are in no evident position to gain from globalization. This culture, however vague, is also not a functional product of capitalism alone, but nourishes off many sources, including the very idea of globality; it makes some sense, therefore, to view it separately from the functioning of global capitalism, even if the latter continues to empower it. Given the power of globalization in reshaping conceptualizations of the world, finally, the effort to grasp the "macrostructuration" of the world independently of its origins has some epistemological value in uncovering how a present situation of globality may differ from its historical antecedents.

These virtues, however, seem to me to be achieved at the cost of an intellectual and political mystification of globalization. Forte observes that "Robertson's approach is 'cultural' in a purely ideational or symbolic sense," resting the evidence of globality on the diffusion of global awareness or awareness of globality (Forte, 1998: 79). Although left-liberal advocates of globalization, including Robertson, concede that globalization has a long history that is coeval with the history of capitalist modernity, there seems to be a reluctance to investigate the implications of the connection between contemporary globality and its context in capitalist modernity, seemingly out of an anxiety about falling back on functionalist explanations, but also because of a possibility that too much preoccupation with globality's relationship to capitalist modernity might reveal globalization as "modernity writ large" (Featherstone, 1996) and the culturalist approach to globalization as a contemporary variant of the culturalism that marked modernization discourse, minus its Eurocentrism. Failure to do so, however, also obviates the need to inquire into the immediate context of globalization discourse within a contemporary global capitalism, where the mere repudiation of Eurocentrism does not in and of itself signify an escape from it, as capitalism even if its globalization carries the stamp of its origins and modern development. This becomes even more evident if we consider that globalization is not of equal concern to all populations globally, but is propagated most enthusiastically from the earlier centers of global power, which continue to shape global economic and political futures.[3] Challenges to Eurocentrism within this context emanate not from populations at large, which may feel the effects of globalization without being players in it, but from global elites empowered by their participation in a global capitalist economy, and may well represent, therefore, the deployment of culture in intra-elite struggles—within a context of shared economic interests. Exemplary in this regard may be the "socialist" government of the People's Republic of China, which in its dealings with the United States (or with Taiwan) consistently insists that negotiations focus on economic issues, leaving aside thorny questions of culture and politics— which does not prevent culture and politics from becoming issues of contention nevertheless.

The failure of cultural globalists to address issues of power mystifies questions of the spatial and social limits of globalization. The elevation of globality to a transcendental status, on the other hand, renders globalization a mystical force that compels all who live under its regime to follow its dictates at any cost— which raises the question of the complicity of this representation of globality with the globalization discourse of transnational capital, the core states of global power, and an emergent transnational capitalist class (in Leslie Sklair's term). It is ironic that globalists such as Ronald Robertson spend such time attacking political economy analyses of capital, such as world-system analysis, while they have little to say about the relationship of globalization as ideology to contemporary structures of power. The compelling power with which globalization is endowed is true to some extent even of analysts such as Giddens who are more cognizant of such a relationship.

Back to the Future: "The Clash of Civilizations"

Interestingly, the most important intellectual challenge to globalization in recent years has come not from the left, but from a political scientist who long has been associated with conservative causes. Samuel Huntington's critique of globalization is in many ways consistent with his earlier criticism of modernization discourse; as he contended earlier that modernization bred not democracy but disorder, he now argues that globalization breeds not global unity but division and disorder. If there is a major difference from his earlier analysis, it is in the hardening of the boundaries of the units of his analysis. Huntington believes that nation-states remain important, and will remain important for the foreseeable future, but shifts attention from nations to "cultural entities" called civilizations. In his seminal article where he first outlined his position, he wrote that "the interactions among peoples of different civilizations enhance the civilization-consciousness of people that, in turn, invigorates differences and animosities stretching or thought to stretch back deep in history" (Huntington, 1993a: 26). The conflicts he perceives between civilizations are products of globalization, which creates not unity—or the erasure of history—but new fractures along historical/cultural legacies. His own understanding of these fractures is exemplary of the ethnicization of learning that has accompanied globalization.

Huntington's point of departure is the premise that in the post-Cold War world, "the most pervasive, important and dangerous conflicts will not be between social classes, rich and poor, or other economically defined groups, but between peoples belonging to different cultural entities" (1996a: 28). He conceives cultural entities at the broadest level in terms of civilizations, which are "culture[s] writ large" (1996a: 41). Huntington perceives a regrouping of the world's peoples around civilizations that in their origins predate modernity. There are seven or eight of these civilizations, of which the most important in his analysis are the Western, the Eastern orthodox (or Slavic), Islamic, and Sinic (Chinese). Language and religion are in his analysis the most crucial defining elements of civilizations, although he views culture most broadly as "the overall way of life of a people" (1996a: 41). Ways of life long assumed to be things of the past are on the resurgence, ironically, as a consequence of modernization, which, on the one hand, has enhanced the economic, military, and political power of non-Western societies, and, on the other hand, has created alienation and identity crises; an expression at once, in other words, of alienation and empowerment (1996a: 76–77). Rather than lead to Westernization, modernization, and the increased contact among peoples that has accompanied it, has intensified the human propensity "to hate" outsiders (Huntington, 1996a: 130).

The problem that Huntington sets out to address is how to secure world order when the Western-dominated world of modernity is being challenged by non-Western civilizations that have made a comeback thanks to modernity, and assert the universality of *their* real or imagined civilizational legacies against the Western. Under the circumstances, "The concept of a universal civilization helps justify Western cultural dominance of other societies and the need for those societies to ape Western practices and institutions" (Huntington, 1996a: 66). This is impossible and unsustainable because the West itself represents a unique civilization with values that are not easily adaptable to the norms of other civilizations (Huntington, 1996b). Worse, it is arrogant and dangerous; "Western intervention in the affairs of other civilizations [not least efforts to export human rights and democracy] is probably the single most important source of instability and potential conflict in a multicivilizational world" (1996a: 312). The best that the West may do is to retreat behind its own boundaries, mind its own affairs, and leave "the primary responsibility for containing and resolving regional conflicts . . . [to] the leading states of the civilizations dominant in those regions" (1996b: 42). The formation of fortress "West" in Huntington's analysis includes control of immigration to the "West" in order to preserve its own unique heritage.

Huntington's civilizational units may seem quaint, if not outrageous, at a time when the "constructedness" of culture has become a matter of faith in Euro-American, especially American, intellectual circles, where intellectuals from other "civilizations" are prominently visible. His discussion of current and impending conflicts between civilizations draws on scattered examples, held together by "common sense" homilies about human propensities of one kind or another. For all its insistence on the power of the past, the argument is deeply ahistorical. Huntington recognizes the constructedness of cultures, differences internal to civilizations, as well as the permeability of boundaries that divide them from one another. And yet these qualifications do not find their way into the argument, which is sustained by an assumption that the values characteristic of civilizations persist against the transformative pressures of time and space. The analysis is marred seriously by his inability to draw clear physical boundaries around "civilizations," which are intermixed in most locations. Having committed himself to "civilizations" as the units of conflict in the contemporary world, he cannot do much better in the end than concede that "the relations between civilizations are complicated, often ambivalent, and they do change. . . . Conflicts also obviously occur within civilizations, particularly Islam. . . .

The relatively simple bipolarity of the Cold War is giving way to the much more complex relationships of a multipolar, multicivilizational world" (Huntington, 1996a: 245). The analysis is also oblivious to the formation of common interests that accompany the globalization of capitalism; he makes little, for instance, of his own quite accurate observation that "the ability of Asian regimes to resist Western human rights pressures was reinforced by several factors. American and European businesses were desperately anxious to expand their trade with and their investment in these rapidly growing countries and subjected their governments to intense pressure not to disrupt economic relations with them" (1996a: 194). Perhaps most important, for all its cultural relativism, Huntington's analysis, as with his earlier work on modernization, is intended to secure global order in accordance with a conceptualization of the world that is rooted in the history of EuroAmerican modernity—minus values such as democracy and human rights that legitimized that modernity.

It would be a mistake, nevertheless, to dismiss Huntington's analysis as a mere reassertion of Eurocentrism or American power, or as an ethnocentrism that borders on racism. His analysis has been received with great interest outside of the United States. The "remaking of world order" that he advocates not only refers freely to U. S. imperialism, but also suggests that the United States should share world power with regional hegemons, in the form of "core states" of civilizations. The appeal of such an arrangement, say to the leaders of "Sinic civilization," should be obvious.[4] Above all, however, I would like to suggest that Huntington's analysis is appealing because it is exemplary of a growing ethnicization/racialization not only in world politics, but also of the ways in which it is conceptualized; it, therefore, speaks to a real situation, as he claims. Huntington himself recognizes that cultures are internally divided, or constructed, which may not matter because constructed or not, faith in their reality leads to the kinds of results that Huntington describes. Faith in all Chinese being Confucian is no less a faith because it may be a construction of the contemporary world. Huntington himself may be engaged in just such a construction with regard to "Western civilization"; the ideological nature of his analysis does not detract from its power to persuade the faithful.[5]

From a critical perspective, what needs to be pointed out are the resistances that are also outstanding phenomena of the contemporary world, about which Huntington has little to say. Not everyone in the world is equally engaged in the remanufacturing of civilizations, although everyone may feel its effects one way or another. In Huntington's analysis, as in culturalist arguments for globalization in general, there is little accounting for the relationship between culture and power; as if globalization or civilizational resurgence were products of invisible processes. The reification of culture in either alternative, mutually contradictory though they are, also disguises the conflicts over life and culture that are embedded not at the offground levels of globality or civilizations, but in everyday struggles for survival and democracy.

PLACE-BASED IMAGINATION

Alternative readings of globalization offer insights into different aspects of globality that are complementary, but in their contradictory conclusions also reveal the complexity of global formations. Political economy analyses point to the context of contemporary globalization both within the history of capitalist modernity, and recent changes in the configurations of capital. World-system analysis which in the post-World War II period challenged modernization discourse to adopt a global perspective still retains its power to reveal structural inequalities built into the capitalist system. On the other hand, these structural inequalities are obscured to some extent both by the decentralization of capital, and an intensified fluidity in its operations that "disorganize" the system on an ongoing basis. The virtue of the "network" analysis offered by Manuel Castells is to reconcile these two aspects of contemporary global formations.

Political economy analyses are not as innocent of questions of culture and agency as culturalist critics maintain, but they do display a bias toward structures and toward the impersonal workings of capital.[6] It is arguable even that political economy analyses have done a better job of formulating explanations that integrate culture and politics than those culturalist analyses that consciously set themselves against political economy. On the other hand, employed wisely, cultural globalism has done invaluable service in pointing out the part played by culture and agency in the dynamics of globalization. What I have described as left-liberal culturalism has reinforced the revelations of political economy analyses in underlining the localization of cultures in the very process, and as a consequence of, globalization. Huntington's culturalism, for all its reductionism, points to the new fracturing of the globe at both the macro- and the micro-levels by a recuperation of historical legacies in response to pressures of globalization.

These analyses are nevertheless lacking in their inattention to still another way of constructing globality; what has been termed "globalization from below" by more than one analyst with reference to the proliferation of place-based movements that cut across the customary East/West, North/South, "civilizational" and national divides. Castells recognizes their importance, but relegates them to a secondary role in favor of ecological and gender-based movements. The recognition is also implicit in left-liberal identification of the local in the global, which stops short however of recognizing the global in the local. Place-based movements are not new, but they have acquired a new significance under the conditions of globalization that, on the one hand, completes modernity's "invasion of the life-world," and, on the other hand, generates "places" as locations for new kinds of politics.[7] The politics of place of necessity differs from location to location in its concerns and constitution; what renders it global is its appearance globally in response to "the unitary framework of experience" of which Giddens speaks. The challenge to radical politics is how to translate reactive politics of place that is limited to resistance to the ravages and uncertainties of globalization into pro-active politics that points to alternative futures; which raises the question of how to coordinate diverse politics of place into a coordinated movement—without abolishing diversity.

To speak of place-based politics as a possible and necessary option requires an "unthinking" of radical politics, much as Wallerstein has spoken of "unthinking social science." The various analyses of globalization previously discussed all share one thing in common: that earlier forms of radical politics have become largely irrelevant under contemporary circumstances. Capitalism is too decentered to permit any realistic option of systemic change, such as envisaged earlier in socialism. Socialism, at any rate, was concretely manifested only in nation-states; both past experience with socialism, and the increasingly problematic nature of the nation-state, rule out as a radical option nation-based movements that may "de-link" from the world-system, and point the way to alternative futures. Labor, women's, and ecological movements, while quite important, also suffer from the fragmenting dynamics of uneven development, as well as the ethnicization of politics of which Huntington speaks. They may be quite crucial, nevertheless, to providing the necessary links between places, which requires new kinds of transnational vision and organizational flexibility.

It is possible to argue presently that even such radical movements may have a hope of success only if they challenge the hegemony of globalization, and seek for ways to ground themselves without giving up their international or global commitments. The nation-state, too, has not yet exhausted all its utility or possibilities, as it may have a protective role to play against the "creative chaos" of globalization. What seems to be clear is that while globalization requires a response that is also national and global, it is necessary most fundamentally to challenge its premise that an offground existence is the fate of humankind, which calls for renewed attention to places; not places as they have been inherited from the past, with their own inequalities and oppressions, but places as they have been worked over by modernity, that in their reaffirmation to everyday life seek also to counter past legacies. Instead of urging places to go global in order to survive, which undermines both economic and political democracy, the crucial task presently may be to create those democractic spaces in which to secure livelihood and to reaffirm the priorities of everyday existence against the visions of future welfare.[8] Places thus conceived are not the givens of history, but projects to be realized. If such projects seem utopian, they are no more so than a globalization with its indefinitely deferred promises. The difference between the two projects lies not in degrees of utopianism, but in their relationship to power.

Unfortunately, a left caught up in visions of globalization, rather than challenge its premises, celebrates its promises of cosmopolitanism or ethnic multiculturalism, and contributes to the very hegemony that it would undermine. Wedded to modernity, left-liberals in our day seem to have hitched their aspirations to the bandwagon of globalization, in which they wishfully perceive not a fulfillment of a program of modernization, but a way to overcome some of its less desirable legacies. It is arguable to the contrary that globalization has finally exposed as an illusion the hope (as much Marxist as it is bourgeois) that the answer to the problems of modernity is more modernization. Although global-ization compromises some of the more valuable promises of modernity, it places beyond the control of everyday life (and even of states and capital), modernity's most destructive consequences. Its celebration by radicals in postmodernism (the contemporary counterpart to modernism) reinforces the ideology of capital in persuading us that we are all condemned to following the dictates of globaliz-zation that emanate not from a single source but represent the cumulative effects of bits and pieces of human progress. Some progress, that in its march continues to negate the very ideas of human welfare and democracy that justify it!

Recognition of the fundamental contradictoriness of globalization might en-able an anti-modernism that may be essential to asking hard questions about capitalist modernity, and formulating alternatives to it. Presently, the most vis-ible protests against globalization, especially in the United States, would seem to bear an unmistakably right-wing character. That they are right-wing is no reason for dismissing them, for they still represent the anxieties and fears of real people who find themselves at the mercy of globalization. At the same time, these protests offer little more than a commitment to preserving accustomed privileges, and are highly limited therefore in their ability to address past leg-acies of inequality and injustice; indeed, they exacerbate them by finding scape-goats for their woes among even less privileged groups.

If the right seems to be addressing problems of globalization more effectively at the present, it may be because the left with its cosmopolitan developmentalist biases has been all too ready to concede places to the political right. The right may be better at it also because it is more willing to affirm particularity against theoretical generalization. Although it may be possible to theorize places, the politics of place is ultimately based on diversity and difference, because each place is marked not only by a particular location but also by a particular legacy. If there is a challenge in that to "unthinking" theory, it is the challenge of everyday political and economic democracy that yet remains to be realized—not just in Chiapas or the Three Gorges of the Yangtze River, but also in Cleveland, Ohio, and Durham, North Carolina.

Globalization is not to be conceived only, or even primarily, as an intellectual problem. It has come to express also hopeful longings for the good life, as well as terrifying uncertainties. Societies and communities around the world seek to place themselves in the pathways of capital by building infrastructures for its operations, hopeful that "if you build it they will come." The efforts are accom-panied by a terrifying anxiety that others might offer more desirable infrastruc-tures, attracting capital away, leaving behind it the ruins of fixed capital and fixed social relationships. The investment in globalization is not abstractly in-tellectual, it is an investment laden with all the hopes and fears of everyday life. To the extent that even the hopes are infused with perpetual anxiety, globali-zation promises to make terror into a condition of human existence. It is this terror that ultimately may be the greatest obstacle to conceiving alternatives to globalization, and to the cultivation of collective subjectivities necessary for their realization.

It may make little sense under the circumstances to engage in abstract critiques of globalization, or to speak of radical alternatives to it. And yet it is precisely for those same reasons that it is necessary to demystify globalization, to show that it is not the product of some natural process of evolution but of human activity that in the pursuit of some goals betrays other goals of equal or greater value. Globalization creates unprecedented wealth only to place it beyond the reach of the majority of humankind. It ushers in democratic forms of governance only to place the most important decisions of everyday life outside the scope of politics. It is more important than ever before, therefore, to create those spaces in which to establish democratic controls over economic as well as political life. Place-based activity may not suffice on its own to achieve those goals, but it needs to be an indispensable ingredient of any radical alternative that hopes to confront the offground abstractions of globalization with the concrete demands of everyday life. The solution to the problems of globalization is not more globalization, or an escape into parochialism, but to ground it so as to comprehend it with greater clarity, and make it accountable to its human constituencies.

NOTES

1. Among the works that are notable for what they reveal about globalization are Martin and Schumann (1997), Barnet and Cavanagh (1994), and Greider (1997). Martin and Schumann, citing globalizationists, point out that globalization is expected to produce a "20:80" society sustained by "tittytainment," that is, a society where only 20 percent of the world's population will benefit from globalization, while the rest will be kept occupied by entertainment. The "20:80" figure was originally forecast by the European Union. See Petrella (1991).

2. Braudel himself drew on Immanuel Wallerstein's world-system analysis, adding to the latter a recognition of other world-systems that predated the emergence of capitalism. He also restricted the definition of capitalism, identifying it not with markets, which exist in all modes of production, or with a particular technology of production, but with the emergence of large enterprises devoted to the accumulation of capital.

3. Noteworthy in this regard is the enthusiasm for globalization of "rational choice" political scientists who, in their very claims to the scientificity of their undertaking, are products of a Eurocentric scientism. A globalized culture, to the extent that it erases cultural particularities, is quite obviously convenient for an approach to politics that assumes the possibility of universal methodologies. Although cultural globalists such as Giddens recognize local permutations of globalization, globalists such as Robertson may have something in common with "rational choice" analysts; the specifically stated goal of dehistoricizing globalization in the quotation cited above is to evolve a "contemporary theory," without telling the reader whose theory it is to be.

4. It is also worth remembering that Huntington's earlier arguments on order were quite popular in the People's Republic of China in the late 1980s in the guise of a "new authoritarianism."

5. It may be revealing that in the concluding part of his book, Huntington states that, "culture . . . follows power" (p. 310). The statement seems somewhat surprising in light of what he has to say about the lasting power of civilization values, but not if we take into account his underlying motivation to reassert EuroAmerican power.

6. World-system analysis does not stand or fall with core-periphery structures; nor does a recognition of the fundamentalness even of technology require obliviousness to questions of culture, agency, and identity. See Immanuel Wallerstein (1996a) for an example of the former, and Castells (1997) as an instance of the latter.

7. For a more thorough discussion, see Dirlik (1999). See also a related symposium on the question of place, in *Development* (1998). The term, "invasion of the life-world," is Jurgen Habermas's.

8. This, too, is a demand that has acquired audibility globally with globalization. References to works devoted to the subject are many, some of which may be found in the bibliography of the essay cited in the previous note. See also Michael H. Shuman (1998) for a recent, and thoughtfully argued, example.

III

FROM NATIONAL STATES TO REGIONAL NETWORKS?

III

9

The Rhineland, European Union, and Regionalism in the World Economy

Michael Loriaux

Globalization, it is claimed, has given rise to a multiplicity of transborder regions of economic activity. Transborder economic regionalism, the argument continues, challenges the economic policymaking competence of the traditional nation-state. In this chapter, I shall set aside the second claim and focus on the first. The example of the Rhineland suggests that some and perhaps many of today's transborder economic regions antedate the borders. Globalization has merely eroded the topsoil of the nation-state system to expose the original regional bedrock. The topsoil of the nation-state is, after all, quite thin. The nation-state system is a recent invention. Although it achieved legal status in Europe in the seventeenth century, it metastasized to the rest of the world only in the nineteenth and twentieth centuries. There is, therefore, no a priori reason to "naturalize" this system. There is no a priori reason to treat the state as the atom or molecule of the international system.

THE RHINELAND AS TRANSBORDER ECONOMIC REGION

By "Rhineland" I refer to that patch of geography drained by the Rhine river, its tributaries, the Neckar, the Main, Ruhr, Moselle, and the two rivers that share the Rhine's delta, the Scheldt and the Meuse.[1] This patch covers three countries—Belgium, Luxembourg, and the Netherlands—and parts of three others—France, Germany, and Switzerland. The Rhineland thus defined is a land that is criss-crossed by a number of international frontiers. It is a curious place to find international political frontiers. This is not to deny that the Rhineland is home to a collection of different nationalities, distinguished by language. The frontiers, however, do a singularly poor job of separating linguistic groups. German is spoken in France, Belgium, and Switzerland; French in Switzerland and Belgium, Dutch in Belgium and (counting Plattdeutsch as a close cousin) Germany. The Netherlands itself is bilingual, since a number of its citizens claim Frisian as their mother-tongue. Moreover, the languages that one currently finds in the Rhineland are, to a significant extent, nineteenth-century constructs. National languages (or spelling and grammar in the case of the Flemish) have been imposed on a variety of regional dialects, some of which bear little resemblance to the official tongue.

Despite such division, the Rhineland is a coherent economic space. It is the heart of the European Union's golden triangle, whose vertices at Milan, London, and Frankfurt encompass a world-class concentration of economic power, and one of the most densely urbanized and populated regions of the world. The Rhine itself runs almost the entire length of this golden triangle. Navigable by oceangoing freighter from Rotterdam to Duisburg and by heavy barge-train from Duisburg to Basel, it links the near-extremities of the triangle like an artery or a nerve. Through its affluents, the Meuse, Moselle, Neckar, and their canals, it draws into its thick web of traffic such cities as Metz and Nancy, Brussels and Antwerp, Stuttgart and Amsterdam. From its seaports at Rotterdam, Amsterdam, and Antwerp, the Rhine extends its reach to southern England and the North Sea. In the south, through Alpine passes—notably the Simplon and the St. Gothard—it reaches out to Milan, Turin, Genoa, and Italy's industrialized north, while the valleys of the Saône and the Rhône link the Rhineland to Lyon, Marseille, and the western Mediterranean. At the core of this Rhineland triangle, Western Europe's steel-producing heartland extends from Lorraine and Hainaut to the Ruhr, including the Saar, Luxembourg, and half of Belgium. It is no accident that the original six countries of the European Common Market belong to this Rhineland fraternity.

The Rhineland's economic fortunes flow largely from a single source, an accident of physical geography that placed a north–south depression across a continent that topography has ordered latitudinally. Topographically, Europe consists of three broad bands: a plain to the north that extends from Dunkirk to St. Petersburg, a band of wooded plateaus and deep valleys that runs from the Massif Central to Bohemia, and finally the high peaks of the Alps and its sister ranges—the Pyrenees and the Carpathians—to the south. Cutting across these three geographical zones are the twin depressions of the Rhine and the Saône-Rhône. These depressions have linked the North Sea to the Mediterranean from prehistoric times, and funneled east–west traffic through bridgeable fords across the rivers. Cities arose at the crossroads—Basel, Strasbourg, Mainz, Cologne— feeding on the commercial and industrial opportunities that geography created, while nurturing the development of a commercial and industrial civilization.

Historical Origins of the Core/Borderland Economy

Thus the Rhineland presents a curious juxtaposition of a core industrial economy and a concentration of international frontiers. It is probably unique in the world in this regard. The origins of this juxtaposition lie deep in history. Rome drew its frontier at the Rhine, and lay the foundation for the Rhineland's urbanization and commercial dominance. The conceptualization of the Rhine as a natural frontier loosened its hold on the social imaginary at times of economic climacteric, as in the early ninth century, the thirteenth century, the late fourteenth century, and the late nineteenth century. But it reasserted itself in the aftermath, as a kind of myth that guided, justified, and energized political action in the region.

The idea that the Rhine is a "natural frontier" emerged fully armored from the ear of Julius Caesar. Caesar designated the Rhine as the terminus of his military intervention in Gaul, the natural dividing line between Celt and German, which, if occupied and defended, would bring stability in perpetua to the empire's northern barbarian march. Caesar's vision corresponded very imperfectly to local realities. Germanophones populated the northern plain on both sides of the Rhine, and Celtophones populated the highlands to the South on both sides of the Rhine. Moreover, the notion of "linguistic appartenance" had little local significance, and much intermingling of the two linguistic groups is evident. The term "German" itself was not used by populations living east of the Rhine to designate themselves, but by populations—notably the Treveri and Tuncteri—living west of the Rhine and generally catalogued as Celts. Nevertheless, the image of a natural frontier served Caesar well by quieting his critics at home who worried that his campaign would involve Rome in a military and political quagmire.

Caesar not only gave rise to the idea that the Rhine was a "natural frontier." His occupation of the left bank lay the foundation for the intense urbanization of the Rhineland that occurred under Rome and laid the foundation of the dense urbanization noted previously. Rome occupied key crossroads along the Rhine, founding colonies at Cologne or Augst (near Basel), and regimental towns at Mainz, Bonn, Xanthen, and Strasbourg. Rome's strong military and administrative presence animated economic activity in the region, and the new cities bustled with merchants and artisans. Cologne, with Lyon, was the greatest city of Gaul and one of the greatest of the Western empire. Trier was promoted to imperial capital in the fourth century. Even as the rest of the Western empire lapsed into economic crisis in the mid-third century, economic activity in the cities of the Rhineland continued strong until the barbarian invasions of the fifth century.

The great migrations that occurred between the fifth and tenth centuries disrupted urban and economic life in the Rhineland. But as populations settled and as the farthest reaches of northern Europe became integrated into the Christian, romanized political community that survived the Empire's demise, urban life in the Rhineland revived. The textile cities of Flanders and Hainaut—Arras, Bruges, Brussels, Antwerp, Louvain—arose along the route between the wool-bearing heaths of England and the ports of Italy, where the spices and silks of the Orient arrived before being shipped north in exchange for Flemish textile. Although this commerce passed initially through the trade fairs of Champagne, war in France and the revival of the cities of the Rhine, nourished by the spread of commerce to the Baltic and beyond, soon diverted it back to its traditional corridor. New cities arose in the foothills of Switzerland—Lucerne, Zurich, Bern—fed by the growth of traffic and the opening of new routes across the Alps. Urbanism and commerce conditioned the rise of Rhineland humanism in the late Middle Ages, exemplified by Erasmus of Rotterdam, Gutenburg of Mainz (and Strasbourg), the Van Dycks, and other Flemish painters who intro-duced the artistic canons of the Italian Renaissance to northern Europe, and even improved on their techniques.

The Reconstruction of the Rhineland Frontier in Modern Times

Throughout the Middle Ages, the notion of a Rhineland frontier faded from the social and political vision of the times, but never completely disappeared. Frankish consolidation united both banks of the river within a single political construct, but the Rhine was still used to separate Teilreiche within the Frankish kingdom. Under the stress of migratory movements, political organization at-omized. The idea of a "natural frontier" had little meaning in early feudal Eu-rope, and was swallowed up by the vast and loosely organized Holy Roman Empire. But it was resurrected again by Louis XIV, who set out energetically to extend his kingdom to its "natural frontier" on the Rhine.

Much of the international politics of Western Europe in subsequent centuries, however, was conditioned by efforts to absorb the Rhineland, the urban and industrial core of western Europe, into the evolving European nation-state sys-tem. The national monarchies arose in regions where cities were weak: France in the plains of the Paris basin; Spain in the forests and deserts of northern Iberia; Brandenburg in the rye fields of Europe's northern plain; England in the wool-bearing heaths of Britain. With the exception of the ephemeral fifteenth century Duchy of Burgundy, the Rhineland never prosecuted with energy its own claim to be the center of political and military power, as it had been in the days of late Imperial Rome or of the "new Rome" of Charlemagne. The typical form of political organization in the Rhineland of the sixteenth century was the city-state or small principality, which the Rhineland shared with its sister-civilizations of Northern Italy and the Hanseatic League. The rise of the national monarchies consigned this form of political organization to obsolescence.

Stein Rokkan sought to elucidate the paradox of state formation at the "pe-riphery of [this] network of strong and independent cities." The political econ-omy of the monarchical states depended on their ability to control and to exploit the movement of goods and persons across their frontiers, whereas the political economy of the merchant city-states was predicated on the ease and openness of such movement. The resultant incompatibility of interests nourished the desire of the monarchs to extend their control, and, wherever "the cities were weak and isolated, the territorial centralizers succeeded." But as the monarchies extended their reach from periphery to core, they bumped up against one another and began to compete for control of this urban space.

The motivations were not entirely material, however. In early modernity, the idea that the Rhine constituted a "natural frontier" was resurrected by the French monarchy. The term natural refers not to the Rhine's geophysical aptitude to define a defensible frontier. Other natural features, such as the Ardennes and the Vosges, could have done as well. Natural was understood rather as it appears in the phrase "natural law." The Rhine frontier was presented as a part of the "natural order" of things, which, if understood and respected, would bring justice and harmony to human affairs. The French monarchy thus resurrected a mythological vision inherited from Rome, that of a revivified Gallia, endowed by the Church with its own monarchy under the reign of Clovis for the protection of Rome. The myth was used as a rhetorical tool in the long contest between Bourbons and Hapsburgs, and—icing on the rhetorical cake—legitimated French conquest of a particularly commercial part of Europe that abounded in coin, arousing the interest of a property-rich but liquidity-poor monarchy that was constantly scrambling after coin with which to pay its troops.

The effort to restore the "natural order of things" made war an endemic feature of life in the Rhineland from the seventeenth to the early nineteenth century. The French definition of "natural" inspired rival definitions, one of which advanced the concept that the "natural," linguistically defined nation was the true bedrock of political order. According to that understanding, which would play a dominant role in the nineteenth century, "Vater Rhein" flowed within the bounds of a "linguistically homogeneous" territory (though in reality the Alsatian dialect and the Plattdeutsch of Cologne are as mutually foreign as, say, Dutch and Bavarian), and gave both symbolic (e.g., the Nibelungenlied) and economic unity to that territory.

As war succeeded war, only the cities of Holland and Switzerland successfully forged a defensive alliance that either held the monarchical aggrandizers at bay, or subjected them to the will of the urban industrial and commercial class (Rokkan, 1975: 576, 579, 589). The Treaty of Vienna, in 1814, completed the integration of the Rhineland within the now triumphant nation-state system. France, though it lost the war, retained its conquests and acquisitions in Lorraine and Alsace. The Hapsburgs retained their waning influence over the principalities of southern Germany. England became the guarantor of the Netherlands (which until 1830 embraced Belgium) as a buffer state. Switzerland had already secured its claim to the headwaters of the Rhine. Finally, the treaty awarded the youngest monarchy, Prussia, with possession of the middle Rhine from Bingen to the Dutch border.

THE FAILURE OF THE VIENNESE SOLUTION

The Vienna conscription of the Rhineland into the nation-state system was short-lived. The industrial era was dawning, and with it the exploitation of riches that had hitherto played only a secondary role in the Rhineland's prosperity: coal and iron. The valley of the Ruhr harbored one of the richest reserves of coal in the world, which was, moreover, of high quality and easily transformed into the coke required by late nineteenth-century steel mills. Coal of lesser quality was abundant in the valley of the Saar, and iron had long been mined in the valley of the Wupper and in the province of Liège. France, which had been calling the Rhine its "natural frontier" since the mid-seventeenth century, had begun to develop interest in its industrial potential during the Napoleonic period. French engineers and functionaries were dispatched to examine the possibility of exploiting the mineral wealth of the region. In the 1830s French and Belgian capitalists spurred investment in Rhenish mines, and French and Belgian workers constituted the first contingent of steel workers in the Ruhr (Niveau, 1970: 92–93).

But it was Prussia that reaped the industrial bounty of the Rhine, since the Ruhr valley lay entirely within the territory awarded to Prussia by the Treaty of Vienna. Prussia worked aggressively to harness the productive capacities of the Rhine to its military ambitions. Levees were raised and canals cut that allowed heavy barges to reach Mannheim by 1830 and Strasbourg by 1890. Prussia pieced together the German tariff union, the "Zollverein," that energized both German commerce and Prussian hegemony. Germany, unified under Prussia's leadership in 1871, financed the St. Gothard tunnel, connecting the Rhine to the Mediterranean by rail. It financed Holland's Nieuwe Waterweg in 1872, giving the port at Rotterdam the infrastructure that propelled it to its present-day status as the world's busiest port. The German government encouraged mine owners to form cartels, of which the most powerful, the Rheinisch-Westfälisches Kohlensyndikat, eventually controlled 80 percent of the coal production of the Ruhr. It also encouraged vertical concentrations that linked mines to steel mills, giving rise to the empires of Krupp and Thyssen (Valette, 1976: 41–44).

The mineral wealth and industrial development of the Ruhr and the Rhenish provinces that surrounded it provided the foundation for the development of other manufactures: automobiles, electrical goods, machine tools, and precision tools. The chemical industry, based first on the transformation of coal and later on the transformation of petroleum imported through the port of Rotterdam, provided the impetus that catapulted Germany ahead of Great Britain as Europe's premier industrial power. German industries produced 24 percent of the world's chemical goods in 1913 and Great Britain only 11 percent (the United States: 34 percent). "Made in Germany" resonated in British ears in much the same way that "Made in Japan" resounded in American ears in the 1980s (Valette, 1976: 5).

Industrial growth stimulated population growth in an era when military power was measured by the number of men conscripted into service. The population of territorial Germany grew from 25 million in 1816 to 36 million in 1871 to 56 million in 1911. The Rhineland provinces of Prussia and Westphalia grew from 2 to 9 million during the same period. But as Germany waxed, France waned. At the time of the revolution, France was the most populous country of Western Europe. But between 1871 and 1911 its population grew by only 2.5 percent. Although it occupied fourth place among the world's commercial powers, its foreign trade grew by only 16 percent between 1895 and 1905, while that of Germany grew by 66 percent.[2] German dynamism and French stagnation conjured the greatest threat to French predominance in Europe since the sixteenth century.

The defeat of Germany in 1919 and again in 1945 created the opportunity to renegotiate the partition of the Rhineland. The efforts to find a solution to the geopolitics of the Rhineland generated a remarkable parallelism in the diplomatic histories of the post-World War I and post-World War II periods.[3]

Following World War I, France sought to detach the Rhineland from Germany and make it a sovereign state, subject to French influence. British and American resistance caused that plan to collapse. Subsequently, the French adopted a strategy that one might call "geopolitical minilateralism." They sought to create, in collaboration with the Germans and without the Americans, some more or less exclusivist arrangement with Germany such that their claims on the industrial wealth of the Rhineland would be given some satisfaction, and German sovereignty over the Ruhr constrained. In 1923 representatives of the French steel industry met with their German counterparts, with the authorization of the French Foreign Ministry, to explore solutions to the reparations problem that might prove beneficial to both parties. They agreed on a plan that involved the transfer of a number of mines to French ownership, a long-term contract guaranteeing the delivery of German coke to French mills, and a second long-term contract whereby German mills would agree to buy a part of the semi-finished goods produced by French industry.

French geopolitical "minilateralism" failed. The occupation of the Ruhr by the French provoked British and American opposition. The House of Morgan and the governor of the Bank of England made it clear to the French that they "could not advance sizable loans to Germany [needed for reparations payments] unless unilateral sanctions were banned" (Blumenthal, 1986: 135). The French, financially strapped and in the grip of a currency crisis, began to withdraw from the Ruhr in 1925. In the interwar period as in the post-World War II period, U. S. involvement in European politics generated new international institutions. The Bank for International Settlements (BIS), established as executor of the Young Plan in 1929, is the dean of contemporary international organizations, and is set symbolically in Basel on the banks of the Rhine, where it materializes as the link between the competition for control of the Rhineland and the development of institutions of economic cooperation in Europe.

The French welcomed involvement by American financiers, given the free fall of the franc on currency markets and the budget deficits that the occupation of the Ruhr had spawned. The Germans, meanwhile, persisted in their strategy of geopolitical internationalism. They had been seeking to enlist American involvement since 1921. In 1924, the Auswärtiges Amt expressed the hope that "the United States could somehow be persuaded to invest large sums of idle and unproductive money in German industry. Not only would Germany's capitalistic system benefit, but its economic recovery and the revision of the Versailles treaty would almost certainly be accelerated" (Blumenthal, 1986: 130–131; see also p. 119).

Having relinquished all unilateral or minilateral claims on the Rhineland, the French now invested in efforts to internationalize it—that is, to contribute to the success of multilateral agreements and institutions that placed constraints on Germany's sovereign power to exploit the wealth of the Ruhr. In other words, the French adopted an attitude of "geopolitical internationalism." But whereas the Germans adopted geopolitical internationalism in order to gain equality of status with the other great powers, the French adopted it in order to institutionalize and confirm international constraints on German sovereignty. The French now looked to the League of Nations and the United States to secure respect of those articles of the Treaty of Versailles that regulated German activity in military matters, and secured the partial transfer of German wealth to the allies through reparations. In 1925 France agreed to admit Germany to the League; in 1927 France and the United States acted together to win adherents to the Kellogg-Briand pact, one of the foremost expressions of the liberal reformism of the period, and when Germany and Austria entered into a trade alliance, the French suggested that the plan be extended to all European countries (Blumenthal, 1986: 140).[4]

Following World War II, the sequence of events was remarkably similar. The French again demanded the dismantling of the German state and the creation of a separate entity for the Rhineland. As in the 1920s, they met with strong American and British opposition, and thus retreated to a strategy of "geopolitical minilateralism." But, whereas minilateralism failed in the 1920s, it succeeded in the 1940s. The United States wanted to reunify the three western zones of occupied Germany to implement its strategy of containment of the Soviet Union. France, one of the occupation powers, resisted. Neither concessions nor Marshall aid swayed them. No compromise was in sight as late as March 1949 when European foreign ministers prepared to meet in Washington to lay the groundwork for the North Atlantic Treaty Organization (NATO). In this context, Secretary of State Dean Acheson appealed to French Foreign Minister Robert Schuman: "I believe that our policy in Germany, and the development of a German Government which can take its place in Western Europe, depends on the assumption by your country of leadership in Europe on these problems" (Milward, 1984: 392).

The French seized that offer, and achieved what has since been recognized as the single most decisive step in the creation of the European Union. They proposed the establishment of a European Coal and Steel Community that placed the entire French and German outputs of coal and steel (along with those of Belgium, Luxemburg, and Italy) under a single European High Authority, and created a common, cartelized market for coal and steel products. The French accepted West German reunification in exchange for secure access to the resources of the Ruhr, multilateral control over the allocation of the industrial wealth of Europe's steel-producing core, and secure European markets for French steel-producing firms. The success of the Monnet Plan of Economic Reconstruction and Modernization was predicated on this diplomatic triumph.

In the beginning, European integration was hegemonically mediated. Working under hegemonic constraint-cum-sponsorship, France pursued its strategy of geopolitical minilateralism in a way that was perfectly compatible with its geopolitical interests. Germany responded by deploying a more inclusive policy of "geopolitical internationalism." The Germans showed generally strong support for mulitlateralism, but only because those arrangements provided the most expiditious way to regain equality of status with the victorious powers and curry Western support for territorial reunification. France, however, continued to work to institutionalize its cartel relationship with Germany and to construct a viable European rival to the Atlantic alliance, because this was the most expeditious way to maximize its control over the way Germany used its resources. In pursuit of that strategy, de Gaulle, who returned to power in 1958, gave strong support to West German claims on East Germany, and, in the first years of his presidency, adopted a decidedly anti-Soviet foreign policy. De Gaulle and German Chancellor Konrad Adenauer signed the Franco-German Treaty of Reconciliation in January 1963, just as de Gaulle vetoed Great Britain's entry into the Common Market and rejected American proposals to participate in the Multilateral Nuclear Force. But de Gaulle's ambitions collapsed at the point of success. The German Bundestag refused to abandon the strategy of geopolitical internationalism in favor of this cartel relationship with France. It voted unanimously to append a preamble to the Treaty of Reconciliation that emphasized the importance of "entente between the free peoples—with a particularly close cooperation between Europe and the United States," and added a pointed reference to Great Britain's exclusion from the Common Market (Grosser, 1989: 185). Adenauer retired soon thereafter and the government of Germany passed to the more liberal and pro-American Ludwig Erhart.

France's strategy of geopolitical minilateralism ultimately failed. France reacted to this failure by adopting a unilateralist, even exploitative orientation in foreign policy. Through brinkmanship in the Common Market, de Gaulle forced passage of the Common Agricultural Policy (which essentially required Germany to subsidize French agriculture), and the formal recognition of the "unit-veto" in Common Market affairs. During this same period, France withdrew its forces from the integrated NATO command structure and adopted a more sympathetic policy toward the Soviet Union.

But Pompidou, who succeeded de Gaulle as president of France, could not sustain the unilateralist thrust of Gaullist policy. Hostility toward Germany left France isolated in Europe. The French responded, as in 1924, by embracing and even championing the cause of internationalism. Pompidou approved Great Britain's entry into the Common Market. He supported the project for Economic and Monetary Union as a means to back France out of the diplomatic cul-de-sac in which de Gaulle had left it.

It is true that the monetary crisis of 1969–1973 delayed implementation of the plan as a bitter feud erupted between France and Germany regarding Europe's response to the breakdown of the Bretton Woods system of fixed exchange rates. But the French altered the general orientation of their monetary policy in 1974 under the leadership of the new president, Valéry Giscard-d'Estaing, and adopted a strong franc policy (for reasons analyzed in greater detail below). France and Germany resolved their monetary differences, solidified their relationship, and assumed joint leadership within the European Community. France and Germany led the campaign to create the European Monetary System in 1978, to admit Greece to the European Union in 1981, Spain and Portugal in 1986, to abolish custom controls at the frontier (the Schengen agreements of 1985 signed with Benelux and Spain), to revise the Treaty of Rome and promulgate the Single European Act in 1986, to establish a plan for Economic and Monetary Union in 1989, to endorse the principle of political union in 1990, to create the Eurocorps in 1991, to reform the Common Agricultural Policy in 1992, and to admit Austria, Finland, Sweden, and Norway in 1994.[5]

CHANGE IN THE HEGEMONIC ORDER AND EUROPEAN ECONOMIC COOPERATION

France and Germany adopted strategies of geopolitical internationalism in response to pressures and incentives created by American actions. But French and German internationalism endures, even though the hegemonic order that spawned it is being gradually dismantled. Enduring Franco-German internationalism and leadership in Europe now constitute, at least in part, a response to American efforts to "alter the terms" of its hegemonic relationship with its allies, efforts informed by American perceptions of decline relative to the rising economies of Europe and especially East Asia.

Monetary integration provides an illustration. The post-World War II hegemonic order was composed of institutions and arrangements that gave states the means to manage and direct capital in a way that preserved political stability within the framework of an open international economic order and export-led growth (Loriaux, 1996). States were empowered to direct capital to accomplish political tasks: neutralize political opposition through subsidies and clientelism; nurture the development of an indigenous industrial and financial elite; and develop a strong industrial base that facilitated participation in an open trade order and contributed to the military strength of the alliance.

France and Germany took advantage of these hegemonic arrangements in different ways. France entered into a thirty-year partnership with inflation. Although inflation did not always manifest itself in consumer price increases, money supply growth was always rapid, even in times of apparent price stability (as, for example, during the post-Korean War recession). Price inflation at other times was held in check by administrative controls. Despite periods of price stability, rapid growth in the monetary base, due to credit expansion, generated endemic inflationary pressures in France that dominated economic policymaking for much of the post-World War II period. To contain and channel those pressures to productive use, successive governments patched together a complex system linking banks to public finance agencies to semi-public lenders to post office checking accounts, all attached to and directed by the Treasury, "the sanctuary inside the temple of the Ministry of Finance, the economic apex" (Zysman, 1983: 114). Through this system, the French irrigated the economy with inflationary money in a more or less controlled fashion. Elsewhere, I describe the development of an "overdraft economy" in which activity, rather than being regulated and directed by market forces, was driven by the growing dependence of industry on credit extended by lending institutions under direct or indirect state control. The state was typically reluctant to impose rigorous standards, fearing the economic and political repercussions of doing so. The overdraft economy thus became a source of "soft constraints," as proposed by Janos Kornai to characterize the former socialist regimes of Eastern Europe.[6]

The institutional constraints of the overdraft economy generally succeeded in containing inflationary pressures. But the dikes gave way on more than one occasion. When the French overdraft economy spun out of control, as it did in 1948, 1954, 1957, and 1969 (to which we could add 1975 and 1981, when France was part of the joint European currency float), the only tool the French could wield effectively was that of external adjustment—devaluation of the franc (or, as in 1954, manipulation of trade restrictions in a way that mimicked the effect of a devaluation). In other words, France's overdraft economy was viable because the international monetary order, structured by a hegemonic United States, made it possible for France to achieve adjustment with the help of (and at the expense of) the international community.

Germany responded differently to the opporunities created by the hegemonic order in international monetary relations. In Germany, economic growth was accorded the highest priority as the means to solve a number of difficult political issues (Hennings, 1982: 479). But Germany's international situation all but ruled out French-style interventionism, while institutional decentralization under the federal constitution—itself the legacy of occupation—complicated state intervention even in the form of Keynesian demand management.[7] The government therefore spurred growth by promoting exports, and promoted exports by pegging the Deutsche mark to an external parity that was undervalued relative to the dollar.[8] The strategy would never have worked had not Bretton Woods conferred on central banks a monopoly on operations on the currency market. Absent that monopoly, the Deutsche mark would have been bid up by traders long before 1971.[9]

But in the mid-1960s the United States began to neglect and finally abandon its hegemonic commitments in monetary relations. It started to indulge in inflationary policy itself under the dual pressure of war in Vietnam and domestic social unrest. American policy aggravated inflationary pressures and monetary instability worldwide. The United States could indulge in inflation, yet ignore the potential trade and monetary effects of inflation, at least for a time, because the American currency was the principal medium of international trade. American policy took advantage of this fact and began to turn predatory (see Helleiner, 1994: 13). Germany reacted to imported inflationary pressures by imposing a rigorous stabilization plan in 1966. As the international monetary system grew more unstable, America's allies called for the devaluation of the dollar. Unwilling to revalue the Soviet Union's gold stock by devaluing the dollar, and increasingly intolerant of the asymmetric trade and monetary arrangements that characterized the hegemonic order, the United States refused to devalue and insisted that other countries revalue. As the crisis worsened, Germany suspended the mark's fixed parity in May 1971, and let the mark float upward as the market dictated. But the French refused that course. They were vehemently critical of American policy. Having devalued in August 1969, they naturally rejected revaluation in 1971. They tried to forge a common European front against American demands that currencies be revised upward, but met with opposition from the Germans, who had coopted floating rates into their war on inflation (Gerbet, 1994: 299–308, 342–50).

The final collapse of the fixed rate system in 1973, however, altered French monetary interests, and initiated a complete turnabout in policy. Floating rates gave rise to the threat of destabilizing spirals of inflation and currency depreciation, notably in the trade-dependent economies of Western Europe (Loriaux, 1991: 24–31).[10] Floating rates, despite the predictions of economic theory, made the defense of the currency more necessary than before, at least for the highly open and trade-dependent economies of western Europe. France opted for a hard currency in 1974, but the overdraft economy's soft constraints on firms rendered ineffective the anti-inflationary policy needed to support a strong currency. Toothless when implemented with sensitivity toward the fragile financial position of French firms, it was devastating when given more bite. Without hegemonic validation, the French overdraft economy was not viable. Persistent currency weakness ended in the near-collapse of the French overdraft economy in the early 1980s. The government, under Socialist direction, effected a dramatic policy U-turn and implemented a series of deep liberalizing reforms designed to give the French economy the means to deploy a strong currency policy.

Monetary cooperation with Germany became essential both to France's efforts to stabilize the franc and reform the structures of its political economy. Those efforts help explain France's current interest in the single currency. Although a system of fixed exchange rates among European currencies would go far toward addressing the problems that floating rates create for open economies, the system would still leave France paying a "risk premium" levied on domestic interest rates for past sins. The single currency would equalize interest rates across member countries (though not across all individual borrowers) and render national economies invulnerable against speculative movements into the mark (which would cease to exist).[11] Inversely, countries that are not in the midst of reforming the structures and mores of their political economy—notably Great Britain—tend not to share France's concerns, and thus attach greater importance to the defense of monetary sovereignty.

German interest in monetary integration fluctuates. The French approached the Germans as early as 1974 with a plan to reform the European currency float in a way that facilitated participation by weak-currency countries. The Germans rebuffed the French proposal, complaining that it asked them in effect to absorb French inflation. That complaint has informed Germany's attitude toward monetary integration on many occasions. Its attitude alters, however, when a drop in the dollar sends speculative money into the Deutsche mark, bidding it up to values that threaten export markets. At such times, Germany shows greater interest in European monetary integration. It is in such circumstances that Germany agreed with France in 1978 to create the European Monetary System (which bore a close resemblance to the French plan of 1974). During the period leading up to the adoption of the single currency, the dollar was high, and German interest in the single currency was low, though political argument was finally able to silence economic skepticism.

Turning from monetary integration to commercial and financial deregulation, we find in other cooperative actions similar efforts to shelter national economies against the stress generated by the dismantling of the hegemonic order. Following the New Economic Policy (NEP) of Richard Nixon and the attendant scuttling of Bretton Woods, the second major shock that the United States unleashed on the world economy was "Reaganomics." Like the NEP, Reaganomics was a reaction to the perception that America was declining as a hegemonic power. It was designed to reanimate the American economy through supply side economics and fiscal stimulus, while generating the funds needed to upgrade the U. S. military, particularly the navy, by stimulating economic growth. But because taxes were cut at a time when the Federal Reserve Board (Fed) was clamping down on inflation, Reaganomics created a sizable budget deficit that the Fed refused to monetize. International capital was siphoned into American Treasury bills by high interest rates. Investors bid the dollar up to record levels as they exchanged foreign currencies to buy U. S. bonds. Europeans responded by deregulating their capital markets in order to compete more effectively for capital's favors. The London Stock Exchange submitted to the "Big Bang" of liberalizing reform, while France, under a Socialist government, introduced the last word in capitalism: a financial futures market on the Chicago model (see Cerny, 1988; Loriaux, 1992).

Deregulation, which occurred on a global scale, endowed capital with a measure of "structural power" that it had lacked during the half century that it was constrained by the rules of the hegemonic order. In this new financial environment, Europeans had to devise ways to make European firms more competitive. Because of financial globalization, a firm's survival depends more and more on the size of its capital base and its ability to realize economies of scale and invest in research and development. Larger firms require larger markets, and the path to larger markets in Europe passes through EU trade liberalization and deregulation (see Hayward, 1995). The single European act, along with other measures, launched the Europeans on the Herculean task of revising and harmonizing their national regulatory codes regarding production and trade.

CONCLUSION

The political economy-cum-geopolitics of the Rhineland is unique in the world, given the military and economic importance of the states that congregate there, along with the close involvement of a hegemonic America in the region and the ambitious experiment in economic and political integration. But it alerts us nevertheless to questions that we might ask in other contexts. The first question has to do with the relationship between the transborder economy, of which there are many in the world, and the borders that intersect them. The history of the Rhineland suggests that the existence of such transborder economies may, in some instances, point to something other than the mere local manifestation of some more general process of "globalization" that is supposedly transforming the world of nation-states. It suggests that in many cases the transnational and international aspects of a regional economy may be closely intertwined and have deep historical roots.

The second question concerns the significance of transborder economies for the evolution of the world economy. The history of the Rhineland suggests that transborder economies are not the consequence of globalization, but that they antedate globalization, and indeed may be the driving force behind the phenomenon that we, rather uncritically, have been calling globalization. In the latter case, what looks like globalization may simply be the consequence of multiple regionalizations—that is, the reassertion of regionally intertwined economies across international borders that were put in place and/or enforced fairly recently, sometimes as late as the early twentieth century. If this is true, then we should not anticipate the advent of a globalized economy, but of a regionalized economy, dominated by regional blocs within which trade is intense but between which trade is of moderate importance. In this regard, it is useful to recall that the European Union as a bloc is only about 8 percent trade dependent, whereas the countries that compose it are individually more than 20 percent and sometimes 30 percent trade dependent. The single market and the common currency will endow this regional bloc, qua bloc, with an autonomy that Europe has not experienced for a half century. The impact of that autonomy on the future evolution of the world economy could be profound.

NOTES

1. The Meuse is not technically a tributary of the Rhine, but shares its delta and generally partakes in the economic and cultural space of the Rhineland.

2. Great Britain's foreign trade grew by 34 percent, and that of the United States by 80 percent.

3. Material in this and the next section is drawn from Loriaux (1999).

4. Blumenthal argues that the French sought to halt and diminish Anglo-Saxon penetration in Europe. But such fears are meaningful only in the context of French fears of growing German power, which, from the French perspective, the Anglo-Saxon powers tolerated and abetted. Compare with the French attitude toward Zollverein in the nineteenth century: see Poidevin and Bariéty (1977: 38–43).

5. The chronicle of European integration can be found in Gerbet (1994). Norway did not ratify the treaty.

6. In the terms of my analysis, the overdraft economy generated "moral hazard" in the French political economy. Loriaux (1991: 90–95, 284–88).

7. Such intervention was difficult despite the relatively large size of the public sector. See Liberman (1977), Chapter 2.

8. Note that the government, not the *Bundesbank*, was accorded the responsibility for determining the exchange rate of the D-mark under fixed rates. The *Bundesbank* was empowered to defend that rate. See Hennings (1982), p. 475.

9. Speculators under Bretton Woods technically bought foreign currencies from the central bank, thus challenging the central bank to satisfy demand for foreign currencies at prices that were fixed by international agreement.

10. Currency depreciation (like devaluation) raised the price of imported goods. If the demand for those goods was inelastic, currency depreciation could result in a vicious circle whereby depreciation and inflation fed off each other. Inversely, attacking inflation could cause the currency to appreciate again, negating whatever commercial benefits were being sought in the first place. Overshooting of equilibrium currency values by an inherently nervous currency market ruled out "finessing" this dilemma through "fine tuning."

11. This observation also applies to other traditionally weak currency countries of the "Club Med," who experience the same need as France to implement a strong currency policy to fight vicious circles of inflation and depreciation. Antonio Guterres, leader of Portugal's opposition Socialist Party, writes: "Interest rates are the fundamental reason why I am a defender of the single currency. This will be the only way to make sure that we stop paying a risk premium, and to have interest rates equal to other countries, like Germany" (*Diario Economico*, 24 August, 1995). Capital flight into the single European currency would create pressures to lower interest rates, whereas, currently, capital flight into the mark creates pressures to raise interest rates in economies that seek to defend a D-mark parity.

10

Slipping into Something More Comfortable: Argentine-Brazilian Nuclear Integration and the Origins of the MERCOSUR

Isabella Alcañiz

In studying the evolution of capitalism and its political configuration, world-system theory has—as a systemic international perspective—concentrated on the north–south divide or, to use the proper terms, the core-periphery divide. But if past political and economic developments in the Third World have taught us anything, it is that within the periphery there is diversity. There is diversity in economic development and in political institutions. And there are also asymmetries that mediate the relationship between countries within the periphery. But global explanations tend to overlook these differences and instead stress the similar ignominies to which developing countries are all subjected by the core. At the most, subsidiary categories are added to explain unexpected specialization patterns or differences in growth rates—that is, semi-periphery.

Globalization, again, threatens to be a new equalizer within most theories explaining the developing world. Of course, it cannot be denied that in the new international context some general economic and policy trends have became a common theme in the Third World: privatization, downsizing, liberalization, and even some political recipes like judicial reforms or anti-corruption legislation have been prescribed to a large number of countries. But the manner and degree to which these countries followed suit, when they did, have been extremely varied.

Given the "shifting geopolitics" of the world, between the end of the Cold War and the beginning of an apparently united and globalized world, it seems more urgent now to unbury the differences among developing nations. If we cannot explain how different countries deal with the pressures of globalization, this phenomenon becomes one totalizing force driving us to accept the doubtful "end of history" mystique. To that end, the next pages tell a different story where national developmental interests, despite being contested from the international system, still drove Argentina and Brazil's strategies in the nuclear sector.

FROM ATOMS FOR PEACE TO ATOMS FOR MONEY[1]

"The exchange was to be American dollars for safeguards"[2] said the former Argentine secretary of the Brazilian-Argentine Agency for Accounting and Control of Nuclear Materials (the ABACC).[3] That is, in order to end economic isolation after the debt crisis, Argentina had to show its good will in the nuclear area. "It was less bothersome, more comfortable," he continued, in order to explain why Argentina and Brazil moved toward nuclear integration instead of directly falling into line with the demands from the United States and the other Non-Proliferation Regime (NPR) members.

In 1985 the democratically elected presidents Alfonsín and Sarney, from Argentina and Brazil respectively, signed the Iguazú Protocol. These agreements established mutual cooperation and supervision in the area of nuclear energy. From that point on, Argentina and Brazil embarked on a process of increasing cooperation, not only in the nuclear sector, but in the trade area as well (creating the Common Market of the South).[4] This new strategy of regional cooperation contrasted sharply with the two countries' previous history of distrust and rivalry. How is it that the first steps toward regional integration were taken in such a sensitive area as nuclear energy? This chapter attempts to answer this question, and in doing so explore the logic behind regional cooperation of semi-peripheral countries.

Throughout the early and mid-twentieth century both Argentina and Brazil followed a developmentalist agenda. That is, their development efforts were characterized by strong state intervention in the industrialization process, which was also typically directed toward import-substitution (Sikkink, 1991). But by the early 1980s the developmentalist model had been generally forsaken in these two countries for it had created overexpanded and indebted states that no longer could sponsor economic growth, let alone development. Furthermore, in 1982 the international debt crisis hit Argentina and Brazil hard, affecting not only their economies but also contributing to their democratization. The emerging trends of globalization and economic liberalization in the world prompted these two middle-income countries to review their development strategies.

The nuclear energy sectors of both countries have always been institutional strongholds of developmentalist ideas and interests. Created in the 1950s in Brazil under President Kubitschek and under President Perón in Argentina, both national commissions of nuclear energy embodied the difficult realities of being semi-peripheral countries: depending on imported technology for development, yet possessing the necessary natural and human resources for the task. In 1985, the year the Iguazú Protocol was signed, this tension was still at the heart of the development of the Argentine and Brazilian nuclear energy programs. But the international order had changed drastically from the times of Perón and Kubitschek, and so had the domestic priorities of these two countries.

Why did rivalry give way to cooperation in the mid-1980s? Why did Argentina and Brazil decide to trade national autonomy, so dear to the developmentalist tradition, for regional subordination? I argue that cooperation in the nuclear energy sector was sought in order to defend precisely Argentine and Brazilian autonomy. That is, both governments pursued regionalization to gain maneuvering room in the face of pressing international and domestic demands. As Theda Skocpol asserted, states are autonomous because they are located at the intersection of the domestic and international arenas, and can play these two orders against each other (1979). Regional cooperation was the way that both the Argentine and Brazilian governments dealt with similar national and international demands.

In telling the story of nuclear energy integration we begin to explore the remainder of the developmentalist politico-economic model under conditions of globalization and liberalization. In Gamble and Payne's words:

Nearly all states now seek, as it were, to ride two tigers simultaneously: they have to respond to the structural power of international capital, which demands the continuing openness of the world economy, and to the continuing pull of national interests of various sorts. (Gamble and Payne, 1996: 16)

The tigers in the Argentine-Brazilian integration were, on the one hand, the members of the Non-Proliferation Regime (NPR) and international creditors, both groups led by the United States, and on the other, the two nuclear energy sectors with their civil and military representatives.

For many years, Argentina and Brazil had been the target of international pressures to sign the Non-Proliferation Treaty (NPT) of 1968. This agreement, led by the United States and western Europe, imposed safeguards on all international nuclear exchanges in order to control nuclear weapon proliferation. The selling of technology to developing countries was strictly supervised by signing members. Upholding their agendas of nuclear independence, Argentina and Brazil had refused to sign the NPT.

Thus, Argentina and Brazil were incited to move toward cooperation from two different arenas: the domestic and the international. First and from "below," both the legacy of the developmental state and the necessity to demilitarize the nuclear energy sectors produced concrete demands on the leadership of Argentina and Brazil. The developmentalist institutions, deeply ingrained in the state apparatus, pressed the newly elected leaders to implement policies consistent with the tradition of autonomy (from international pressures) in the energy sector. The urgency for democratic stability moved Alfonsín and Sarney to shift the control of nuclear policy from military to civilian agents (Redick, Carasales, and Wrobel, 1995).

Second and from "above," the necessity to end economic and technological isolation defined the timing and regionalization of the nuclear policies followed by the governments of Alfonsín and Sarney. In 1985, at the time of the signing of the Iguazú Protocol, both Argentina and Brazil were under intense international pressure to open up their economies. Attending to the demands from foreign creditors, these countries promised reductions in government spending and major economic reforms that would dismantle previous developmentalist policies. The energy sector in general, and the nuclear area in particular, would be affected by these measures. The regionalization of the Argentine and Brazilian nuclear energy programs allowed the two governments to ease the political pressure on them without having to compromise their autonomy.

TOWARD THE IGUAZÚ PROTOCOL: SEPARATING MILITARY GOALS FROM THE DEVELOPMENTALIST AGENDA

When discussing the nuclear energy programs in Argentina and Brazil, one must consider the developmentalist agenda and the role of the military in both countries. The development of these state programs, although with different technological outcomes,[5] was done by closely scrutinizing the advances in the other country. As Adler states, "Their competition to be number one in this crucial area led to an action-reaction pattern" (Adler, 1987: 280). By 1985 developmentalist ideas, characteristic of the 1950s and 1960s, were strongly challenged as a viable economic model, but their political and ideological force was still informing some state institutions. While in general the developmentalist model has had much more enduring and supportive advocates in Brazil than in Argentina, the nuclear energy sectors of both countries had been shaped by this agenda and, given their institutional coherence, continued under the spell of this model in 1985 (Sikkink, 1991).

The development of energy sources was crucial to the industrialization effort in the Third World. Both Argentina and Brazil as semi-peripheral countries financed most of their industrial policies by using cheap energy supplied by state-owned firms. Thus, energy issues in both Argentina and Brazil were tied to notions of autonomy and industrial growth. Self-reliance in the nuclear energy sector was a goal held by both countries, even though Argentina was more successful than Brazil in creating sustainable nuclear energy industries (Adler, 1987; Solingen, 1996).

Under Perón's administration in the 1940s and 1950s, Argentina emerged as a growing industrial economy. During World War II the potential of this country had been demonstrated on the political and commercial front. It was time, Perón thought, to demonstrate that this nation could also be powerful on the industrial-technological front. The first steps taken in the direction of nuclear development were faulty, though. Perón hired a German scientist, Ronald Richter, in tune with his admiration for nationalist Germany, and put him in charge of Argentina's nuclear development. At that point in time, the development of this energy sector would not only be for industrial purposes; military concerns were also part of the nuclear equation.

The German scientist was unable to deliver, and Perón suffered national embarrassment for he had announced to the world that Argentina was on its way toward nuclear grandeur. After this fiasco Perón decided to empower the recently created National Commission of Atomic Energy (CNEA) by hiring the best technicians regardless of their political (and ethnic) backgrounds. In this way, and throughout the following decades, the major body of nuclear energy in Argentina remained nonpartisan (Adler, 1987). In a country where politics have been described as an "impossible game" (O'Donnell, 1973), the CNEA produced not only doable projects, but remained a coherent and consistent unit under different regimes.

The cohesiveness of the CNEA was cemented by the belief in certain shared objectives: "The development of nuclear power as a national project, and the CNEA's nonpartisan character" (Adler, 1987: 296). The ideological glue that brought all members of this body together was the belief in the ultimate goal of autonomy. In addition, the leeway given to the CNEA in hiring and, more important, in policy-making helped centralize even more the nuclear program in the hands of these—some civilian, some military—technicians. This quest for technological autonomy, as Adler describes it, made the CNEA an eager recipient of developmentalist ideas.

In Brazil developmentalist policies, initiated under the second administration of Vargas (1951–1954) but crystallized with Kubitschek (1956–1961), have marked the political economy until the present. Many authors agree that this has been due to the relative autonomy of the Brazilian state and its political leadership from societal pressures (Kaufman, 1990; Sikkink 1991). Still, strategies for nuclear development in Brazil, while oriented toward self-sufficiency, were not as successful as in Argentina.[6] Furthermore, in contrast with Argentina, nuclear policy-making was not centralized in one body. The power to decide over nuclear issues was scattered throughout many state organisms, and as Adler argues: "The (Brazilian) National Nuclear Energy Commission—CNEN—created in 1956, was no equal to the CNEA and its undertakings" (Adler, 1987: 281).

In 1975 the Brazilian government signed an agreement with West Germany by which the latter was able to exploit part of Brazil's uranium in exchange for technology, infrastructure and nuclear reactors. Adler illustrates some of the dependency problems that arise when a developing country needs foreign technology:

As part of the 1975 agreement with West Germany, Brazil also purchased its own uranium enrichment technology. First choice was the centrifuge system used by Urenco, but West Germany's partners opposed the transfer of this sensitive technology. So Brazil had to settle for jet-nozzle, or Becker, technology, similar to the centrifuge but requiring larger amounts of electricity, and at that time still untested at the industrial level. Gaseous diffusion, the third enrichment technology, which the Americans used, was unavailable for purchase by Brazil. (Adler, 1987: 304)

Thus, advanced technology for peripheral countries was conditional on the core's interests. These interests were both security-oriented, due to the rationale of the Cold War in Latin America, and material, given the prosperous nature of the nuclear business for the technology-selling country. The case of the Brazilian-German contract shows us the political and economic reasons behind the Argentine and Brazilian goal of autonomy. Ideas of self-reliance were upheld and furthered in both countries because the political leadership of the two nuclear programs understood that if they continued to be dependent on foreign technology, their programs would never prosper. Independence was desired not only from certain domestic political forces, such as political parties or labor organizations, but also—and as important—from international control. As the presence of the ABACC demonstrates, this sentiment is still alive today in both nuclear sectors.

Another institutional legacy of the developmentalist model was a military with invested interests in the state-led industrial production of arms, energy, and technology. Demilitarization of the CNEA and CNEN was the second domestic factor pushing presidents Alfonsín and Sarney toward nuclear cooperation. The precarious relations between the military and the democratic administrations can explain why both presidents were willing to renounce any claim of absolute sovereignty (by creating a "regional sovereignty") on their nuclear policies. By setting up mutual controls in this sector, Sarney had a greater chance of demilitarizing it and Alfonsín had a new political instrument to keep the (once in control) military at bay.

The involvement of the military in the nuclear development plans was great in both Argentina and Brazil, and both shared one fear: that the other country would go nuclear first. Even when neither country really saw the development of nuclear weaponry as a viable alternative (for international, political, economic costs), they nevertheless comprehended the potential for arms that the nuclear cycle provides. Until the Iguazú Protocol, Argentina and Brazil remained wary of each other. A student of South American geopolitics describes the situation for Brazil as the following:

Brazil must consider the dangers of Argentina going nuclear first, and, while it can tolerate the possibility of an Argentine first, Brazil would probably not accept a long-lasting situation where Argentina is nuclear and Brazil is not. Thus, Brazil feels the need to be ready to go nuclear as a reaction to Argentina, or, possibly, to preempt its southern neighbor. (Child, 1985: 102)

At the time of democratization, the military strength of the two countries differed. The Argentine dictatorship under Galtieri had been defeated in a war against the United Kingdom (the Malvinas/Falkland War), thus losing the support of all major economic and political players in the country. Furthermore, the seven years of military rule had led the country to its worst economic crisis since the 1930s Depression. In addition, the 1982 nationalization of the private sector's foreign debt placed the military as one of the biggest liabilities in Argentine society. The political situation in Brazil was different. After two decades of military rule (1964–1985), Brazil had emerged as the most dynamic and largest economy in Latin America. In contrast to Argentina, foreign lending in the early 1970s had gone to support the industrialization efforts of the country.

The differences between the Argentine and Brazilian military and nuclear sectors are important, but it is among the similarities of these two cases where the explanation for nuclear cooperation lies. The CNEA and the CNEN and like organisms were all composed of civilians and military technicians and bureaucrats. It is true that in Argentina the CNEA had been able to secure, more than in Brazil, independence from domestic political forces, including the (often) ruling military. But what was the same for both Argentina and Brazil was that as long as the country was under military rule, its nuclear sector would be more prone to follow strategic guidelines. In other words, from 1964 to 1985 in Brazil and from 1966 to 1983 in Argentina (excluding the Peronist interregnum of 1973–1976) geopolitics was the norm.

The imperative of demilitarizing the nuclear sectors was only one of many demands that the leaders of these new democracies had to face. In the case of Argentina, the pressures that Alfonsín encountered are summarized in the following passage:

Alfonsín wanted to end Argentina's diplomatic and economic isolation and assert civilian control over the nuclear energy program. He also wished to preserve Argentina's independent nuclear policy while reducing international pressure on his country to fall into line with the nonproliferation regime. Consequently, a new Argentine initiative to Brazil, which was emerging from a two-decade twilight of military government, seemed opportune. (Redick, Carasales, and Wrobel, 1996)

Thus, democratization in Argentina and Brazil was an important factor in the shift of the bilateral relationship. Military dictatorships had characterized their foreign policies as geopolitical; the democratic governments of Alfonsín and Sarney followed a conciliatory course of politics. These two administrations had to act in order to achieve the "balancing of military interests against the demands of demobilization, economic reform, and democratization" (Hunter, 1996: 2). This explains in part the change from competition to cooperation.

Still, this is not the whole story. If the cooperative agreement between Argentina and Brazil was solely a result of democratic forces, then the changes in nuclear policy of both countries should have been absolute. That is, the bilateral arrangement should have entailed an immediate and unreserved entry to the Non-Proliferation Regime. This did not occur in the 1980s, and it is only recently that both countries have taken concrete steps toward the final ratification of the NPT.[7] Demilitarization as a natural consequence of democratization was an important factor explaining Argentina and Brazil's change of behavior toward each other. But the fact that neither immediately signed the NPT or the Tlatelolco Treaty (the NPT's equivalent exclusively for Latin America) supports the argument that national imperatives of autonomous development were also part of the Iguazú equation.

Hence, in this section we have seen how the goal of autonomy inherited from the developmentalist agenda and the imperatives of demilitarization brought by democratization converged in a particular way in the two nuclear energy programs. The new leadership of Argentina and Brazil had to meet the challenge of these two domestic demands. However, they were not the only sources of pressure related to nuclear issues. From the international order—more specifically, the Non-Proliferation Regime—Argentina and Brazil had been the steady recipients of demands to comply with the International Atomic Energy Agency (IAEA) safeguards and to sign the NPT.

For decades, the two countries had separately opposed the interference of any other country in the development of their nuclear programs. Argentina and Brazil had systematically used arguments of energy autonomy and national sovereignty to fend off the attacks of the United States and other industrialized countries. Why were Argentina and Brazil compelled in 1985 to go beyond declamation and produce concrete evidence that they were not pursuing an arms race in the Southern Cone? Were the Iguazú Protocol and the creation of the ABACC a political maneuver to convince only each other that there were no hidden intentions in their nuclear operations? Or was it intended to reach a greater audience, going beyond regional politics? The Iguazú Declarations and the Bilateral Agreement were clearly oriented toward the international community. In the next section I present my argument of how and why this was done.

THE FINAL DETERMINANT: INTERNATIONAL ORDER AND REGIONAL SOVEREIGNTY

The signing of the Iguazú Protocol in 1985 marked the beginning of a new era for the nuclear programs of Argentina and Brazil. For the first time in the history of bilateral relations, these two countries committed themselves to: (1) collaborate in the effort of developing nuclear energy, (2) provide a series of visits to the nuclear facilities of both countries, (3) supply formal assurance of the peaceful nature of their nuclear programs, (4) set the basis for future collaboration in the research and development of nuclear energy. The message sent to the core economies was one in which these two countries were taking formal steps toward greater openness and transparency in the development of nuclear energy. But why did the governments of Alfonsín and Sarney decide in 1985 to respond to international pressure? Beyond domestic political motivations, Argentina and Brazil's cooperative agreement was also a result of economic demands from the international system.

Students of Argentina and Brazil's foreign nuclear policies agree that the Iguazú Protocol was devised as a response to international pressure. In particular the United States, as the leading Western member of the NPR and hegemonic power in the Americas, attempted to coerce Argentina and Brazil into joining the NPR. In a conference on Argentine-Brazilian nuclear cooperation, one speaker stated the situation:

I cannot go into the tortuous history of relations between Washington and Buenos Aires and between Washington and Brasilia in detail here. I can, however, summarize it in one sentence: as far as it was able to, the US government attempted to hold the balance in the complicated relationship between Argentina and Brazil.

He then continues:

I even dare to say that were it not for the insistence of the US government that Buenos Aires and Brasilia sign the Nuclear Non-Proliferation Treaty, both countries would not have felt the need to co-ordinate policies in the face of pressures that affect them equally. (Leventhal and Tanzer, 1992: 63–64)

Redick, Carasales, and Wrobel also state that Argentina and Brazil started to cooperate in the nuclear area in order to improve relations with the advanced nuclear countries, while being able to remain independent from them in their own nuclear programs. Moreover, these authors argue that because Argentina and Brazil had historically maintained the same position before the NPR—of noncompliance to the international safeguards dictated by the United States and western Europe—they began to visualize a bilateral agreement. A shared "enemy" made these two countries aware of the possibilities of creating a common front.

Argentina and Brazil rejected the Non-Proliferation Treaty as an inherently unequal and unacceptable treaty, and neither was a contracting party to the Treaty of Tlatelolco, which created a Latin American nuclear-weapon-free zone in 1967. Both nations had avoided full-scope International Atomic Energy Agency (IAEA) safeguards and had certain unsafeguarded nuclear facilities with military potential. (Redick, Carasales, and Wrobel, 1995)

Solingen asserts that the Argentine and Brazilian states were able many times to get around the conditions set by the industrialized (nuclear) world. Furthermore, she argues that the restrictions on the availability of certain technology did not have such a profound effect on the technological development of the two nuclear programs. This author holds the two countries' collaboration with West Germany (an occasional detractor from the NPT) as an example (Solingen, 1996). In a similar vein, Kenneth Johnson states:

Argentina, as a politically unstable nation of great hemispheric importance, is more susceptible to US influence in the economic sphere than in the diplomatic, cultural, or strictly military sphere. (Johnson, 1982: 53)

This is not to say that the weight of the NPR on domestic nuclear policies was negligible. The pressure existed; the purchase of nuclear technology or infrastructure could only be done under IAEA safeguards. That is, even though Argentina and Brazil had refused to abide by these rules, they were forced to do so in their purchasing of foreign assistance. This in turn could make them follow one particular technological path, which perhaps was not their first choice. The case of Brazil not being able to access American technology (mentioned in the previous section) stresses this last point. Thus, political pressure from the NPR was strong, yet Argentina and Brazil had been able to continue on their nuclear paths despite it.

The early 1980s were not only marked by the democratization of South America, but also by the eruption of international recession and the debt crisis. Brazil, and even more so Argentina, had at the beginning of the decade their economies severely in debt. In 1982, with Mexico's unilateral decision to postpone payment of the principal and interests of its foreign debt, the financial problems of developing countries in repaying their loans became an international crisis.

When Alfonsín and Sarney took office their main task was, besides carrying out the political transition successfully, to straighten the economy. Both countries were heavily in debt, both internally and externally. Since 1982, with the Mexican crisis, the international club of creditors had started looking for common solutions for the Third World debt. International creditors addressed the general crisis as such and offered the same remedies to different countries. Orthodox monetary policies were recommended, in addition to financial and trade liberalization. In order to pay the debt, foreign creditors (and the "Washington Consensus") expected these developing countries to clean house by reducing the size of the state and consequently augmenting the private sector participation in the economy (Bianchi, 1985; Frieden, 1991).

Argentina and Brazil both had state-coordinated economies. Therefore, this meant that Alfonsín and Sarney had to carry out an institutional reform, as well as economic and political transformations. International recommendations made to these recently democratized countries to liberalize the economy were tied to the promise of continuance (or discontinuance) of loans. Because of this, in Latin America dependence on the World Bank, the IMF, and other international lenders was high. These states had to make amends (such as liberalization of financial and capital markets, privatization, etc.) in order to continue receiving fresh foreign currency to solve both large state deficits and balance of payment deficits. As the economist Pastor asserts:

Since 1982, the International Monetary Fund has played a major role in managing the international and intranational conflicts caused by the nearly half trillion dollars of Latin American debt. (Pastor in Frieden and Lake, 1991: 320)

Many Latin American countries realized that the only way to receive foreign resources was to be in good standing with the IMF and the World Bank. This in turn would allow them to keep financing their foreign debt, through the extension of IMF (conditioned) loans, such as the standby loan or extended fund facility. In Argentina and Brazil, economic reform was pursued in order to solve the internal deficit and the growing inflation. In the first years of government, Alfonsín and his finance minister Sourrouille produced the *Austral* plan, President Sarney, on the other hand, came up with the *Cruzado* plan.[8] Both plans were a somewhat heterodox version of the dictates of the IMF.

Without a doubt, the nuclear sectors of Argentina and Brazil were affected by the debt crisis. These energy programs had been the recipients in the past years of a great part of the foreign loans. In 1985 the Argentine CNEA was indebted by $800 million or 1.7 percent of the total foreign debt of this country. Of Brazil's $102 billion total debt, the state nuclear enterprises owed $2.1 billion (Adler, 1987). Thus, the economic crisis affected the nuclear sector and was an important factor in the changes produced in Argentine-Brazilian bilateral relations. Still, the economic crisis did not move Argentina and Brazil to shut down their nuclear programs. As Adler states for the case of Argentina in 1985:

Nevertheless, most of the autonomy project's goals remain intact. The project has proven to be too advanced, the technological, industrial, and strategic achievements too numerous, and the national pride payoff too important, for even a deep economic crisis to halt the project entirely. (Adler, 1987: 294)

Brazil also remained firm on its path of nuclear development. Despite the economic situation, it would have been more costly in political and economic terms to dismantle the program. Thus, both countries, while reducing the budget allocated for nuclear development, continued with their projects. Cost reduction has been a priority for the governments of Argentina and Brazil beginning in the mid-1980s until the present day. Yet this imperative only informed the formalities of the new arrangements between both countries.[9] Cost reduction did not dictate the terms of the new bilateral policies in nuclear energy.

Therefore, international forces of political and economic liberalization, brought about by the world recession and the debt crisis of the early 1980s, had a great influence on the outcome of the nuclear negotiations of Argentina and Brazil. Still, political and economic liberalization did not liberalize nuclear policies in Argentina and Brazil. These two countries did not dismantle their nuclear programs, nor did they immediately join the NPR. Because Argentina and Brazil still needed to respond to the demands of the international financial system, the political demands from the NPR became more pressing. The new bilateral safeguards between Argentina and Brazil made Washington and its allies diminish their pressure. Thus, the leaderships of Argentina and Brazil were able to continue with their own strategies for nuclear development, while at the same time ending the political and economic isolation in which their military predecessors had put them.

CONCLUSION

The Iguazú Protocol (and the creation of the ABACC) implied a signaling to the international community. The message was clear: we will meet you halfway. Argentina and Brazil would give in to international pressure without forfeiting control of their nuclear programs. Alfonsín and Sarney had to respond to pressures originating from the developmentalist mandate for autonomy in the energy sector, the democratization pressure to reduce the military influence in critical sectors, and the fiscal crisis that resulted from the international debt crisis. Nuclear cooperation was, I argue, a mechanism to answer to those pressures. The costs of nuclear integration were few, given that both countries shared similar goals of autonomy and development in this area. The benefits could be significant, both in diplomatic and economic terms.

The case analyzed here shows the new role of regional politics in the semi-periphery. Given the globalization of national economies and the economic-political liberalization that this entailed, domestic developmentalist models were no longer viable. Argentina and Brazil's reincorporation into the world market in the 1980s under these conditions produced the internationalization of development strategies. The Iguazú Protocol showed their intention to converge toward the world market without a belief in the miracles of the market. It was the old developmentalist spirit without the developmentalist agenda. Developmentalism, with its strong nationalist and military elements, was transformed from a national ideology into a regional agenda. The nuclear energy sector gave Argentina and Brazil a niche to exercise *regional sovereignty*.

These emergent forms of regional sovereignty within the semi-periphery provide a new research horizon to old international problems. Will expanding regional cooperation to other areas, such as trade, allow Argentina and Brazil to escape similar domestic and international pressures—coming from "below" and "above"—as those that triggered the nuclear integration process? Until now the MERCOSUR has not evolved beyond providing a buffer zone to a broader economic integration to world markets. Yet, because of the momentum the MERCOSUR has gained in Latin America as a trade zone, Argentina and Brazil have increased their negotiating power with the United States. Witness to this are the events of 1997, when Argentina was named a major non-NATO ally by Washington, and Brazil became the (unofficial) candidate for regional representative to the United Nations Permanent Security Council. These two offerings can only be explained as a delayed gesture of the regional hegemon attempting to finally recognize the significance of its semi-periphery "getting comfortable."

NOTES

1. This chapter has benefited from the comments of Edward Gibson, Michael Loriaux, Michael Hanchard, Ben Ross Schneider, Susan Bloom, Michael Bosia, and Ernesto

Calvo. This research was financed by the Institute for the Study of World Politics, the National Science Foundation, and the Center for International and Comparative Studies (CICS) at Northwestern University.

2. Interview with Dr. Coll conducted in Buenos Aires, Argentina, August 1997.

3. Created in 1991 by bilateral agreement and based in Rio de Janeiro, Brazil, the ABACC supervises and verifies that all nuclear activities and materials are only used for peaceful ends in the two countries. The same year it was created, the ABACC and the International Atomic Energy Agency (IAEA) signed a Quadripartite Agreement. This connection with the IAEA highlights the important role international actors played in the whole Argentine-Brazilian nuclear integration process.

4. Better known as MERCOSUR, the founding treaty was signed in 1991 by Argentina, Brazil, Paraguay, and Uruguay. The Common Market began in 1995.

5. Among many differences between the two nuclear programs, such as the degree of autonomy achieved in this sector from domestic political pressures (which was greater in Argentina than in Brazil) together with the greater or lesser involvement of foreign and state assistance (greater for both cases in Brazil), the technological paths chosen also differed. Argentina oriented its nuclear industry toward heavy water reactors and natural uranium production. Brazil, in contrast, produced enriched uranium and light water reactors. The political account of the development of these programs attests to the key role played by nationalist ideologies of development in determining the technological outcomes (see Adler, 1987, and Solingen, 1996).

6. Argentina's early nuclear strategies proved more ingenious in the long run. The initial major nuclear project carried out in this country was the construction of the first nuclear research reactor. Instead of seeking out the assistance of the technologically advanced countries, the Argentine CNEA (under the direction of its president, Quihillalt) decided to build the reactor with the available domestic resources. "Many people called the decision crazy and irresponsible; but Quihillalt and the *guerrillas* were not after efficiency; instead, they wanted to learn how to build a reactor by themselves" (Adler, 1987: 296).

7. Argentina finally signed and ratified the NPT in 1995. Brazil has ratified the treaty in 1998.

8. *Austral* and *Cruzado* were the names for the new currencies in Argentina and Brazil respectively.

9. Cost reduction has been an important consideration for the Argentine and Brazilian governments only in recent years. Both countries attempt to minimize and evenly share the costs of running the ABACC. In the late 1990s plans for privatization of the nuclear sector in the two countries also pointed to the economic concern.

11

Mutual Benefit? African Elites and French African Policy

Scott L. Greer

Decolonization defied expectations in francophone Africa. As new states appeared across Africa and Asia and asserted their sovereignty and autonomy, France and its former African colonies began to construct a peculiar relationship that stood somewhere between formal and genuine sovereignty. This relationship has continued to repeatedly defy international norms and, often, logic. French African relations have their glamour and subterranean mysteries—French foreign legionnaires and intelligence operatives manipulating politics and staging coups in Africa, French mercenaries doing the dirty work of the French state, or the mysterious power wielded by seemingly private individuals over whole countries. The relationship between France and francophone Africa almost mocks the normal functioning of sovereign states in a state system, as when the president of Gabon decided who his ambassador from France would be, or when Radio France International announced the overthrow of Jean-Bedel Bokassa's regime in the Central African Empire before it happened (Wauthier, 1995: 309). The relationship questions normal understandings of diplomacy: the francophone African states even have their own French ministry, colloquially known by its address on Paris's rue Monsieur, which has changed its name often but has always remained willing to service African heads of state. Meanwhile, French secret services traditionally ran the telephone company of Niger and tapped what they liked (Golan, 1981). This relationship questions the processes of decolonization in Africa—Gabonese elites tried at the last minute to swap their prospective independent state for full integration into France (Péan, 1983), and the long-time rulers of Senegal and Côte d'Ivoire were formerly French politicians of note. It questions the basic relationship between rulers and their states: Bokassa himself retained French citizenship and his military pension until he died.

Finally, this relationship between France and its former colonies questions understandings of the politics of and relations between independent states. Francophone African states might be dependent in a global sense, but there is no obvious systemic reason for them to make themselves dependent on one middling power. French relations with Africa so thoroughly minimize sovereignty on both sides that they constitute a limited case of the power of individual networks, transnational forces, and the messy intrusion of the complex organizations known as states into the antiseptic world of diplomacy and strategy. Although the private dealings and secretive interventions of France in Africa— and Africa in France—will probably never be clear to scholars, the contours of Franco-African relations are visible from a distance. It is on the distribution of resources and their political determinants and effects that this chapter will focus (see also Andereggen, 1994; Chipman, 1989; Greer, 1999; Manning, 1998; Wauthier, 1995).

Resource flows and policymaking in French African relations show a pattern. During the 1950s France faced the Cold War imperative of decolonization. However, French policymakers tried to escape the effects of decolonization. Building a bloc of African client states appeared to be a useful means of maintaining power and prestige in a state system. The leaders of new African states, mostly unconstrained by powerful nationalist movements, understood the situation and entered into a virtual compact of dependency with France. France would stabilize state structures in return for the elites' support. In France, African policymaking remained opaque, unaccountable, and remarkably personalistic—the better to maintain the president's ability to develop the French position in Africa.

By the 1990s, after three decades, the failure of the Soviet Union, and the appearance of a new generation of French politicians, the relationship became unstable. Francophone Africa's position in the world was deteriorating—formerly peripheral, it was becoming hopelessly marginal. France was turning to the project of European integration as its old quasi-colonial grand strategy became obsolete. Facing the end of French attention, African elites moved to preserve and expand the networks and institutional ties that supplied their resources. The very lack of French interest in African affairs made this possible, as elite French politicians thought about topics other than the administration of relations with minor clients. Whether this situation of French involvement in Africa can last, however, is doubtful. French engagement at its apogee was sustained by a peculiarly personalistic form of government and a nineteenth-century understanding of state power based on alliances. Now, it survives based on little besides the machinations of those who benefit.

FORMS OF FRENCH INVOLVEMENT

French African policy has gone through two stages since decolonization, stages as markedly different in content as they are similar in style. France has constantly focused aid and attention on its former colonies and some states that it courted and that joined the French bloc later in their histories (Schraeder, Hook, and Taylor, 1998). Close ties, a rhetoric of complementary vocations, familistic reunions, personalistic relationships between heads of state, and a strong affective link characterize the relationships between the governments of these states and the French state (Golan, 1981). Emotions do not equal policy, however, and rhetoric underdetermines outcomes. That African affairs *can* and often do summon emotional responses in France is unequivocally true, but the content and occasions of those responses cannot be directly derived from the passion of the actors involved. The content of policy is best understood by looking at the institutional and personal relationships of the actors involved, and studying the content of policy need not entail any denigration of the powerful emotional and cultural links that tie many Africans and French or the strong links made in French political discourse between African prestige and national status.

After decolonization and until the 1980s, French policy was nakedly self-interested, patronizing, and generally corrupt. It was also, however, centralized in the president's office and therefore could be organized according to French strategic interests. Virtually all French policy fell under presidential control. As long as French policy remained centralized in the hands of the president, the pursuit of French ends remained relatively coherent. During this era, Presidents de Gaulle, Georges Pompidou, and Valéry Giscard d'Estaing all sought to gain and keep African allies for France, thereby ensuring French great-power status and high international profile. French policy also sought to maintain French economic dominance. France, having lost its status as a major power in a world dominated by the United States and the Soviet Union, gained prestige and its own field of dominance from this bargain with African elites.

Resources

The extraversion resources that matter and mattered most take three forms: aid, military engagement, and tutelage (Greer, 1999). France has been one of the largest donors to the continent and narrowly concentrates its aid in the Francophone states. Often, the French state simply transfers funds to governments to cover their budgets. Much of the aid to governments and nongovernmental organizations has functioned more as a prop for the governments and elites than as actual development assistance (Cumming, 1995; Grey, 1990; Péan, 1988).

Second, the extensive French military presence in Africa includes thousands of troops stationed in six countries, bases on French possessions around the continent, and a special rapid-reaction force posted outside Paris that includes interventions in Africa as part of its duties (Chipman, 1989; Rouvez, 1994: 117–32). The troops posted in Africa have occasionally intervened in the affairs of the countries; either actively, by supporting contenders for power, or passively, by withdrawing support from leaders who had depended upon such support.

Less obtrusively, the French military trains many African officers, assisted in the creation of the armies, and arms them still. The French secret services also played a major role in training and organizing the states' secret services at their creation. Little evidence suggests that the links between the French intelligence services and their African colleagues ever weakened.

The third form of French intervention is tutelage. Tutelage refers to the practice of using French citizens or the French state to directly administer policy on behalf of African states. After independence, many French citizens stayed on in their colonial posts or came to Africa to serve as high-level bureaucrats and cabinet ministers or lower-level civil servants. *Coopérants*, French youths doing their required national service, teach, administer, and assist governments across Africa. Tutelage sometimes provides extra resources that African states could not supply (such as technical expertise unavailable in states emerging from colonial rule). It also removed resources from internal political competition; French advisors were relatively impartial in domestic political activities and usually were firmly beholden to the chief of government (Boone, 1992). Tutelage was a serious compromise for any nationalist and deprived elites and many educated Africans of jobs. It accordingly declined over time and as Africanization programs continued (Boone, 1992: 177–79; Guth, 1991). The CFA franc, a common Francophone African currency pegged to the French franc, constitutes the most durable form of tutelage.

FRANCE AS STABILIZER: PRESIDENTIAL POWER 1958–1981

Dependence in general does not imply dependence on a single state. In fact, a risk-averse client seeks as many patrons as possible. Francophone African leaders, however, opted instead for a strong bilateral relationship with France. The reasons for this original decision lie in the relationships established at decolonization. Despite the French official ideology of colonial improvement and assimilation, the new states created at decolonization lacked trained cadres and were poorly equipped to maintain basic functions (let alone attempt development). Unlike other former colonial powers, however, France signaled its interest in maintaining a significant presence in the former colonies (Bourgi, 1980; Lavroff, 1980). Alliance with the French offered significant benefits from the perspective of elites who were already in commanding positions of the new states. Stability, revenue, and to a lesser degree international acceptance were interests of state elites in Africa. If elites gave France support in international organizations and a position of remarkable importance in their political economies, France would provide all three through its aid, tutelage, and military involvement. Francophone states were indeed more stable than most, and even in coup-prone countries the state and social structure usually survived the turnover at the top (Grey, 1990).

It was also possible to refuse the bargain with France, but at a high price.

Guinea was the only colony to vote for independence over association, and it provoked an immediate French pullout (even to the point of ripping telephones off the walls of government buildings as they left). The shock to Guinea demonstrated the dependence of their former colonies on a French-operated administrative and economic infrastructure. No other African leaders opted to pay that price; aid, tutelage, and military support were preferable. The assimilation, or at least integration, of some prominent African leaders into the French political classes helped; it was easy for former colleagues of major leaders to keep personal relationships with them after they had become rulers. Some leaders, such as Leopold Senghor (of Senegal) or Felix Houphouët-Boigny (of Côte d'Ivoire) had been in French cabinet posts; some leaders such as Leon M'ba of Gabon so preferred French ties that they lobbied to become fully integrated parts of France rather than independent states (Péan, 1983: 40–41).

The price African elites paid for French support was, from their perspectives, relatively small. They had to support France in international forums and participate in the familistic organizations and events that mark and marked French African relations (arguably, this was an attraction of close association rather than a price; see Golan, 1981; Martin, 1985; Prunier, 1995). French firms had to remain dominant in the new states' economies. African leaders also provided considerable funds to French political parties, which are chronically weak and underfunded and therefore receptive to donors and donor influence (Mény, 1992). Most important, the states had to continue to grant France pride of place as their greatest international friend, benefactor, and protector.

African elites rapidly learned that they could manipulate these relationships with France. France was essentially attempting to monopolize the functions of the advanced industrial world in relation to these states, an unstable situation in a world that contained capital of many (or no) national origins and a variety of potential patrons, including the Soviet Union. Thus, African leaders could extract concessions from France by threatening to leave the French bailiwick. To build a link with the Soviets or Americans would deal a simultaneous blow to French foreign policy, commercial interests, and self-image. In a relationship that was based on African affirmations of French power and importance, any African disparagement of French power and importance could created a serious problem for French strategy. Omar Bongo of Gabon acidly summarized: "Le Gabon, croyez-moi, est une belle fille, très jolie, très belle, à qui tous les hommes veulent faire la cour. Alors, c'est là qu'il faut faire attention, parce qu'un ami de perdu, dix de retrouvés"[1] (Bayart, 1984: 61). Resources were useful but not determinate in carrying out such strategies—anybody in francophone Africa with a claim to sovereignty could stake a claim on French prestige. Thus, while mineral-rich Gabon certainly extracted more concessions from Paris than other states, indigent Chad became a quagmire for France almost entirely due to the French need to defend their prestige and credibility.

French economic and political dominance required policies that helped stabilize elite power in Africa. The stability (generally purchased at the price of repression) and close economic ties to France that were in the interests of the French state were also in the collective interests of incumbent elites in the francophone bloc states. The collective benefits for elites of French stabilization existed in tension with the vulnerability of individual members of the elites. As some francophone African leaders learned, it was perilous to be seen by Paris as a threat to stability or economic relationships, for that might lead Paris to support a change of leader. The centralization and freedom of French policy allowed it to perform a useful stabilizing function in its African allies, but that very freedom and stabilization meant that France might intervene to end the career of a person who threatened the stability of the arrangement. The individual and collective self-interests of most francophone African elites thus stood in tension, and the paths that French resources followed in Africa were the objects of their political strategies. French President François Mitterrand observed that France deals with states, not with their individual governments. Mitterrand mischaracterized the relationship: France dealt with elites at first, but during Mitterrand's presidency it began to deal with individuals.

This pattern of French involvement depended to a remarkable degree on the personalities of presidents. The French presidency is, in constitutional terms, comparatively weak (Hayward, 1993; Keeler and Schain, 1996). In practical terms, however, the president is a dominant figure in much of foreign and often in domestic policy. Since de Gaulle, who largely created the Fifth Republic, the president has had considerable abilities to intervene in politics and retains almost complete control over some areas of policy. African affairs is the most important of the areas reserved for the president. Division of labor permitted close attention to Africa. The presidential staff usually numbered around fifty, but of those, ten were usually full-time Africa specialists (Elgie and Machin, 1991). The informal networks maintained by Jacques Foccart, the presidential advisor for Africa under de Gaulle and Pompidou, further centralized power and were closely integrated with the French intelligence agencies. This personalism of French policy defined and made possible the functioning of the Gaullist system of French African relations.

Overall social stability did not, therefore, mean that individual leaders held unconditional French support. The French record of supporting or turning a blind eye to coups as well as interventions to sustain governments and regimes demonstrates the vulnerability of an individual African leader in this framework. Stability sometimes required overthrowing individuals. France supplied an appealing range of extraversion resources and supported the maintenance of a status quo that benefited France while leaving individuals exposed. French private interests, African leaders, and individuals of the African elites all had incentives to find more *individually* secure means of sustaining themselves. Collectively, having France as an external regulator was useful, but for individuals it could be disastrous.

FRANCE AS SABOTEUR: CORRUPT DECENTRALIZATION
1981–1998

The relationship between the French state and African elites rested on the integrity of the French state and its ability to play a role as a unitary actor. French African policy was extraordinarily deinstitutionalized and dominated by the president until Mitterrand in the 1980s. Ministries and parastatals that dealt with Africa (especially the Ministry of Cooperation and to some extent those of Defense, Education, Foreign Affairs, and the Treasury) had little or no autonomous policy while the president's informal networks gave the president even more latitude to pursue his goals. This policy model depended on the presence of a president who would spare the energy to develop a single French policy as well as presidential advisors who were able to maintain control over French African policy in its many forms. An uninterested president meant drift.

The Mitterrand years saw just such drift. Although he had been an architect of the original model in the 1950s, during Mitterrand's fourteen years he lost interest in African policy. Despite promises of significant changes in African policy with the Socialist victory of 1981, Mitterrand (who had overseen French African relations in a 1950–1951 cabinet post) reverted to personalistic and deinstitutionalized relationships (Bayart, 1984; Whiteman, 1983). He did not make many policies, unlike his activist predecessor, and pointedly demonstrated his interest in African affairs by limiting discussion of the continent to a half-hour weekly briefing during his second term (Marchesin, 1995). *Cohabitation*, or two-party government, left ministries charged with African policy in the hands of opposition Gaullists for two years. This sped fragmentation by giving well-connected Gaullist barons in France opportunities and resources to build their networks in Africa.

Meanwhile, Mitterrand's African advisors (including his son) concentrated on maintaining the status quo—their private business deals and relationships with various members of African elites (Bayart, 1984, 1990; Krop, 1994). To fill the vacuum in instructions from the presidential palace, the ministries and units of government involved in African affairs developed their own groups of Africa specialists and comparatively autonomous policies (Bayart, 1996). Political barons such as Charles Pasqua and Jacques Chirac, who had extensive links in Africa, used their new autonomy to expand and reinforce their own networks on the continent. The result was drift from the 1980s onward in African relations. The president's policies were carried out when they existed, but often there was no policy. Instead, many more individuals within the French state made policies in the breach. Meanwhile, the presidential office generally supported the status quo in all its details.

This administrative decay came at the same time as changes in the French strategic calculus. In strategic terms, the end of the Cold War, the decreasing importance and autonomy of the French state in the world economy, and the economic decline of the francophone bloc began to reduce the resources that France could and would dedicate to Africa. The disappearance of the Soviet Union sharply reduced the ability of African states to play off other powers against France. Although those states that had important natural resources or long-standing American involvement could still manipulate the French, the range of possible patrons shrank and African state's dependence on the sole Western state interested in them increased. Without the Cold War, Africa lost much of its previous strategic interest. The Cold War French strategy was based on "l'Afrique et la Bombe"; as such, it needed major adjustments after both atomic weaponry and Africa had become marginal in international politics and much less important in French politics. African leadership was worth much less, just as it was becoming more expensive.

The reduction in the economic and strategic importance of both France and francophone Africa also meant that French resources for Africa became harder to procure. The states of the francophone bloc had always been a poor fit for the French economy (Chipman, 1989; Coquet, Daniel, and Fourmann, 1993; Marseille, 1984; Rouvez, 1994), and from the 1970s onward French trade with francophone Africa declined increasingly rapidly. Strategic materials such as uranium, which had been concerns of the French due to their atom-based do-mestic energy policy as well as international nuclear strategy, lost their high profiles (Martin, 1989). Meanwhile, Nigeria outstripped the rest of francophone Africa combined as a French trading partner, and West African economic flows inexorably centered on that vast country. Despite this strategic development, it proved difficult to reshape the webs of contacts that excluded Nigeria while so tightly linking France with its old colonies.

Not only did francophone Africa diverge further from France; it also regressed economically. The progressive economic decay of the francophone African states made them increasingly expensive allies. During the 1980s, therefore, France began to "multilateralize" its relationships with Africa, referring the states to the Bretton Woods institutions. The international organizations pre-scribed structural adjustment, and France agreed (although its debt forgiveness and aid policies cushioned the blow somewhat). Involvement in Africa became steadily more difficult to justify, and the number of French politicians and busi-ness figures involved in Africa also declined. Compared to the resources that African elites and states required to maintain themselves, French assistance was small.

Furthermore, as African economies and state capacity declined, elites de-pended more on extraversion to maintain their resource flows just as extraversion resources of all types declined. Individual Africans and interested French indi-viduals faced increasing incentives to multiply their personal links within the French state in order to gain more secure patrons. Without a central policy, the French officials charged with allocating resources of military and civilian aid and technical assistance had to make numerous decisions and found many members of the African elites as well as French civilians who included them in Franco-African networks. The networks increasingly allocated resources.

The practical implication of this state fragmentation is that the French state has gone from being a relatively autonomous stabilizer to being an unthinking saboteur. Resources directed by mid-level officials, who have extensive contacts in the elites of francophone Africa, go to sustain individual Africans and French private interests within their networks. Corrupt decentralization reduces the degree of control and accountability in policy. It thus separates the common interests of the French state and African elites (stability and close economic ties) from the actual effect of French policy, which is to stabilize individuals' careers and incomes (often at the expense of a stable social or political structure). High-profile events such as the 1997 collapse of Congo-Brazzaville or the Rwandan genocide can prompt French intervention. Without high-level attention, however, the type of routine French interventions to change or support governments and regimes that characterized French policy for decades are unlikely. France simultaneously strengthens various sections of African elites without any significant strategy or coordination, and then does not intervene unless a state collapses. Two examples show these dynamics at work: French involvement in Rwanda up to the start of the 1994 genocide, and the devaluation of the CFA franc.

The Devaluation "That Changed Everything"

The CFA franc was a common currency of two central banks for regions roughly approximating the old French Equatorial and French West African colonial federations (Godeau, 1995). Pegged to the French franc, the currency was guaranteed by the French government. On one hand, this meant that countries of the franc zone had stable monetary policy; there was no potential manipulation of macroeconomic policy for short-term political or economic ends, and the central bank was guaranteed to be free of serious corruption. Given the economic records of some states in the franc zone and the disasters that states with independent monetary policies visited on themselves (such as the hyperinflation of Mobutu's Zaire, or Ghana's monetary travails), this means of establishing a stable currency was not indefensible as an economic policy.

On the other hand, the CFA states had French monetary policy, and France was under no obligation to make its macroeconomic policies with the welfare of Africa in mind. The 1980s plainly demonstrated this: the French after 1983 tied the franc to the German deutschemark, and the result was that the obsessively anti-inflationary policies of the German central bank were directly transmitted to Burkina Faso and Madagascar. Given the divergent sectoral profiles of the franc zone countries and their collective difference from the French (and European) economy, such an arrangement possibly required forgoing opportunities for a more growth-oriented macroeconomic policy. To elites in francophone Africa, the stability and immunity to manipulation of macroeconomic policy seemed worth the loss of sovereignty and monetary autonomy. (Mali abandoned the zone and reapplied four years later, and Spanish-speaking Equatorial Guinea joined.)

The CFA franc was also an important resource to African elites. Through it France performed a regulatory function in Africa, reducing the ability of elites to choose macroeconomic policies destructive of their economies and themselves. The CFA did not cause extraversion, but did shape it. Devaluation disrupted mechanisms of extraversion by at least temporarily eliminating arbitrage opportunities. Beneficiaries of the CFA parity, which included many well-connected members of francophone African elites, could not be expected to support devaluation. However, France devalued the CFA in January 1994, halving its value with almost no warning. The reason this draconian policy change could and did happen lies in three important facts.

First, CFA policy was (unlike military or economic aid decisions) relatively immune to network penetration. Institutionally, CFA policy was made by a small circle of high-level French politicians and bureaucrats. Treasury officials hold some of the most prestigious bureaucratic posts in France. They are much better integrated into elites of mainland France than into the circles that deal with Africa (their professional interests are in France and Europe and not the CFA). This limits the opportunities that extraversion networks can use to change policy. Further, the centralization of policy means that these officials are rare (macroeconomic policy, unlike aid, requires relatively few managerial staff). In other words, monetary policy in a system with functioning macroeconomic institutions (clearly including France) is almost inherently centralized and it is difficult and generally unsatisfying to construct networks within it.

Second, no interpretation of French or African interests, sentiments, or strategy circa 1994 could justify spending money to maintain the CFA parities. The time and issue were singularly unpropitious for subsidies to the CFA. After the Cold War, the cheap international prestige of African engagement seemed less appealing to many French. Eleven years after France itself was humbled by capital flows, thirteen years after the World Bank's Berg Report arguing for structural adjustment, two years after France committed itself to stringent macroeconomic targets for the European Monetary Union, and in the middle of a surge of media "Afro-Pessimism," symbolic resources to argue against devaluation were seemingly absent. Few argued that France had an obligation to support the regimes and distort the economies of its African allies. Meanwhile, the pressures of European economic and monetary integration were increasingly forcing a choice between Africa and Europe. Thus, when the cost of the CFA finally forced the issue on French policymakers, retrenchment seemed the obvious option.

Third, the decision to devalue came from a high-level politician without African networks. Prime Minister Edouard Balladur decided to devalue the franc by 50 percent against the French franc, setting a new fixed rate at which France would defend the parity. Balladur was part of a younger generation of the French elite. A graduate of the *grands écoles* whose alumni dominate France, he knew little about African affairs and preferred not to deal with them. His priorities were in the areas for which he had been trained and in which he had experience—European affairs and French public policy. In this he was typical of the French elite's younger members. The older style of Gaullist or Socialist politician, with colonial experience and diverse international contacts, has largely given way to technocratic politicians with similar domestic careers, networks, and bases of support. The development of a French political elite that is ignorant of and uninterested in African affairs obviously threatens stable relationships of extraversion (Hibou, 1995).

The lessons of the CFA devaluation are thus twofold. First, French commitment to francophone Africa is declining as Africa becomes more expensive and less obviously important. Generational changes within French elites reinforce this trend. Second, engagement varies with visibility. Crises aside, French engagement remains most likely when it need not be justified outside the small circles of African policymakers and interested parties. Comparison with Franco-Rwandan relations between 1990 and 1994 highlights this point. In Rwanda, France *did* assist an African regime. Extraversion took the form of networks that penetrated the middle levels of the French and Rwandan security forces and states. This form of extraversion integrated people with control over resources (aid officials, military advisors) into networks. It thereby tied them into the regime.

RWANDA, 1990–1994

It was Valéry Giscard d'Estaing who first built links with the former Belgian colony of Rwanda. Superficially, the small Great Lakes state was an island of stability, despite the fault line that colonialism had created between Hutu and Tutsi and a bloody series of massacres upon independence. France treated Rwanda as one more state in its bloc; it directed aid and military advice to Rwanda in return for allegiance. Mitterrand's governments carried on French involvement, but only in 1990 did France become deeply engaged with Rwandan affairs. In that year the Hutu regime of Juvenal Habyarimana began a publicity offensive and caught Paris's attention with a loudly prodemocratic speech just as France was beginning to speak of democracy in Africa. More important, however, 1990 saw an unexpected invasion by the Tutsi guerrillas of the anglophone Rwandan Patriotic Front. France responded to the Habyarimana regime's request for assistance, sending paratroopers to defend the capital. The RPF withdrew.

After 1990, however, the decaying Rwandan regime increasingly manipulated ethnicity to maintain its position (for histories of this period see African Rights, 1995; Braeckman, 1994; Chrétien et al., 1995; Guichaoua, 1995; Prunier, 1995; Reyntjens, 1994; Verschave, 1994). Ethnic tensions rose as cliques within the regime sought to use ethnicity to maintain themselves in power. Finally, when unknown assassins shot down Habyarimana's airplane, a genocide was not only possible but had already been organized.

Within hours of Habyarimana's death the first Tutsis (and opposition Hutu leaders) were killed, and over the next weeks Hutus killed Tutsis in a well-organized massacre (usually led by local civil servants). Almost immediately the Tutsi refugees of the RPF began to advance across the country with some urgency. This created waves of Hutu refugees linked to the regime and the genocide. The refugees fled mostly to Zaire, where they proved a destabilizing force. Finally, France intervened, sending troops under UN auspices to secure a safe area for refugees and presumably to stop the genocide.

The French role in Rwanda *prior* to Operation Turquoise, the 1994 intervention, demonstrates the new contours of French policy. Invocations of Franco-African solidarity justified French support for the regime to the relatively few who asked (Habyarimana's loud support for democratization also helped French supporters of his regime defend their actions). Studying justifications, while important in explaining Turquoise, is of limited usefulness in explaining antecedent French policy. Apart from the 1990 deployment of paratroopers, Rwandan policy had been largely left alone by higher levels. Policy responded to the intents and concerns of the networks of French businesses, government officials including secret services and armed forces members, and groups within the Rwandan elite seeking security and resource flows (see especially Smith, 1995; Verschave, 1994).

The French secret services, involved in Rwanda and maintaining extensive links to the Rwandan government and security apparatus, trained Rwandan state security employees and apparently offered intelligence services to the state. More directly, the SDECE did not apparently gather intelligence on, or seek to warn Paris of, the clear threat that their allies in the Rwandan state might engineer even larger-scale ethnic violence. Even without accusing them of directly assisting the genocide planners, they did not show any signs of attempting to head off the visibly approaching events (Braeckman, 1994). The French military trained, supplied, and supported the Rwandan military as per their orders from Paris, but went beyond their official obligations. Within the relevant Parisian ministries, Rwandan affairs officials pressed for and received steadily augmented shipments of weapons to Rwanda until the genocide began (African Rights, 1995; Human Rights Watch, 1994). There is no evidence that French military advisors sought to discourage their Rwandan (Hutu) trainees from participating in and organizing ethnic violence, either during the sporadic outbreaks in the early 1990s or during the preparations for the major genocide. Instead, French military advisors continued to train and equip the military (for examples, see Prunier, 1995: 108–13).

Both the French military and French intelligence officers on the ground in Rwanda faced similar conditions: they were in constant contact with the Rwandan regime's security forces, were posted to defend the country against a Tutsi military threat that they associated with the "Anglo-Saxon" powers, and were given few incentives to warn of threatening signs in the country (and who would they warn?). Their situation produced a considerably greater commitment on their parts to the existing Rwandan regime of Habyarimana than to the Rwandan state or people. Further, the democratic, republican ideologies of the French military stressed majority rule. French republicanism has long had a vaguely Rousseauian taste for sovereign national wills, which has made life difficult for minorities (Hoffman, 1995; Prunier, 1995: 111). To defend a Hutu regime, in a majority-Hutu country, against minority invaders seeking to take power by force could seem thoroughly acceptable to French democrats.

In addition to the partially intentional and partially spontaneous over-identification of French armed forces and intelligence services in Rwanda with the Habyarimana regime, the circuits of Franco-Rwandan relations included many private actors. These individuals, almost all linked with some element of the French state, government-tied French aid organizations, or the French military services, often profited from Rwanda. Since the country produces few export goods, such profits stem from monopolies that are sometimes maintained through illicit political activities (Krop, 1994; Verschave, 1994). These private companies could and did lobby to defend and increase French aid to the Habyarimana regime that had given them their benefits. Rwanda received the favor of the Ministry of Cooperation, and France directed large sums of foreign aid to French nongovernmental organizations (NGOs) operating in Rwanda and the Rwandan state.

The role of the president, or the prime minister, is strikingly absent between the 1990 and 1994 emergencies that threatened the Hutu regime's existence. In this less exciting period, different clans of French and Rwandans organized policy with the acquiescence of the president's son. The minutia of Franco-African relations, details often decided at middle and low levels of policy, diffused accountability and decentralized decisionmaking. It thus made possible a system of corrupt decentralization and prevented the emergence of any strategy. Thus, the combination of private actors, military and intelligence networks, and Rwandan regime members made policy—albeit policy that was sometimes disrupted by executive attention.

The result of such policies is that Rwanda has lost as much as a tenth of its population and is now ruled by a group of anglophones whose links to Paris and French business are tenuous. By the standards of "French interests" the policy of Rwanda in France was a failure, and the elites whose interests were so close to French interests are now mostly in exile. The micropolitics of French engagement in Rwanda had created a catastrophe not only in human terms, but also for "French interests" in Rwanda. As Paul Kagame, the new (anglophone) leader of Rwanda observed, "If they wanted people [in Rwanda] to speak French, they shouldn't have helped to kill all those people here who spoke French" (Gourevitch, 1997: 48).

THE POLITICS OF EXTERNAL INTERVENTION IN THE PERIPHERY

French engagement once stabilized. Now it sabotages. In devaluing the CFA franc the French state showed how little it is willing to commit of its declining resources to an increasingly marginal group of states whenever it is pressed and easily able to decide. In Rwanda the French state showed the degree to which its officials can support malign groups with very little regard to strategic considerations of even very basic kinds (such as preventing genocide). Devaluation showed that when significant expenses from Africa intruded in French politics, the first concern of French politicians was to reduce the expense. Rwanda, on the other hand, showed how without a coherent policy the French could massively contribute to destabilizing a country through resource allocation that is explicable only through corrupt decentralization. Rather than acting as a suppressor variable in African politics, French engagement has made it both less predictable and less stable.

During decolonization France went to unusual lengths to ensure that it would have a dense web of interaction with its former colonies (compared with Britain, which did little to preserve ties). Nevertheless, the implication of the French experience is that disengagement for any former dominant power is not as easy as it might appear, whether it is Russia withdrawing from parts of the old Soviet Union or the United States casting off its Cold War links with Central America. Interest groups, transnational networks, and mutual transparency can leave many political actors equipped to exploit the relationship between the two states. Global flows of persons and capital can expand and reinforce links at every level, from migrant communities to highly placed business transactions. Strategic attention to an area can decrease much more quickly than the extent of these interpersonal ties and engagement. Thus, interested French parties continue to shape French policy, even as French interests turn elsewhere.

Even when there is no argument for a state to prolong its interventions in the affairs of another state, the resourcefulness and ingenuity of many people in both states can preserve the engagement. Imperial disengagement—from America in Latin America to Russia in the former Soviet Union—will require more than a shift of strategic interest at the top. Important links still bind power and periphery: it will ill serve analysts to accept that a strategic decision to turn away, or strategists' tendencies to ignore the periphery, will lead to disengagement. The mere renunciation of a state's interest in a part of the world is no guarantee that the state will not continue to have dramatic and possibly disastrous effects there. It will also require a deliberate effort to break ties between states. Such a policy might seem deeply unappealing to pressured state leaders. Those leaders would usually prefer to ignore the dependent country and leave policy to their subordinates, who are, after all, interested and knowledgable.

NOTE

I would like to thank Randall Collins, Georgi Derluguian, and Christina Nyström for their comments on this chapter and Jane Guyer for valuable discussions of the subject.

1. "Gabon, believe me, is a beautiful girl, very pretty, very beautiful, whose heart all the men seek. So they must court her, because for every boyfriend lost, ten can be found" (author's translation).

12

The Geoeconomic Reconfiguration of the Semiperiphery: The Asian-Pacific Transborder Subregions in the World-System

Xiangming Chen

The guiding idea or general proposition for this chapter is that the Asian-Pacific transborder subregions that have emerged and expanded in the 1980s and 1990s have begun to reorganize a major part of the semiperipheral zone of the world system, with important implications for the study of the world system. To evaluate this proposition, I will begin by locating the origin of the transborder subregions in a temporal conjuncture of interdependent historical, economic, political, and sociocultural factors. These factors, which reflect geohistorical continuity and geopolitical change in the Asia-Pacific region, will be crystallized into a geoeconomic model of transnational (sub)regional formation. Then I will develop the argument that the transborder subregions, once taking shape, are capable of (1) mediating the impact of globalization on local economic development by creating both opportunities and constraints, and (2) altering the horizontal relationship between nation-states and the vertical relationship between central and local government by challenging the conventional principles and practices of national sovereignty, exclusive territoriality, and regulatory capacity. These consequences could reorganize and even revitalize the Asian-Pacific semiperiphery of the world system.

This chapter is organized into four sections. The first section conceptualizes the transborder subregion as a new unit of analysis for studying the world system. Section two traces the historical and contemporary conditions for the emergence of the transborder subregions, and then accounts for it theoretically. Section three illustrates the analytical issues regarding the transborder subregions with three cases. The last section draws the implications for the reconfiguration of the semiperiphery in the Asia-Pacific.

CONCEPTUALIZING A NEW UNIT OF (SUB)REGIONAL ANALYSIS

The transborder subregion provides an unconventional unit of analysis for the study of the world system. The transborder subregion occupies a distinctive rung in a relational hierarchy of six conceptual levels and analytical units: global, continental/regional (e.g., Asian-Pacific), *subregional*, country, nation/ethnicity, and locality/city. In Scalapino's definition, transborder subregions are Natural Economic Territories (NETs), which are "economic entities cutting across political boundaries that combine natural resources, manpower, managerial skills, capital and technology, depending on the private sector for survival and growth, and varying greatly in size, shape and number of parties involved, without a formal institutional structure" (1995: 101).

The most salient feature of the transborder subregion is its very own geo-economic composition. Territorial boundaries are not only a necessary basis of national autonomy and political unity (Gilpin, 1987), they define both the inside and outside of nation-states by leaving no empty space between them in the global political space (Javis and Paolini, 1995: 4). A transborder subregion, however, wedges a new economic space between the borders of two or three states and takes on an in-between status. Consisting of multiple subnational units—cities and their hinterlands on and adjacent to both land and sea borders—the transborder subregion links and articulates selected localities to the global economy despite and bypassing the countries involved. The transborder subregion truly exemplifies James Rosenau's domestic-foreign frontier "as a widening field of action, as the space in which world affairs unfold, as the arena in which domestic and foreign issues converge, intermesh, or are otherwise indistinguishable within a seamless web" (1997: 5).

Oriented primarily toward economic development through cross-border cooperation and competition, the transborder subregion is largely driven by private enterprises of local (indigenous) and foreign (multinational) ownerships. The state, especially the national government, plays a limited and often lagging role in either promoting or preventing the emergence of a transborder subregion. And the local government is much more involved than the central government in a transborder subregion, given its spatial composition. Some transborder subregions exhibit resurgent cultural and ethnic regional identities that have undergirded and permeated the shared border areas historically but have been dormant or suppressed until recently by the lack of economic ties and contentious political borders.

This discussion leads me to conceptualize a transborder subregion as a relatively large (although generally smaller than the conventional cases of cross-national regional economic integration) transnational spatial-economic entity that combines: (a) the participation and integration of contiguous and/or adjacent subnational, border areas with varying degrees of economic complementarity; (b) a hierarchy or cluster of cities with or without a central node; (c) transnational production systems with uneven ties to the global economy; (d) private-sector-driven economic activity with limited and targeted state intervention at the local level; and (e) spatially based historical connections, ethnic affinity, and subcultural identity.

The formation of a globalized subregional transborder economic space challenges the conventional unit and logic of world-system analysis. The transborder subregion reflects a greater differentiation and more complex interaction of the conditions and processes that constitute the world system. Although economic exchanges (e.g., trade and investment) used to be sufficient in differentiating countries into general types of unequal positions in the world system, stronger geographic proximity and cultural affinity in a transborder subregion could help create a more cooperative and balanced economic relationship among the countries. More specifically, most Asian-Pacific transborder subregions contain varied combinations of semiperipheral and peripheral economies at one level and the core and peripheral parts of these economies at another level. This defies the traditional analytic logic of world-system analysis for dealing with the relational structure of national economies and calls for a new approach to integrating a more complex hierarchy of levels of analysis.

ORIGINS AND CONDITIONS OF THE ASIAN-PACIFIC TRANSBORDER SUBREGIONS: HISTORICAL ANTECEDENTS AND RECENT VARIANTS

First, the location and configuration of the transborder subregions today could be traced back to the Sinocentric tributary system and the geographic structure of maritime Asia influenced by that system. The China-centered tributary system was "the external expression of hierarchical domestic relations of control, extending downward and outward from the imperial center" (Hamashita, 1997: 114). This system covered much of maritime Asia that stretched from Northeast Asia to East Asia and then from Southeast Asia to Oceania in the form of a series of seas and the landmasses. More important and relevant to the transborder subregions today, historically "the states, regions, and cities located along the periphery of each sea zone were close enough to influence one another but too far apart to be assimilated into a larger entity" (Hamashita, 1997: 115).

The involvement of China's coastal and northeastern and southwestern land borders in anchoring several transborder subregions bears some resemblance to the external relations of the traditional, Sinocentric tributary system. Overlaying Map 12.1 onto the map of the maritime zone of Asia in Hamashita (1997: 116), one is struck by the remarkable similarity between the old and new spatial structures. Different localities and regions in the international political economy at any particular time not only depend on their historical geography and accumulation of assets and liabilities but on their ability to adapt to changing circumstances (Agnew and Corbridge, 1995: 6). Although the Sinocentric tributary system and its geographic orbit of maritime zones were resilient, the overseas

Map 12.1

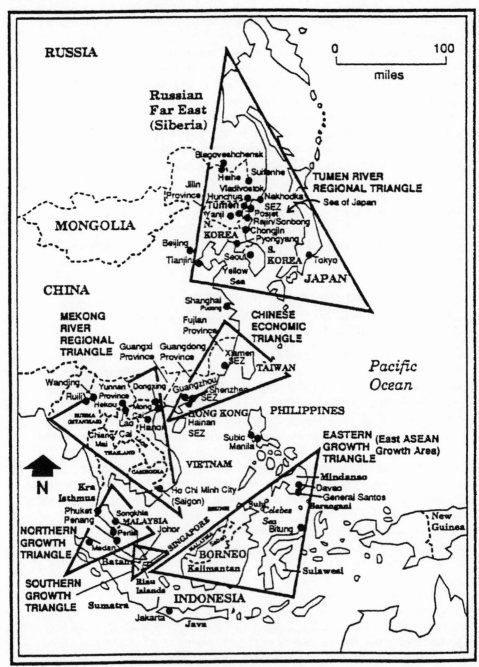

Source: This map was originally produced and published in Xiangming Chen, "The Evolution of Free Economic
Zones" (IJURR, 1995). By permission of Blackwell Publishers.

Chinese diaspora of traders and merchants who helped sustain that system were severely weakened and cut off from the Chinese mainland by a series of political and military events before and after 1949, such as Japan's takeover of China's coastal regions, the defeat of the Chinese Nationalists by the Communists, and the U. S. embargo against China during the Cold War (Arrighi, 1998b).

To understand the interruption and the subsequent resurgence of the geo-economically based transborder subregions, we must be aware of the external and internal changes in the Asia-Pacific political economy. World War II and the Korean War bifurcated the Asia-Pacific into the capitalist and socialist camps, headed by the United States and the Soviet Union, respectively. The two camps were based on the important strategic and economic ties between the United States and Japan, between the Soviet Union and China (in the 1950s), and close links between the smaller capitalist states (South Korea and Taiwan) and the United States/Japan and between smaller Communist states (North Korea and later North Vietnam) and the Soviet Union/China. Although the relations between the Soviet Union and China, between the United States and China, and between China and Japan changed drastically, the overall political bifurcation continued to define Asia-Pacific regionalism as an aggregation of bilateral interstate relations into the 1970s.

These power positions and norms in the regional international system and their associated development ideologies and strategies, according to Katzenstein (1997) and Selden (1997), have accounted for the absence of formal multilateral regional integration like the EU in the Asia-Pacific. Katzenstein also attributes this outcome to the historical and contemporary domestic structures of East and Southeast Asian states characterized by the legacy of universal empires, regional kingdoms, fragmentary polities, ritual sovereignty (instead of legal and effective), hierarchical order, and intricate networks.

Although these scholars have provided excellent historical and regional contexts for studying the transborder subregions, their explanations are too early in the causal chain. Why did most of the transborder subregions not emerge until the 1980s? I suggest that the spatial continuity underlying maritime Asia and the transborder subregions today has resurfaced largely because the political bifurcation of capitalism and communism that once shaped Asian-Pacific regionalism has largely disappeared. Although the historical and regional contexts have become conducive to the emergence of the transborder subregions, it still must be theoretically explained as an empirical phenomenon.

LINKING GLOBALIZATION, LOCALIZATION, AND TRANSNATIONAL PRODUCTION

The globalization literature provides the most general backdrop and framework for studying the emergence and consequences of the transborder subregions. From this complex and diffused literature, I have identified and isolated three useful perspectives. First, I draw on James Rosenau's turbulence theory to understand the mutual penetration and reinforcement between economic globalization and transborder subregionalization. Rosenau (1997: 80–81) defines globalization and localization as "processes and forces that compel individual actors and collective entities to engage in similar behavior and participate in encompassing and coherent organizations or systems as opposed to narrow their horizons and withdraw to less encompassing organizations or systems." The interaction between globalization and localization has both integrating and fragmenting processes and outcomes. This logic suggests that the transborder subregions could be analyzed as a "local response" of subregional scale that both accommodates and resists economic globalization. At another level, a transborder subregion can either strengthen or weaken the impact of economic globalization on localities in a border region and can either facilitate or constrain the latter's adaptation to the global economy.

Second, Saskia Sassen has focused on the uneven local and national impacts of economic globalization on creating a new geography of power and weakening the regulatory power of the territorial state. The former is exemplified by the emergence of global cities (New York, London, Tokyo) that exercise a disproportionately large financial influence worldwide as the central nodes of the global economic hierarchy (Sassen, 1991). The strategic functions of the global cities, coupled with their ironic location within national territories, undermine the exclusive sovereignty of the national state through the decentering of regulatory regimes (Sassen, 1996). Extending this perspective, I expect to find, within the transborder subregions, dominant regional cities of global status and functions (Hong Kong, Singapore, Shanghai, Kaohsiung) that link the global and national economies within a transborder space. The supposed incompatibility between the functions of the emerging Asia-Pacific world cities across and within national spaces may create both economic integration of an entire transborder subregion and political fragmentation on the various sides of the national borders within that subregion.

Third, the transnational production systems and commodity chains call for a perspective on the industry and organizational level dynamics that structure the transborder subregions. As Scott (1995: 52) and Storper and Harrison (1991: 411) define it, a production system involves a functional division of labor through a network of input-output linkages set in a relational context of power and decision-making. Conceptualizing production systems as global commodity chains, Gereffi (1996) argues that such organizational variables as the types of production and distribution networks are very important in creating overlapping and at times conflicting regional divisions of labor and determining export growth and industrial upgrading in East Asia. Since transnational production systems and commodity chains span and materialize in the transborder subregions differently, the local industrial configuration and firm structures that ground the macro-level intra-subregional trade and investment ties will have a strong influence on the transborder subregions.

REGIONS WITHIN AND ACROSS BORDERS

"Regions are once again emerging as important foci of production and as repositories of specialized know-how of technological capability, even as the globalization of economic relationships proceeds apace" (Scott, 1995: 59). Much of the earlier theorizing of regions dealt with regional economic differentiation and development within national borders. The German geographer Christaller (1972) formulated the central place theory (CPT) based on the regional hierarchies of towns in southern Germany in the 1930s. The French economist Perroux pioneered the notion of growth poles that are foci or centers "from which centrifugal forces emanate and to which centripetal forces are attracted. Each center being a center of attraction and repulsion, has its proper fields, set in the fields of other centers" (1950: 50). Growth poles may produce either "backwash" (negative) or "spread" (positive) effects on the regional hinterlands (Myrdal, 1957). These intra-national models of regional structure and processes could be extended to the transborder subregions.

The limited theorizing of cross-national regions has focused almost exclusively on regional economic and political cooperation and integration as reflected in the EU and its various antecedents. The level of integration was the most common dependent variable to be explained, while the typical independent variables included national goals, size of regional groupings (number of member countries), perceived costs and benefits, and extra-regional factors such as superpower influence (Axline, 1994). Focusing mostly on the U. S./Canadian and the U. S./Mexican borders, the borderlands literature (e.g., Konrad, 1991; Martínez, 1986) has examined the shared characteristics of people and activities in border areas and how the former make the latter distinctive regions or contiguous zones of frequent and intensive interactions and transactions that both blend the nation-states into each other and temper their central tendencies. Recent research on European cases (Corvers, Dankbaar, and Hassink, 1996; Reid and Church, 1996) shows that although the move toward the Single European Market (SEM) and the removal of trade barriers, coupled with political and administrative decentralization within the nation-states may facilitate international cross-border cooperation, the peripheral location of border regions and large economic disparities among the constituent parts may hinder their development.

The transborder subregions may also be linked with a new phase and type of Asian urbanization. Moving beyond an earlier model of Asian urbanization as characterized by extended regions of intensive agricultural and nonagricultural activities around and between large city cores, McGee (1995) identifies an expanding city-state model, characterized by Singapore expanding its economic activity and leisure needs into the adjacent regions of the Riau archipelago (Indonesia) and Johor state (Malaysia). Chia (1993: 3) labels this process "a metropolitan spillover into the hinterland." On the regional scale, the continued growth of within-country mega-urban regions, the expansion of selected port

cities and other coastal locations, the emergence of Hong Kong and Singapore
as Asian world cities, and the more frequent and intensive transborder transactions are creating network-based urban growth corridors in the Asia-Pacific
(Douglass, 1995: 54). The rapid expansion of air travel, container shipping, and
fiber-optic telecommunications links and flows across national boundaries make
borders more of an opportunity than a barrier.

Finally, some Asia-Pacific transborder subregions are rooted in and bounded
by spatially distinctive historical ties, ethnic identity, migration circuits, and
linguistic similarities. This regional aggregation of individual and group social
capital and closure (Coleman, 1994) promotes multilateral trust and greater interdependence among the various constituent units of a transborder subregion.
Recent studies (Chen, 1994, 1996, 1998; Lever-Tracy, Ip, and Tracy, 1996;
Selden, 1997) show that the Chinese diaspora communities play a crucial role
in channeling investment to southeastern China and parts of Southeast Asia,
contributing to the formation of some transborder subregions.

A DESCRIPTIVE ANALYSIS OF THREE TRANSBORDER
SUBREGIONS

The preceding theoretical discussion suggests important dimensions and variables for the empirical study of the transborder subregions. To illustrate these
dimensions and variables, I offer preliminary and descriptive comparison of
three transborder subregions. The three cases are selected from a list of ten
transborder subregions (see Tables 12.1 and 12.2) for three main reasons. First,
they reflect important variations along the analytical dimensions. Second, they
include all the key semiperipheral economies located in three strategic parts of
the Asia-Pacific region. Three, they are generally more developed and mature
than the other subregions, making data more available.

Size, Spatial Boundary, and Economic Complementarity

As Table 12.2 shows, the three subregions have a relatively short history,
which confirms that they are a new phenomenon of transnational economic
development. The three subregions differ considerably in sizes of both population and area. A distinguishing feature of the subregions is that they consist of
three political units of uneven status and weight. The *Sijori* Growth Triangle
and the Chinese Economic Triangle (hereafter the *Sijori* GT and the CET)
are similar to each other as both consist of both national and subnational economies. All three members of the Tumen River Triangle (hereafter the TRT) are
different-sized subnational economic units. The contiguous/adjacent borders of
the *Sijori* GT and the CET refer to the similar separation of Singapore from
Riau Islands (province) and southeastern China from Taiwan by ocean. Although
the physical boundaries of the CET and the TRT may be drawn more broadly
to include other contiguous and adjacent national or subnational economies (see

Table 12.1
The Transborder Subregions in the Asia-Pacific

Subregion	Current Status	No. of Countries Involved	Component Countries and/or Areas
1. The Greater South China Economic Zone*	Existing	3	Guangdong and Fujian Provinces (southeastern coastal China), Hong Kong, Taiwan
2. The SIJORI Growth Triangle*	Existing	3	Singapore, Johor State (southern Malaysia), Riau Province (Indonesia)
3. Southeast Asia's Northern Growth Triangle	Existing	3	Southern Thailand, Northern Malaysia, Western Indonesia (Sumatra)
4. East ASEAN Growth Area	Existing	4	Eastern Malaysia (Sabah), Northeastern Indonesia (Borneo), Southern Philippines, (Mindanao), Brunei
5. The Tumen River Triangle*	Existing	3	Jilin Province (Northeastern China), Khasan Region (Russian Far East), Northern Border Area of North Korea
6. The Tumen River Regional Development Zone	Emerging	4	Northeastern China, Khabarovsk, Sakhalin, (Russian Far East), Northern North Korea, Niigata region (Japan)
7. The Northeast Asian Greater Region	Existing	6	Northeastern China, Russian Far East, Japan, North Korea, South Korea, Mongolia
8. The Greater Mekong River Subregion	Existing	5	Yunnan Province (Southwestern China), Laos, Thailand, Vietnam, Cambodia, Myanmar
9. The Yellow Sea Rim Economic Zone	Existing	3	Liaoning and Shandong Provinces (Northern Coastal China), Western South Korea, Kyushu (Southwestern Japan)
10. The South Asian Economic Coopeation Zone (BIST-ECZ)	Under Discussion	4	Bangladesh, India, Sri Lanka, Thailand (Myanmar is expected to join)

Note: *denotes the three illustrative cases in this chapter.

Source: Compiled by this author.

Table 12.2
Characteristics and Dimensions of Three Transborder Subregions in the Asia-Pacific

Characteristics and dimensions	Transborder Subregions		
	SIJORI Growth Triangle	Chinese Economic Triangle	Tumen River Triangle
Location	Southeast Asia	Southern China	Northeast Asia
Time of establishment	Late 1980s	Late 1980s	Early 1990s
Constituent Members		(See Table 12.1)	
Area (sq. km.)	● 639 ■ 18,914 ★ 500	● 300,000 ■ 1,080 ★ 36,000	● 5,200 ■ 4,130 ★ 1,000
-total	- 20,053	- 337,080	- 10,330
Approximate Population	● 3 million ■ 2.3 million ★ 150,000	● 99 million ■ 6 million ★ 21 million	● 190,000 ■ 47,000 ★ 131,000
-total	- 5.5 million	- 126 million	- 368,000
GDP per capita (US dollars)	● 13,000 ■ 3,600 ★ 500	● 500 ■ 13,000 ★ 11,000	● 400 ■ 400-500 ★ 1,000
-total GDP	- 40 billion	- 263 billion	- 12 billion

	Singapore	Hong Kong	Hunchun?
Central node (city)	● Singapore	■ Hong Kong	● Hunchun?
Key cities and localities	● Singapore* ● Jurong Town* ● Johor Bahru ■ Pasir Gudang* ■ Senai* ■ Sri Gading* ★ Batam Island* ★ Bintan Island ★ Bulan Island	● Guangzhou ● Shenzhen* ● Xiamen* ● Fuzhou* ● Dongguan ● Putian ■ Hong Kong* ★ Taipei ★ Kaohsiung*	● Hunchun* ● Tumen ■ Nakhodka* ■ Vladivostok* ■ Posyet ■ Slavjanka ★ Rajin* ★ Sonbong* ★ Chongjin
Major industries	◆ Textiles ◆ Food ◆ Electrical components ◆ Oil exploration and Refining ◆ Financial services ◆ Transit shipping ◆ Tourism	◆ Electronics ◆ Footwear ◆ Bicycles ◆ Plastics ◆ Food and beverages ◆ Toys ◆ Financial services ◆ International trade	◆ Timber and lumber ◆ Oil and natural gas ◆ Minerals and mining ◆ Fishing ◆ Shipbuilding and repair ◆ Transit shipping ◆ Tourism
Border type	Contiguous/adjacent	Contiguous/adjacent	Contiguous
Ties to the global economy	Strong and direct	Very strong and direct	Weak and indirect

Notes: ●, ■, and ★ denote the different-sized geographic units of the same economic and political systems.

◆, ◆, and ◆ denote the major industries in each transborder subregion.

* denotes export processing zones (EPZs), special economic zones (SEZs), or industrial estates (IEs).

Sources: The statistical information, which pertains to the early 1990s, was derived from Chia (1993, p. 18), Tang and Thant (1994, p. 10), Yu (1994, pp. 13-18), and this author's estimates. The rest of the table was also compiled by this author.

Chen, 1995), I have delimited their boundaries as such to reflect the more tightly integrated economic activity among the identified units.

Economic complementarity holds the key to understanding and potentially explaining the growth and performance of the transborder subregions. The *Sijori* GT and the CET have higher levels of economic complementarity than the TRT. The average GDP per capita masks the disparities among Singapore, Malaysia (Johor), and Indonesia (Riau), and between Hong Kong-Taiwan and southeastern China. GDP per capita for the three members of the TRT, however, fall within or very close to the U. S. $400 to 500 range. In both the *Sijori* GT and the CET, Singapore, Hong Kong, and Taiwan have been experiencing high and continually rising land and labor costs and industrial upgrading, which have been pushing their labor-intensive, low-value-added industries into Johor, Riau, and Guangdong and Fujian provinces. In 1991, the monthly wage for an unskilled worker in Singapore was U. S. $350 per month, compared with U. S. $150 in Johor and U. S. $90 in Batam of Riau, respectively. This wage differential facilitates a regional division of labor: Singapore hosts the headquarter offices and R&D centers; Johor is suited for mid-level manufacturing, while Batam provides the most cost-competitive workers for labor-intensive operations (see Anwar, 1994: 25). Likewise, the abundant and cheap labor in Guangdong and Fujian provinces make them the "industrial backyard" for Hong Kong and Taiwan. In the TRT, although wage differential is much smaller, the labor shortage in the Russian Far East has been drawing surplus Chinese and North Korean workers over the border (Kim, 1994).

Local Agglomeration and Regional-Local Ties

Economic activity within the subregions is unevenly distributed spatially, focusing on a few major cities or localities. There are differences among the three cases with regard to the type and degree of local agglomeration. In the *Sijori* GT, Singapore investment in Johor is not concentrated in Johor Bahru, the capital city of the Johor State, even though it is located across the causeway between the two countries. In comparison, Singapore and Indonesia jointly established the Batam Industrial Park (BIP) on Batam Island to concentrate manufacturing-based investment from Singaporean companies and TNCs. The less developed Bintan Island has recently become the second location for Singaporean investors. The CET has more vertically differentiated agglomeration among the Chinese cities. Guangzhou and Shenzhen, as second-tiered cities below Hong Kong, have heavily concentrated investments from Hong Kong and Taiwan in a wide range of industries, whereas the lower-tiered cities of Xiamen, Fuzhou, Dongguan, and Putian (see Table 12.1) have attracted investment in more specialized industries, such as electronics in Dongguan and athletic shoes in Putian (Chen, 1994). In the TRT, the lack of external investment, coupled with a flat urban hierarchy (no dominant city), allows the cities to maintain their original type and degree of industrial specialization, such as fishing and ship repairing in the Russian port cities of Posyet and Slavjanka.

Local concentration and agglomeration in the *Sijori* GT and the CET, especially the latter, amount to a sort of "regional localization." The locational advantages and disadvantages contribute to intra-regional variation in economic growth. This preliminary comparison shows that the three subregions are grounded in uneven regional-local ties through local agglomeration, which is expected to influence the development of the entire subregions.

The Regional City as Anchor

Similar to the role of the global city as a central node in the globally integrated financial system (Sassen, 1991), the three subregions are anchored to dominant cities that exercise powerful economic influence on a distinctive regional scale. The abstract conception of the growth pole of Perroux (1950) makes it flexible enough to be transferred from an intra- to a transnational regional context. The regional city as the growth pole transcends national borders by playing an integrative and coordinating role.

Singapore and Hong Kong are clearly the regional cities for the *Sijori* GT and the CET (Table 12.1). Singapore has the more dominant influence over the *Sijori* GT than Hong Kong over the CET, partly due to its superior physical infrastructure. Singapore's Changi Airport is the largest international airport in the Asia-Pacific with the largest cargo handling capacity. Singapore's physical proximity to Johor, Batam, and Bintan reinforces its locational advantages as the regional center. Investors in Singapore can drive over a 1,038-meter-long causeway to Johor Bahru, while a ferry ride from Singapore to Batam and Bintan takes only thirty and forty-five minutes, respectively. The excellent infrastructure in Singapore and its convenient access to nearby low-cost land and labor have recently prompted such TNCs as BMW, Motorola, Rockwell, and Sharp to strengthen and expand their regional hub activities and operations in Singapore (Singapore Economic Development Board, 1995).

Although Hong Kong is not the dominant population center in the CET (Guangzhou is), it clearly functions as the central economic node whose influence also spreads beyond southern China. In regional theoretical terms, the hinterland of Hong Kong stretches to include much of China. This close pole-hinterland relationship can be measured by the number of overseas companies using Hong Kong as the hub or the so-called "gateway" for conducting business in and with China. A 1994 survey showed that during the 1990s, more than fifty new regional headquarters have opened in Hong Kong each year, up from only twenty per year in the 1980s. In 1994 a total of 714 overseas companies had regional headquarters in Hong Kong (Hong Kong Trade Development Council, 1995). Bordering on Guangdong, Hong Kong's physical connections with the mainland province have been improved through more efficient transportation. A recently completed super highway and newly opened express train service between Hong Kong and Guangzhou cut travel time from over three hours to little over one hour. Hong Kong-based Cathy Pacific Airways has begun a major project to develop the infrastructure of Xiamen International Airport. Following the recent opening of Hong Kong's new H.K. $155-billion airport, the Hong Kong Special Administrative Region (HKSAR) government has unveiled another ambitious infrastructure plan (costing H.K. $200 billion) for opening up more the New Territories in the north of Hong Kong near the border. A key project is to build a new "super bridge" linking north Lantau Island with the northwest New Territories. And the new bridge's central span may surpass that of the Tsing Ma bridge, keystone of the Lantau Link that connects Hong Kong's new international airport with the rest of the HKSAR (Hong Kong Trade Development Council, 1998).

Unlike the *Sijori* GT and the CET, the TRT lacks a dominant center. The Chinese border city of Hunchun, however, has the potential to be the regional growth pole (see Table 12.1). Although Hunchun has a small population of 175,000, it combines several advantages. First, Hunchun is centrally located at the joint borders of China, the Russian Far East, and North Korea, close to the mouth of the Tumen River on the Sea of Japan. Second, the strategic location of Hunchun makes it a hub and terminal in the cross-border water and rail transportation systems. This gives Hunchun convenient access to a cluster of Russian and North Korean ports such as Posyet, Zarubino, and Rajin. Third, in 1992, Hunchun was designated an open border city and China's first border economic cooperation zone, which accorded the city special financial incentives (e.g., lower taxes) for foreign investors. This status gave Hunchun economic advantages similar to those associated with the free port and trade zone status of Singapore and Hong Kong. Given the very short existence of the TRT, it will take future research to show whether Hunchun can develop into the economic center of the subregion.

Regional Production Systems and Their Ties with the Global Economy

Although the preceding characteristics and factors could influence the development of the transborder subregions, a more critical determinant is whether they have developed an integrated cross-border production system that is favorably tied up with the global economy. Such a production system cannot develop without significant external and internal manufacturing investment that takes place in response to the emergence of a transborder subregion. There are major differences among the three cases in the volume and type of cross-border investment and the resultant production systems.

In the *Sijori* GT, Singapore accounted for 22.7 percent of the approved investment in Johor during 1981 to 1990, whereas Singapore's share of investment in Malaysia as a whole was about 10 percent (Anwar, 1994: 25). During that period, Singapore had 466 approved projects, far ahead of Japan's 119 and Taiwan's 107. The volume of Singapore's investment, however, ranked second behind Japan, indicating that Singaporean investors were small and medium-sized firms engaging in labor-intensive manufacturing (Ho, 1994). Moreover, investments from Singapore and foreign companies grew in a parallel fashion during 1981 to 1990. When Singapore's investment in Johor peaked during 1988 to 1990, averaging M$150 million per year, foreign investment also peaked with an annual average of M$600 million. These investments involved many joint ventures between Singaporean firms and European or Asian partners in such industries as textiles, rubber, food, and low-value electrical components (see Table 12.1). The semi-finished or finished products are shipped back to Singapore for completion and export to world markets (Parsonage, 1992: 310). Since the establishment of the Batam Industrial Park (BIP), a number of TNCs, including AT&T, Philips, and Sanyo, have entered the BIP as tenants. Thomson Consumer Electronics, based in France, has recently strengthened its Singapore operations with the goal of making the city-state a regional hub for supporting its Asian business, which includes a factory in the BIP (Singapore Economic Development Board, 1995).

The cross-border investment flows within the CET are more balanced than in the *Sijori* GT. Hong Kong's cumulative investment in Guangdong province is estimated to be close to U. S. $30 billion, over half of Hong Kong's total investment in China. An estimated 80 to 90 percent of Hong Kong's manufacturing industries have been shifted across the border, providing about five million direct and indirect jobs in Guangdong. Although Hong Kong has invested much less in Fujian province, together the two Chinese provinces account for approximately two-thirds of Hong Kong's total investment in China (Chang, 1995; Chen, 1994). Taiwan investment is heavily concentrated in Guangdong and Fujian, especially in the cities shown in Table 12.1. About half of the foreign investment in Fujian has come from Taiwan. A recent estimate by the Hong Kong Great Chamber of Commerce put the cumulative investment from China in Hong Kong at U. S. $26 billion, more than the United States and Japan combined (Hamlin, 1995). Although fluctuating from the mid-1970s on, Hong Kong's cumulative investment in Taiwan had reached U. S. $800 million by the early 1990s (Chang, 1995).

The heavy Hong Kong and Taiwan investments in Guangdong and Fujian provinces have created cross-border production systems similar to the *Sijori* GT. Yet the production systems in the CET exhibit more formal characteristics of what Gereffi (1995) calls "triangle manufacturing." This arrangement involves U. S. and other overseas companies placing orders with Hong Kong or Taiwan manufacturers who in turn shift some or all of the production to affiliated factories in Guangdong and Fujian provinces. The triangle is completed when the finished goods are shipped to the overseas buyers and markets.

In the TRT, very little cross-border investment and production currently exists. Almost all economic exchanges involve bilateral trade among the three parties and some labor movement among them. In 1991 the former Soviet Union and North Korea were Jilin province's third and fourth largest export destinations. Jilin accounted for 15.2 percent of China's total trade with North Korea (Liu and Liao, 1993). By the end of 1993, the number of Chinese workers in the Russian Far East reached 30,000, most of whom were sent by Heilongjiang and Jilin provinces. In 1993, 90 percent of the foreign workers in the Russian Far East cities of Khabarovsk and Amur were North Koreans (Kim, 1994). Twenty Chinese-North Korean joint ventures have been set up on the Chinese side of the border, including restaurants, sauna parlors, and real estate operations (Chen, 1995). As regards extra-regional investment, a handful of American TNCs, including American Airlines, Coca-Cola, and General Motors, have visited the Ragin-Sonbong special economic zone in North Korea with investment ideas, but no construction of any facility has started (*Asiaweek*, 1995).

The comparison shows that the *Sijori* GT and the CET have developed cross-border production systems closely integrated with the global economy through alliances with TNCs and "triangle manufacturing." The TRT, on the other hand, has little cross-border production and TNC investment, which isolates the subregion from the global economy. Bunker (1989) argues that it is more difficult for extractive industries to develop linkages and create diffusion because of the fixity of natural resources in space and physical isolation. The major industries in the TRT are of the extractive type (see Table 12.1). The TRT's less accessible location, reinforced by low economic complementarity among the three members, contributes to its weak ties with the global economy.

IMPLICATIONS FOR THE EVOLVING SEMIPERIPHERY

The emergence and expansion of the Asian-Pacific transborder subregions have three implications for the semiperiphery in the larger region. First, the geoeconomic foundation of the transborder subregions points to a need for reconceptualizing the structure of the Asian-Pacific semiperiphery that has been based on cleanly bounded national economies. The transborder subregions may exert two restructuring effects on the Asian-Pacific semiperiphery. At the broad regional level, the transborder subregions make all the semiperipheral economies more differentiated and less distinctive as they have become more integrated with their neighbors to varying degrees. If we used to view the semiperiphery in the Asia-Pacific as primarily consisting of the newly industrializing economies (NIEs), the transborder subregions now embed them in larger and more connected economic systems. The transborder subregions also make the large semiperipheral countries of China and Russia more internally differentiated as China's coastal areas and Russia's Far East are drawn deeper into the increasingly globalized Asian-Pacific economy. This uneven growth may allow some of the previous peripheral parts of these countries (i.e., border areas) to gradually become core regions both internally and for the transborder subregions where they belong.

Second, the transborder subregions have created new and more convenient opportunities for the semiperipheral economies to cooperate with their neighboring periphery, thus sustaining their development. The *Sijori* GT and the CET provide the most illustrative examples. The Yellow Sea Rim (see Table 12.1) has opened up a similar opportunity for South Korea to invest in the geographically proximate Bohai region of China's Shandong and Liaoning provinces. This geoeconomically based new alliance between the semiperipheral and peripheral countries could generate both cooperation and competition within and between the transborder subregions. Depending on the particular mix of economic complementarity and other factors involved, the transborder subregions could reenergize the stagnating semiperipheral economies and pull their peripheral neighbors along through cooperation. The competitive aspect of the new ties, on the other hand, could create frictions and conflicts between the semiperipheral and peripheral partners and subject them both to a loss-loss bind. In the light of the current and almost region-wide financial crisis affecting all the economies, the transborder subregions may provide some limited and uneven space for some countries to revitalize through effective subregional networking.

Finally, the distribution and shape of the transborder subregions, with China anchoring and being involved in several of them, may suggest a true realignment of geopolitical, geoeconomic, and geocultural power within and across all three zones of the world system in the Asia-Pacific. This claim is rested on the evidence that the transborder subregions are helping to restore the historical core position of China in the region. By drawing Hong Kong, Taiwan, and South Korea into two of the transborder subregions along its coast, with a more distant involvement of Singapore, China may be reaping double benefits from the four key semiperipheral economies in the Asia-Pacific. The heavy investment from the NIEs has allowed China to grow its own export-oriented industries and become more competitive in labor-intensive exports on the global market. At the same time, China is pressing the NIEs on its periphery to upgrade their industries to stay ahead of its cheap-labor industries and develop their own high(er)-technology industries. Although the transborder subregions are not the key to China's ascent to the core, they could facilitate that process by keeping its chief semiperipheral competitors on their toes.

NOTE

An earlier draft of this chapter was presented at the 22nd annual conference of the Political Economy of the World-Systems Section of the American Sociological Association, Northwestern University, March 22–24, 1998. I thank Georgi Derluguian for useful editorial comments. The research and writing for this chapter was supported in part by a Faculty Scholarship from the Great Cities Institute of the University of Illinois at Chicago during 1999.

13

The Process and the Prospects of Soviet Collapse: Bankruptcy, Segmentation, Involution

Georgi M. Derluguian

Russia . . . is merely logistics attached to an arsenal.
Alexander Herzen in the early 1850s

The dates on the tombstone of the USSR, 1917–1991, mark the true beginning and end of the twentieth century. It was the century of turmoil, grave fears, and enormous hopes, but above all it was the epoch of gigantic corporate agencies. The current globalization originates largely from the reactions to the past attempts of applying the historically unprecedented power of states and parties toward the presumably rational channeling of every kind of social action. Thus globalization cannot be properly understood without accounting for the nature and the outcomes of socialist experiences that were a major variety of state-bound reformism—perhaps an extreme variety, but nonetheless no more than a variety within the range of modern state practices.

The successful seizure of state power by a tightly organized group of radical intellectuals (which is what actually happened in Russia in 1917) established the precedent that for the rest of the twentieth century remained the dominant pattern of antisystemic contestation worldwide. The second Soviet revolution was unleashed from above during 1929 to 1938 in reaction to the market failures. It was a ruthless bid to break up the peasantry and subordinate every kind of social action to the mobilizational state. The success of Stalinist industrialization, validated by the victory in World War II, showed the further potential as well as the stringent limits of socialist experiments within the capitalist world-economy.

Here we encounter the intersection of systemic possibilities with Russia's specific position within modern geopolitics and geoculture. Hypothetically, the Bolsheviks could have won political power only in the Russian heartland and avoided the reconquest of ethnically non-Russian borderlands. The Russian empire would then likely follow the common pattern of the Habsburg and Ottoman disintegration. In real history the victorious Bolsheviks did not stop before creating the unprecedented Soviet federation of national republics that could not possibly exist without the overarching bureaucratic apparatus and the futurist ideology of the communist party. Falling short of the projected world socialist revolution, the USSR nonetheless established a tightly organized geopolitical power base of continental proportions. For largely the same reasons, the fragile New Economic Policy (NEP) and the relative social diversity of the 1920s had to end in calamitous industrialization. Without the second Soviet revolution Russia would most likely have remained just another predominantly peasant semi-peripheral state ruled by a populist bureaucratic organization like the contemporary party-state of Mexico or the Kemalist army-state of Turkey.

The trajectory of the USSR was exceptional due to the state's size, the long tradition of previous state modernizations since before Tsar Peter the Great, and its position in immediate proximity to Europe. In the morphology of the modern world-system Russia always compensated for her relative economic weakness with the strategic importance of her land armies situated on the edge of the European core. Russia's stature was the highest in the periods of anarchy within the core. For the first time this happened in the early 1700s when the emergent empire of Peter the Great wrestled control over the Baltic resources from Sweden, the erstwhile mercenary pillar in the declining trade network of the Dutch. The glorious entry of Russian soldiers into Paris in 1815 and Berlin in 1945 twice saved the capitalist world-economy as a historical system that Napoleon and Hitler threatened to subsume into the despotically unified world-empire.

In the aftermath of both victories Russia was politically alienated by the new hegemonic powers, respectively Great Britain and the United States, that grew weary of the former ally's sheer size. For the same reason, however, during the periods of alienation the Russian state was never pushed too hard by the contemporary hegemonic power. Russia always retained an honorable status in contemporary world politics disproportionate to her economic weight. In *Pax Britannica* and in *Pax Americana* Russia remained in fact a special partner in enforcing conservative order over the volatile eastern and central parts of Europe (Bunce, 1991). Both times the ritualized rivalry between Russian empires and world hegemonic power thus had to be relegated to the areas outside Europe. In the nineteenth century it was the Anglo-Russian *Great Game* fought over the tribal frontiers and the enfeebled empires of Asia; after 1945 the Soviet-American competition in the post-colonial Third World reproduced an analogous rivalry on a larger scale and considerably higher ideological pitch.

Geopolitical peculiarity made the Russian state at the same time vulnerable and exceptionally important. Its highly ambiguous sense of cultural belonging to Europe translated into the perceived obligation of the educated elites both before and after 1917 to bring the country up to modern European standards. Acting with their trademark vigor and ferocious devotion, the Bolsheviks overcame the social and cultural contradictions of old imperial Russia by establishing a radically more centralized state, sharply reducing the social diversity and systematically destroying the potential bases of opposition (including their own comrades who were too reluctant to embrace the new apparatchik code). The unparalleled concentration of power was applied to transform the Soviet production base and the society itself into a centrally administered industrial machine whose design was determined by the overriding goal of defense against the hostile capitalist environment.

In the process the socialist state has indeed achieved substantial social homogenization by recasting its citizens into an educated, urbanized, and overall proletarianized pool of industrial labor. The social homogenization, substantial vertical mobility in the earlier periods, and obtaining (indeed, obsession with) the markers of modernity, which were essentially the result of unremitting war effort, produced a strong impression of validity of the founding socialist ideology. The promise of a better material life became central only later, in the declining phase of socialist trajectory, when the war effort and patriotic ideology could no longer serve as sole justification for the enterprise, and when in the late 1950s the Soviet state reached the limits of proletarianization and had to face the increasingly demanding expectations of its newly urbanized and homogenous citizenry.

State socialism cannot be reduced to ideological or military dictatorship. It was more than that. The ideological apparatus, the military command, and the industrial management always remained separate from each other and vertically subordinated to the political leadership through the mechanisms of Communist party control over the key appointments (the lists of *nomenklatura* positions) and the subordinate institution of secret police that pervaded every domain under the norms of state vigilance. The net result was a peculiarly fused form of developmentalist dictatorship that in the ascendant war preparation phase very successfully emulated the contemporary industrial base of capitalist core states. It later spanned its own emulations, which for the lifetime of a generation appeared to be a world socialist system in the making—a claim that the world-system analysts always doubted (Wallerstein, 1974a). Randall Collins actually predicted the Soviet collapse in terms of geopolitical theory (Collins, 1978 and 1995). Immanuel Wallerstein never made an explicit prediction, likely due to his personal and political allegiances, although he argued on numerous occasions that the Soviet bloc could not sustain its own achievement over the long run.

In retrospect the general cause of Soviet failure seems clear. It had little to do with its official socialist ideology, which was in practice (if not in rhetoric) just a more activist and colorful version of typically twentieth-century modernizing reform. The USSR disintegrated because it overspecialized in preparing for industrial-age warfare, in building the bureaucratized mobilization state; generally it overadapted to the geopolitics of the twentieth century. Such over-specialization grew from the earlier overconcentration of efforts and resources that was probably the only way a semiperipheral state could hope to match the core in the arenas that were symbolically important in its times. The Soviet model became irrelevant and eventually extinct once the patterns of world-system began shifting under the impact of the American crisis of 1968–1973 in the direction generically called globalization.

Analysis of the Soviet demise also helps to understand the resilient power of capitalism and the true advantages of hegemonic power, for it was the United States that in the early 1970s first faced a set of problems very similar to those that later brought down the USSR. These problems included the geopolitical overstretch expressed in the permanent deployment of large garrisons and navies far away from the home base; a bloated military-industrial complex that practically excluded market pressures; accumulated bureaucratic rigidities within the state, the private capitalist apparatuses, and basic social arrangements (what neo-liberal critics later called the age of entitlements); a fabulously expensive military that proved incapable against Third World guerrillas; an embarrassing economic crisis arriving after the period of unprecedented expansion that the ruling elite once proclaimed the result of its scientifically informed wisdom; and, finally, the reformist, future-oriented, universalistic official ideology coming in blatant discord with its own promise of equality and ever increasing prosperity for all.

The United States, however, did not collapse in the wake of its defeat in Vietnam, the dollar devaluation, the oil shock, the domestic ethnic conflicts and democracy movements, the Watergate scandal, and so on. The United States was not a mono-organizational entity like the USSR (Rigby and Fehér, 1982). It combined the logic (and therefore the problems) of imperial territorialism with the logic (and therefore the resources) of capitalist accumulation. This combination was a major advantage that made the American state much wealthier and less homogenous than the socialist USSR state. At no moment did the United States experience a crisis spreading through every sector or a clear-cut distinction between the entire citizenry and the entire elite, the situation of us versus them that made the East European revolutions of 1989 so sudden and sweeping. Furthermore, the United States could benefit from its hegemonic advantages by forcefully drawing on the wealth and political loyalty of its allies, something that Moscow could never do with the unruly and oversubsidized East European satellites.

Globalization itself may be traced back to the efforts of the U. S. ruling elites to deal with the crisis of the early 1970s. Let us note that the current globalization started from the undoing of bureaucratic rigidities and social contracts of the post-1945 period; the shift from social-democratic Keynesianism to more stringent neo-conservatism in ideology and economics; the vastly increased transborder mobility of capital; the cultivation of new middle classes; the reforms of policing and the military; perhaps even the proliferation of new social movements with their profound divisions and one-issue focus. The Soviet demise—more exactly, the bankruptcy of its military-industrial machine—was another consequence of this global transformation.

THE SOVIET DECLINE: IRRATIONAL, DOGMATIC, OR PATH-CONSTRAINED?

Several events in the trajectory of the Soviet Union could qualify for the signal crisis, that is, the turning point at which an historical entity exhausts its mechanisms of reproduction and begins to decline but temporarily recovers and for a while continues moving along the same vector. This could have happened as early as in 1962, when the brutally suppressed general strike in Novocherkassk showed the limits of Stalinist despotic industrialization, or in the aftermath of the Prague Spring of 1968, when Brezhnev's leadership gave up on attempts at reinventing Communism and shifted instead to the taming policy that combined selective coercion, corporatist redistribution, and the acceptance of mass consumerism instead of ideology.[1] The easy petrodollars and international credits of the seventies helped to subsidize the Soviet bloc for another decade, while the political crisis of U. S. hegemony was wishfully presumed in Moscow to be its own success. The sharp reversal came in the early eighties when the costs of comfortable stagnation became insupportable with the decline in oil revenues, the spread of middle-class consumer aspirations among the Soviet citizenry, the increasingly evident bureaucratic corruption and the generalized atmosphere of cynicism, the USSR's embarrassing inability to extinguish the rebellions in Poland and Afghanistan, and the American shift from détente to renewed Cold War in reaction to the perceived Soviet gains of the previous decade.

If the signal crisis of the USSR could be dated to several events stretched between 1962 and 1980, its final crisis arrived in the succession of three sharp jolts. In 1989 Moscow abdicated from its external empire in Eastern Europe and dumped its Third World allies. In 1991 President Yeltsin, installed as the new ruler in Moscow, acknowledged the loss of control over the former Soviet republics. In 1996, five years after the formal dissolution of the USSR and its cementing Communist party, Russia suffered an unmitigated military debacle in Chechnya. The Chechen war made apparent the collapse of the last pillar of Soviet state power—the Red Army. The secession of Chechnya further signified a secular discontinuity in the geopolitics of northern Eurasia. The area has been dominated by the succession of ever-expanding Russian land empires marked by the 1553 conquest of the Volga Tatar khanates by Ivan the Terrible; the 1721 opening a window to Europe by Peter the Great; the 1921 Bolshevik recovery of the former realm of the Tsars and therefore inheriting its geopolitical position; finally, the crowning achievement of superpower status in the aftermath of 1945.

The greatest army in Russian history was forged in World War II and remained ever geared toward its frightening and glorious experience. Indicatively, the nuclear factor did not significantly change the thinking of Soviet generals about future wars, which they still imagined along the lines of blitzkrieg, only even bigger, faster, and more mechanized.[2] The maintenance of a huge standing army long after 1945 was neither the collective folly of generals and megalomaniac bureaucrats nor a peculiar idiosyncrasy of Russian national psyche. Least of all was the Red Army maintained in the expectation of world socialist revolution—this vision had perished shortly after the Bolshevik victory, in the stark realities of the mid-1920s, and even its rhetoric had been dropped long before the formal dissolution of the Comintern in 1943. The Soviet strategy was rather driven by the logic of territorialist accumulation that was enshrined in the peculiar architecture of the Soviet state, in its symbols and discourse, and in its very geopolitical position.

In this case the analytical separation of endogenous from exogenous factors seems particularly meaningless. During the five centuries since its emergence in the late 1400s the Russian state was only an occasional participant in the capitalist world-economy but it has always been part and participant of modern European geoculture and geopolitics. Ironically, Russia moved into the center of capitalist geoculture and geopolitics precisely between 1917 and 1989, when ideologists on all sides loudly claimed that the Soviet bloc had become a separate system in every respect. This will perhaps remain in modern history as the biggest example of ideological misrepresentation ever.

The Soviet experience grew from and, in its turn, re-shaped the two processes that were central to the modern world-system. The first source was the twentieth-century geopolitics determined by the wars of British (and generally European) succession: the two devastating conflicts involving the entire core between 1914 and 1945 that were known as the World Wars, and the scores of attendant anti-imperialist rebellions that started shortly after 1917 and continued to rock the peripheries of world-system until the 1970s.

The second source of Soviet experience was the geoculture of progress interpreted in the practices of industrialism and social reformism. The key agents of the epoch became the new bureaucratically organized corporations: the industrial enterprises, the social movements, and the modern states. State socialism attempted to maximize the effectiveness of the three types of corporate agents by forcefully merging them into one supercorporation. Therefore it would be more useful to analyze the rise, bankruptcy, and breakdown of the USSR as an historical instance of a particularly big bureaucratically fused corporation specialized in territorialist accumulation and the practices of modernization.

The Bolshevik founders of the USSR considered central planning an immensely more rational form of economic and social regulation than the perennially disruptive chaos of the markets with their wasteful duplication of economic functions by competing firms. State planning and prevention of competition were not an exclusively socialist idea. Bureaucratic regulation was continuously attempted by large private businesses in their struggles for control over markets and by practically all governments, especially during wartime or in preparation for wars. The Bolsheviks admired, at least no less than they

loathed, the American trusts and the German bureaucracy. Recall Lenin pro-
claiming in 1915 financial capital and imperialism as the last necessary step in
the historical progression toward socialism.

All revolutionary attempts to use state power in overcoming underdevelopment showed that the fusion of political, administrative, and economic power
produced in the medium term the strengthening of state capacity but at the same
time invariably led to the phenomena that the Hungarian economist Janos Kornai
described as the problems of soft budget constraints and the attendant economy
of shortage (Kornai, 1980). This was neither a mistake nor a logical aberration.
It was rather the outcome of a distinct logic that Giovanni Arrighi called territorialist (Arrighi, 1994). Although the logic of territorial state power historically
predated the cosmopolitan logic of capitalist accumulation, it did not disappear
with the birth of capitalism. Territorialism was reproduced in the capitalist
world-economy by the continued existence of multiple states and therefore geopolitics (Chase-Dunn and Hall, 1997).

The Soviet version of territorialism obtained its opportunity in the geopolitical
configurations of the twentieth century. At first, the grave turmoil of the two
world wars isolated the USSR and made it a key ally against Germany. After
1945 the Soviet bloc was accommodated in *Pax Americana* as the honorable
and unavoidable foe. These were the necessary conditions. To survive in the
epoch of industrialized warfare the USSR had to emulate the industrialism of
core capitalist states.

The very success of Soviet militarized industrialization, however, proved to
be its undoing. The USSR emulated the contemporary industrialism short of the
commercialization of warfare as practiced by the core states. The Soviet
military-industrial complex was simply not designed to pay for itself. It was
built in the expectation of European continental wars and victory regardless of
the human and material costs. Besides, the Soviet ideological eschatology predicted that the inevitable end of capitalism would pave the way to the proper
Communist society where money would disappear and material goods become
plentiful. In a prolonged peaceful period the combination of mobilizational state,
exclusion of markets, and the symbolical sanctioning of such a situation as
normal resulted in the decreasing effectiveness of management (suitable to operate only in the wartime emergency mode), pervasive shortages, and in the
general inability of the Soviet state to deliver on its bold ideological promises.

A concomitant problem of Soviet-style industrialization was the notoriously
shoddy (more precisely, uneven and generally declining) quality of state socialist
production. It was in fact a perverse triumph of socialist workers that should be
attributed to the institutional design of the Soviet state at least, no less than to
its ostensibly proletarian ideology. By creating shortages of every kind, including the shortage of labor, while denying its employees the political possibility
to bargain for higher wages, the socialist state forced itself to accept the creeping
tendency toward lowering the labor inputs. The workers were tacitly allowed to
decrease their efforts in order to prevent the politicization of their demands. We

have relatively sparse documentation of workers' protests under state socialism except for the most spectacular instances such as regularly happened in Poland, but there is little doubt that the state socialist managers constantly felt the need to appease their employees. The outcome of this perverse class struggle was equally perverse. The wry East European joke "They pretend to pay, we pretend to work" meant in fact demoralization that damaged the work ethics and crippled the ability of workers to pressure the rulers through collective action.

The specific diagnosis is well known. Liberated from the market pressures, the Soviet managers were left with three major tasks: to insure themselves against removal by superiors; to strengthen their bargaining positions in the central allocation of supplies; and to maximize their administrative control over the relatively unruly and increasingly scarce workforce (Burawoy, 1985; Filtzer, 1992; Ticktin, 1992). All three tasks were best achieved through accruing the political-ideological prominence to the enterprises and their administrative locations (which was called in the insider jargon of Soviet planners "securing highly reportable projects"). Socialist administrators were also induced to forge mutually binding networks within the state apparatus. Hoarding, bartering resources, shrouding the operations in bureaucratic secrecy were essential to this pattern of managerial behavior within the centrally administered framework. In the end what appeared rational strategies from the standpoint of individual actors amounted to systemic irrationalities.

ALUMINUM AS THE MIRROR OF SOVIET EXPERIENCE

At this point it would be useful to make an illustrative digression and, using the example of the Soviet aluminum sector, show how this industrial system emerged, expanded, and evolved after the end of state socialism.[3] In the 1980s the USSR produced around 3.5 million tons of aluminum a year. It was estimated to be roughly three times above the peacetime internal demand. The huge excess was stockpiled in strategic reserves and simply squandered. This explains the puzzling piles of aluminum kitchenware all over the Soviet bloc that were inferior to cast iron utensils, yet often the only available of its kind. The project of using aluminum for canning beverages ran into the need to spend precious hard currency for importing the production lines and to the generally low priority accorded to consumer products. The logical suggestion to export the redundant aluminum failed because of a combination of Western protectionism and the lack of initiative from the Soviet Ministry of Foreign Trade that had no incentive to fight an uphill battle on the world market for metals. The Soviet aluminum producers had no interest in promoting their exports either. Most of them were not even allowed to travel abroad because of security clearance. Meantime the USSR continued to expand its aluminum industry, which became a strong lobbying agency on its own. Additionally, the aluminum makers had prominent allies in the hydropower sector that always needed to justify the construction of yet another world champion dam on a Siberian river.

The original impetus, however, was military. Since the beginning of Stalinist industrialization, aluminum production has been listed as top strategic priority. Aside from the obvious application in building aircraft, the innovative (and very expensive) use of aluminum alloys for engine parts made possible the famous T-34 tank, arguably the best tank of World War II, which combined an impressive speed with heavy armor. When in 1942 the German command was considering the new generation of armored vehicles, they had to opt for bulky monstrosities like the *Tiger Panzer* because of the sheer shortage of aluminum in Nazi-occupied Europe. In the 1970s the calculations of Soviet General Staff, drawn from the worst-case scenario of simultaneous war against NATO and China, showed that during the first two months of such conflict the Soviet army would need to replace up to fifty thousand tanks. The combined institutional weight of the military, the aluminum producers, their allies in the energy sector, and the fact that sizable towns in Siberia and Central Asia depended on the local metallurgical plants assured that the Soviet Politburo continued to pour resources into an otherwise patently redundant industrial sector.

After the Soviet disintegration the Russian neo-liberal reformers tried to pull the plug on the aluminum industry, drastically reducing state orders. The aluminum plants scrambled to export their production on the world markets at any price, often illegally. The price of a ton of aluminum in the early 1990s tumbled from over $4,000 to just above $1,000. Nevertheless the sudden monetization of the Russian aluminum industry offered the possibility of instantaneous fortune to the people who controlled it. The struggle for control was fierce and often deadly. For instance, in 1995 the employee shareholders of Krasnoyarsk Aluminum Plant (KrAZ), one of the biggest in Siberia, elected a new CEO, nicknamed the Bull, who was previously a boxing coach and since 1990 proprietor of a private security agency. The KrAZ export contracts were secured by a shady London-based firm founded by two Soviet émigrés to Israel (*Russia Business Review*, April 1999). By the same token, much of the brutal civil war in the former Soviet republic of Tadjikistan was in fact the struggle among various warlords for the control of the Tursun-Zadeh Aluminum Combine, the main hard currency earner in this impoverished Central Asian state.

The postscript to the aluminum story is developing as I am writing these words. The charismatic former General Alexander Lebed, who succcessfully ran in 1997 for the governor of Krasnoyarsk province, moved to tax the KrAZ and force it into paying its local suppliers. Lebed made no secret that it was his rehearsal for the Russian presidential campaign. Aluminum could generate fabulous fortunes only because its masters shared very little with the energy suppliers, who in their turn did not pay the railways and the coal miners, and everyone did their best to avoid paying taxes and workers salaries. It is unclear how long such a cannibalistic scheme can endure without causing a major social and political backlash or permanently crippling the export markets.

Aluminum isn't too exceptional. In a similar instance of fabulous overproduction, the USSR used to manufacture almost three times more tractors and pesticides than the United States and still had to import American grain. The industrial base designed for the tank and chemical warfare could not save Soviet agriculture. Or, in the most macabre applications of soft budget constraint, it was revealed that the USSR stockpiled nearly forty-five thousand nuclear warheads—three times more than the CIA's estimates and surely more than enough to destroy the whole planet. What kind of market reform can deal with all those tractor/tanks, pesticides, nuclear bombs, or aluminum plants?

The story of Soviet aluminum clearly shows that the standard criticisms of state socialism were wrong in attributing its pathologies to the socialist ideology. The critical (soft budget constraint) part of the analysis developed by the neo-classical economists is perhaps persuasive, but the ideological devotion of the critics—as well as the die-hard advocates—of state socialism obscured what simultaneously was the true achievement of the USSR and the source of its implosion. It was the creation of a heavily industrialized territorialist superpower in an economically weak semiperipheral location.

TRIUMPH AND IMPASSE OF THE SOVIET TERRITORIALIST MONOPOLY

The expression military-industrial complex perhaps described the USSR better than any other state of the twentieth century (Zaslavsky, 1994). Or it deserved the label USSR, Inc. at least no less than Japan. In the United States the nonmilitary private capitalist interests could politically challenge the exclusiveness of the military-industrial complex. It was what in fact happened during the presidency of Eisenhower who originally made current the expression military-industrial complex. The USSR failed to demobilize after 1945 despite the recurrent political attempts to rationalize the regime during the periods of ideological relaxation and economic reform. The USSR largely eliminated competitive pressures from within, but as long as the Cold War lasted it remained under tremendous competitive pressure from without that was channeled through the arms race. Moscow was kept extremely anxious about upholding superpower status with all its ideological, political, and military attributes. Rulers who came to power after Stalin were perennially torn between the urge to rationalize their mechanisms of power and the fear of losing control precisely because their power rested on an institutional setup that over time became self-defeating and looked quite irrational.

The Red Army at the historical summit of its might, achieved in the 1970s, overshadowed the German Wehrmacht. It was a splendid industrial machine relying on a heavy mass of armor, a harshly disciplined corps of professional officers, and millions of conscripted boys. Admittedly, it was fabulously expensive and wasteful. But above all, it was redundant. In the language of business consultants, the Soviet military was an extraordinary case of bad investment rooted in the incorrect assessment of previous success and sustained by an inertial and comfortably insulated corporate culture. Meantime, the U. S. hegemony excluded wars among the core states and rendered territorial conquests an obsolete strategy. No less important from the Russian standpoint, after 1945 the centers of world political and economic power were no longer situated on the European continent, where the Russian land armies traditionally played a major role.

The USSR tried to compensate for its eroding advantage in conventional land armies by putting valiant efforts into developing a nuclear arsenal, a strategic submarine fleet, and pioneering space program. These were arguably the most amazing feats of Soviet central planning that in less than a decade (1948–1957) undid the splendid oceanic isolation of the United States. The achievement of symbolic parity in strategic weapons bolstered Soviet superpower status for three whole decades. It induced in the Soviet leadership a momentous sense of triumph, but it also placed on them a tremendous burden of maintaining pace in the contest with a much wealthier rival. This achievement in hindsight appeared part of the Soviets' undoing. Even in the areas of its previous success such as space flights, Moscow had no prospect of matching the billions of dollars poured by the United States into the moon race. In the most conspicuous arena, the nuclear arms race, the USSR ended up deadlocked. Despite their exclusive symbolic value, nuclear weapons were an impasse in interstate rivalries. The USSR was forced to accept competition in the nonmilitary fields—economic, political, cultural, and ideological production—where the huge American advantages left it no chance. Neither the Soviet Olympic team nor the Bolshoi ballet could detract from the sweeping effect of Western mass culture on Soviet urban youths. In a fundamental sense the Red Army was defeated by rock music and blue jeans. The newly accessible Russian archives reveal that the Soviet leadership felt deeply inferior and embattled far more often than triumphant.

PERESTROIKA: REINVENTING THE SOVIET STATE

Meanwhile, the large conscript armies of the industrial age appeared increasingly anachronistic as the core states moved to the new forms of production and social organization (let's tentatively call it post-Fordism, which is at least clearer than the postmodernist formulations). The problem became apparent already in the sixties when it was first reflected in the Soviet attempts at economic reform. The reformist movement was aborted after 1968 when it became no less apparent that the fused character of state socialism left almost no space for maneuver. Due to the functional fusion of state socialist governance and ideology, the effects of pending bankruptcies in the symbolically crucial but now obsolete industrial branches would have inevitably spread throughout the entire corporation, affecting the military that remained the major consumer of industrial outputs. Meantime the state socialist planners could no longer rely on the Stalinist methods of sacrificing enormous amounts of material resources and human lives to achieve their goals. The goals themselves became far more complex than simply to build up an arsenal of industrially produced armaments. The most intractable goal became maintaining the loyalty of Soviet populations whose sociodemographic profile had vastly changed in the course of state socialist development. The population was no longer predominantly peasant with high birth rates and low consumer expectations but rather urban workers and cadres with very low birth rates and consumer expectations rapidly approaching the well-advertised patterns of mass consumption in the capitalist core.

The military-industrial machine that earned the USSR its superpower status now itself posed the perennial Russian problem—looking backward compared to the West. Not unlike economic corporations operating on the capitalist markets, the USSR, an expressly territorialist corporation, found itself constrained by the ideological aura and the sheer enormity of its past investment. The Soviet superpower militarization was underpinning domains as diverse as industry, academia, space research, patriotic ideology, the nationalities policy, sports, education, and male socialization. As happens in the periods preceding systemic crises and collapses, both the advocates of change and their conservative opponents were right. The Soviet bloc and its central unit, the USSR, could not be transformed without immediate damage to its symbolic stature and organizational coherence, yet it had to be transformed or face extinction.

Khrushchev's attempt to downsize the Red Army and rationalize Soviet economic and political management cost him dearly. The ruling *nomenklatura* of the USSR, which largely owed to Khrushchev its autonomy and safety from the state terror, instead opted to follow the least-effort principle and reap the fruits of de-Stalinization. The subsidized hedonism of Brezhnev's reign, however, did not succeed in muffling its critics and widespread misgivings. In 1969 Soviet dissident Andrei Amalrik argued in the darkly prophetic pamphlet *Will the Soviet Union Survive until 1984?* that the USSR had completely lost its erstwhile ideological enthusiasm, and imperial inertia was driving it toward a violent end, which Amalrik envisioned in imminent war with Mao's China (Amalrik, 1970). Amalrik's underground pamphlet was certainly known and privately discussed among the Soviet elites. Yet, the autonomous corporatist nature of the Soviet bureaucracy mightily hindered its own self-reflecting capacity. Individually, most members of the ruling *nomenklatura* realized that something had gone rotten in their kingdom, but they could not dare to specify and discuss these vague sentiments because of the *nomenklatura*'s peculiar organizational existence as a rigidly ranked and unified bureaucratic caste. The USSR avoided Amalrik's horrific prediction of war against China; nevertheless the dissident critic was proven correct when even a leadership as fearful of consequences as was Brezhnev's couldn't resist the temptation of using the costly idle army to score what seemed an easy gain in Afghanistan.

The energetic party youngsters like Gorbachev inherited the messy situation that still looked reparable to almost everyone. The USSR appeared solid, only a little too stolid. Gorbachev's ideas were borrowed from the dissident critics of a 1968 generation who had engaged in a dramatic dialogue with the Communist rulers and eventually came close to being their alter ego. Still *uskorenie* (acceleration), *perestroika* (restructuring), and, later, *glasnost* (public debate) remained campaign slogans that fell far short of a reflected program.

Whether the Soviet system was indeed reparable would remain a theoretical question. Gorbachev's faith in his ability to fix the USSR and renegotiate its positions within the world-system proved sufficiently stabilizing and allowed the Soviet empire to crash land without a major calamity. A less optimistic last (for invariably he would have been the last) General Secretary could have turned for the discourse and program to another kind of dissidents—the radical nationalists. In fact, this is what the Serbian Communist bosses did in 1989. At a steep social and economic cost, by improvisations leading to mounting confusion, Gorbachev achieved the political and ideological delegitimation of the entire Soviet coercive apparatus and thus assured a remarkably peaceful shedding of imperial burden. At the circumstantial level, he was unwittingly helped by three factors: the failure of the Soviet invasion of Afghanistan, which failed to produce publicly recognized war heroes who could evolve into patriotic icons; the emergence of the irrepressible national democratic movements within the Soviet republics and in Eastern Europe; and the boisterous glasnost-era press, which was dominated from the outset by the celebrity intellectuals aspiring to wrestle symbolic and later the state power from the bureaucracy.

Gorbachev's downfall is commonly blamed on these very factors—the momentous immobilization of coercive apparatus; the attack on the bureaucratic institutions by the radical factions of intelligentsia under the slogans of democratic access and accountability; and the politicization of nationally-structured civil societies within the Soviet realm. This explanation is insufficient. The popular movements unleashed from the top by Gorbachev's perestroika primarily challenged the mid-level ruling *nomenklatura*. In fact, the introduction of new controls over the self-contained Soviet bureaucracies by subjecting them to the tests of elections and market competition appear in retrospect the strategic goals of Gorbachev's reform (Urban et al., 1997). The futile activist coercion of Andropov demonstrated that the sustainable governability of the Soviet Union required a profound restructuring of social controls and not just the invigoration of the apparat through purges.

Before Gorbachev could create the new regime, the subordinate factions of *nomenklatura* defected and reneged on the two fundamental taboos of the *nomenklatura* behavior—engaging in nationalism and private accumulation. The reaction of Soviet bosses to the tumult unleashed by perestroika was no less improvised, but it worked because the actual power had already moved to the mid-level bureaucratic bodies due to Brezhnev's toleration of "stability of cadres." Instead of reversing the results of Brezhnevism, perestroika in fact accelerated and completed the process of imperial decay and diffusion of central power.

The collapse of state socialism was neither a revolution from above nor from below; it was rather from the middle. After 1989 the mid-ranking managers of the Soviet state rushed to insulate themselves from central government, to suppress or co-opt the internal challengers, and reconsolidate their power within the corporate spaces that they administered. Arguably a few of them perished, yet the majority, especially among the younger generation of *nomenklatura* that was formed in the Brezhnev-era atmosphere of opportunism, survived the new navigation in lifeboats.

The radical changes at the levels of rhetoric and symbols of power should not obscure the fact that the economic, social, and political trends of the post-Soviet nineties grew from the notorious "aberrations" of the Brezhnev period: corruption and the maturation of bureaucratic cliques, criminal entrepreneurship, ideological and moral decay. This does not mean that social change was minimal. The major new condition was created by the elimination of central ideological and political mechanisms. This exacerbated the contradictions of state socialism and brought them into the open. The key new condition was segmentation and the elite appropriation of the formerly unified spheres of bureaucratic control. The Soviet bloc literally fell apart and remained in this awkward situation through the nineties.

THE TWO MODES OF POST-SOVIET SEGMENTATION

Before the end of the USSR its ruling *nomenklatura* were found in two kinds of corporate bodies. The first kind were various territorial subunits: fifteen national republics and over twenty lesser ethnic autonomies and nearly a hundred regular provinces predominantly situated within the huge Russian Federation. The second kind of corporations were the nonterritorial enterprise agglomerations (state trusts and combines) and various ministries that supervised a panoply of economic branches and state institutions ranging from defense to education. The distinction between the territorial and nonterritorial units of Soviet power is crucial to explaining the divergent strategies pursued by the ruling elites in the wake of central state collapse.

The Soviet Union fell apart when various bureaucratic cliques defied and defected from the central government that they judged unpredictable, unable to deliver on the previous promises of corporate redistribution, and often downright threatening. Gorbachev's attempts to neutralize his opponents by immobilizing the mechanisms of ideological and police coercion (which was a sensible move given the fate of Nikita Khruschev) invited all sorts of popular pressures that directly challenged the mid-level bureaucracies. After a moment of hesitation and bewilderment (that provided the brief window of opportunity to the nascent East European democracies) the groups of *nomenklatura* began to transform their particular domains into autonomous units. The social and political controls let go by Moscow were reconsolidated locally.

Learning from experience and mutual emulation, the *nomenklatura* cliques dropped the ineffective Communist ideology and appropriated the rhetoric and symbols of their challengers, purged the unreformable hardliners, and, only under pressure, incorporated some figures of the 1989–1991 rebellions. This mutation occurring in the huge expanses of the former Soviet bloc was fraught with a myriad of circumstantial conflicts, fleeting alliances, and bewildering political episodes. The general pattern of segmentation, however, remained the same, and the outcomes emerged within a range that appeared rather limited on careful examination. The core of Soviet-era elites prevailed everywhere except in extreme cases like Chechnya, where the very bases of power were literally destroyed, or the instances where the fractured state apparatus was forced into cohabitation with upstart new leaders and criminal warlords (the mercurial President of Belorussia, Lukashenka, provides an outstanding example, as do many businessmen emerging from the black markets and teenager street gangs of the late seventies). Furthermore, the character of mutation and the particular outcomes were often determined by the previous reconfiguration of power in 1956 through 1968. This was no less true of Uzbekistan and Azerbaijan than Poland and Estonia.

On 25 December 1991 the previously unified power and assets of the former USSR were neither destroyed nor transformed. Emancipated from central control, power and assets were fractured and divided (privatized) among the bureaucratic corporations along existing institutional lines. The two kinds of Soviet-era corporations (territorial and nonterritorial) engendered two patterns of *nomenklatura* privatization. The second determining mechanism was the relative value of privatized resources on the world market and in the interstate system that conditioned the immediate fortunes and the politics of new rulers and entrepreneurs.

Those nonterritorial (industrial and financial) *nomenklaturas*, which were particularly lucky to preside over the readily marketable assets, easily evolved into trading monopolies. These elite factions had an obvious interest in promoting the monetization of exchanges, privatization of assets, and access to the world markets, but they would also seek to constrain the radical marketization advocated by the neo-liberal ideologues because it no less obviously threatened the new mercantile capitalists with increased competition. The leading example of this kind is Yeltsin's long-standing premier Chernomyrdin of 1992–1998, who came to the government from a lucrative position in the export-oriented natural gas industry and used the powers of state office to provide his branch with preferential export quotas and huge tax breaks.

The less fortunate former "red managers" whose assets were undervalued or redundant on the world markets would clamor for state subsidies and protection on the grounds of social justice and national pride. Using the advantages of rural control, the collective farm bosses, for instance, united into the influential Agrarian party that specialized in lobbying for subsidies. The political opposition, particularly the neo-communists and nationalists, would compete for constituencies within these depressed sectors. By far the most successful was the populist mayor of Moscow Yuri Luzhkov who deftly applied the centrality of his office to tame the Moscow-based mass-media and accrue enormous popularity as the collective lobbyist for troubled enterprises. The example of mayor Luzhkov spun off numerous emulators among the Russian provincial governors.

A different though intrinsically very similar strategy was pursued by the groups of *nomenklatura* that presided over the territorial units of the USSR. The territories with internationally recognized claims to national self-determination (the fifteen union republics of the USSR including Russia) offered their elites the opportunity to transform their corporations into newly independent states. The bureaucracies of new states merged to various extents with the select outsiders from the local intelligentsia who provided them with new symbols and ideology. Invariably it was some blend of nationalism with capitalist reformism. The actual proportion could vary greatly, but generally it reflected the assets found within the territories and their proximity to the core and the global flows of capital. With the notable exception of nationalism, the rest of the anti-systemic programs of 1989–1991 (environmentalism, human rights, reform socialism, various brands of anarchism, and religious fundamentalism) were rapidly marginalized everywhere in Eastern Europe and the former USSR as the reconstituted elites consolidated their power and tamed the outbursts of popular movements.

The territorial units without any plausible nationalist claim (i.e., regular provinces) still followed the same pattern under the discourse of federalism and decentralization. The most contested proved to be the in-between cases of the territories with some degree of ethnic specificity, but less than a full array of sovereign state institutions. Here we find the instances as dire as Chechnya, Karabagh, Abkhazia, Transnistria, or Serbia's Kosovo.

Following the general pattern of post-Soviet segmentation, Boris Yeltsin in 1991 brought to the control of the core Soviet republic a typically circumstantial bloc of the lesser-rank *nomenklatura* and the politicized intellectuals. Yeltsin inherited severely limited state power and a much bigger mess than the one that had once challenged Gorbachev but, paradoxically, the first president of Russia was in less danger than his predecessor and foe in the Kremlin. The Soviet empire had already crash-landed and fallen into the constituent parts. The revolutionary popular mobilizations had subsided before the end of 1992, self-exhausted and extinguished by the localized factions of *nomenklatura*. With the end of the Soviet Union political conflicts were reduced to the intra-elite rivalries for the spoils. For a moment the runaway confrontations of 1992–1993 within the victorious blocs threatened the severely fractured post-Soviet elites with self-destruction, but soon the new norms and compromises ensured a weak form of political stability through the opportunistic, continuously renegotiated power-sharing between the central bureaucracy and its counterparts entrenched in the industrial sectors and provinces. The new party system and an anarchic form of parliamentarism emerged as the political expression of consensus among the segmented elites. To this list of actors we should add the mass media, seized in the aftermath of glasnost by the competing cliques of journalists—arguably, the biggest innovation in the arsenal of Russian political struggle and the sustained outcome of Gorbachev's attempt to create the field of public politics.

Where are the Red Army and the KGB in this picture? Quite astonishingly given their previous aura and positions, these pillars of Soviet power were major losers on every account. These enormous organizations could convert their power and assets into neither territorial sovereignty nor economic capital. Arguably a few corrupt generals succeeded in individual enrichment and many KGB officers became successful entrepreneurs in the new and booming market of industrial espionage and private protection, but if anything this inflicted further damage on the institutions of state coercion. After 1991 the mighty coercive apparatus of the USSR found itself politically disunited and demoralized after a series of military defeats and the years of public humiliation under Gorbachev's glasnost. The single most important defeat was arguably the shameful failure of the conservative coup in August 1991 that largely removed from power the old imperial hardliners. Yet, there was a heftier structural reason for the decline of the Soviet coercive apparatus. The effective subordination of the military and the secret police to the political leadership of the USSR was the major condition and achievement of de-Stalinization in 1956–1968. (Khrushchev was toppled not by the generals but by fellow Politburo members who rightly feared the further normalization and rationalization of the Soviet state.)

The Red Army was a truly professional institution in the sense of its strict subordination to civilian control and its years of preparation for external combat against other regular armies. Unlike the Third World militaries, it was institutionally and morally unprepared to take over the government on its own. The military hypothetically could be used by the radical political forces, but the Russian nationalists dismally failed to advance in the new historical setting a credible alternative to the existing regime. The amazing endurance of Yeltsin's regime despite the economic ruin, the thunderous Chechen fiasco, and personal failings may seem utterly improbable unless one realizes that its opponents were even weaker. The combination of these factors rendered the Red Army and the fractured relics of the KGB politically inert and docile institutions dependent on the new state rulers.

The decommissioned coercive apparatus was still an economic burden but no longer a major political problem. For this reason the immobilized giant was simply left to decay. The military's debacle manifest in Chechnya buried the hopes to restore the Soviet coercive capacity and reconquer the empire. Although the prospects of democracy remained uncertain in Russia, the prospects of a militarist regime intent on restoring the empire became even less certain. It has been assured that the territorial segmentation of the former Soviet realm will endure. In the place of Soviet Union emerged a vast region contested by the scores of overlapping territorial sovereignties and non-territorial monopolies.

THE SPIRAL OF INVOLUTION

The aftermath of Soviet collapse was proclaimed the period of transition from state socialism to the capitalist market economy and liberal democracy. Viewed less teleologically, the main vector of the post-Communist drift appears rather an involution, the process by which the historical system undergoes shrinking, segmentation, and decrease in its normal operations rather than substantive change in its organization. The post-Soviet states exhibit the familiar irrationalities and pathologies of state socialism, only in an exacerbated form. To put it in simpler words, the post-Soviet Russia and most CIS republics behaved like the old USSR, only smaller and worse. Michael Burawoy demonstrated how the involution operated in Russian factories, where the patterns of managerial control, the production processes, and labor relations remained unchanged, while the breakup of the Soviet central planning produced an even more uncertain environment (Burawoy, 1996).

The post-Soviet segmentation gave new prominence to various kinds of intermediaries that included the trading monopolies and banks formed on the basis of former ministries and state trusts, the territorially based political patrons and lobbyists in the elected organs, and, last but not least, the criminal groups. The cumulative effect of organizational segmentation and monetizaton of post-socialist economies, quite contrary to the expectations of self-regulating markets, in fact strengthened the hierarchical industrial integration, barter among the enterprises at the horizontal level, and the ruthless expropriation of surplus and even the necessary stocks from the enterprises by intermediaries. The sight of such an inglorious transformation may indeed invoke the hero of Giuseppe di Lampedusa's novel who, describing Sicily in the epoch of liberal reforms, noted: *"Everything must change in order to remain the same."*[4]

After a spate of radical reforms proclaimed during the initial chaotic period of his presidency, Boris Yeltsin found himself relying on the familiar patterns of Soviet rule. The first president of Russia recreated the deliberately convoluted system of bureaucratic checks and balances, including a virtual central committee apparatus (the sprawling Presidential Administration that doubled the government functions) complete with the quasi-politburo of trusted courtiers; he mediated between the rivaling governmental bureaucracies, enterprises, and territories that competed for a slice of the federal budget (the latter remained the major redistributive mechanism); and, when in the end of 1993 his new regime matured in the battles with the transitional parliament, Yeltsin jettisoned the ambitious liberal ideologues and fell back on the traditional imperial ideology and strategy. The Chechen fighters proved Yeltsin's return to territorialism no more feasible than the neo-liberal plan of rapid conversion to capitalism. Meanwhile, the imminent presidential elections of 1996 showed that the basis of Yeltsin's rule had shrunk dangerously, even within the Russian power elites. At this point he dumped the erstwhile palace clique, embraced the recently created financial oligarchy along with their mechanisms of media manipulation, and made tenuous ad hoc deals with select political outsiders and territorial governors.

The expansion of the regime's base in 1996 earned Yeltsin a miraculous re-election, ended the war in Chechnya, prevented challenges from the humiliated military and the neo-imperial opposition, and resulted in a more convoluted scheme of power sharing that oddly resembled the functional illogics of European *ancien régime* or, more immediately, Brezhnev-era corporatism. But the attempted regime of Yeltsin's "stagnation" was obviously too dependent on the world markets of finance and raw materials to maintain the redistributive pattern of governance. In less than two years it was undone by the internecine scrambles among new oligarchs and the sweeping effects of world financial crisis. After two tumultuous decades Russia still faced the dilemmas that beset the Soviet leadership in the twilight of Brezhnev's reign.

The collapse of the USSR removed the superpower burdens but at the same time accentuated Russia's downward mobility within the evolving world-economy. The control of central government over the regional and sectorial bureaucracies dissipated to problematic extremes verging on outright separatism. Bargaining for the state redistribution remained in the core of governance, but the source became overtly external and beyond the control of Moscow, while the domestic redistributive fights grew extremely vicious, including the dirtiest blackmail and assassinations. The deeply unpopular political establishment and the dramatically downgraded intelligentsia were deadlocked as always between the reactionary isolationist and the westernizing wings, with an aloof tsar-like figure presiding over the panoply of differences; only this time the struggles became politicized in the new anarchic parliamentarism and widely publicized in the mass media that mightily contributed to the popular revulsion against any ideology and politics. The industrial park and infrastructure continued to deteriorate at accelerating rates. The army remained still huge, impractical, and after Chechnya provenly incapable. The lines between the state and the private and the criminal security enforcement blurred to form an undifferentiated sector of violent entrepreneurship.[5] State ideology became an even bigger void than before, despite the regular invocations of patriotic values and the "traditional religions of the country." International leverage of Russia was reduced to ritualistic acknowledgment of her great power status.

The sharp decline in real wages, which allowed the preservation of an odd semblance of nearly full employment, drove large segments of the population into semi-subsistence, petty trade, moonlighting, as well as theft from the workplaces and rampant alcoholism (once again, the all too familiar phenomena of the Brezhnev period reemerging on a vastly magnified scale). Even so the popular efforts to cope succeeded in no more than mitigating the crisis while the social subsidies to the essentially untouched bureaucratized agriculture, to the bankrupt industries, and to the huge decrepit urban sector remained ever unbearable burdens on state finances. Russia's enormity and cold climate provide an enduring reason for maintaining a centralized administrative apparatus capable of absorbing the costs of energy consumption.[6] Unlike the tropical Third World, the industrial cities of Russia would starve and freeze without at least an intermittent supply of basic utilities.

Will the involutionary cycle persist? It may. A complete collapse bordering on physical extinction is the least likely possibility. The system has shown con-

siderable capacity to reproduce itself along its glaring insufficiencies and contradictions. Furthermore, the post-Cold War geopolitics help to stabilize Russia's
involution in three crucial respects. First, unlike the imperial collapses of past
epochs, the former Soviet republics are not in danger of external conquest.
Global capital is not about to invade them either. Under the existing conditions
foreign investors have to cooperate with the Russian trading monopolies at the
level of circulation, only in the exceptional instances reaching into the levels of
production. The Russian trading monopolies would continue to incorporate or
destroy both the foreign capital and the emergent smaller businesses.

Second, the optimistic comparisons of the Russian trading monopolies to the
East Asian business conglomerates miss the crucial difference in the class structures and position of East Asia within the post-1945 capitalist world-economy.
East Asian monopolies were manufacturing giants that enjoyed the combined
benefits of neo-mercantilist states, a tame and inexpensive workforce with privileged access to the largest capital and consumer market in the world, the United
States. The post-Soviet trading monopolies have none of those advantages and
(except the exporters of raw materials and hi-tech armaments) stand little chance
on the world markets. Their state has all but surrendered, their productive base
is outdated and inefficient, their workforce is neither tame nor powerless. Although the power of post-socialist workers is rooted in their control over the
shopfloor operations and exists in the unstated contract with management, it is
nonetheless quite effective.

In another important difference from the Third World, workers in Russia and
elsewhere in Eastern Europe firmly aspire to the Western European standards
of living. On the one hand, this makes Russian labor costly; but on the other
hand the combination of workers' social power at the shopfloor (which is the
overlooked reason why they so stubbornly refuse to desert their workplaces)
and the established expectation of decent wages generate the internal demand
that supported a "normal" degree of market operations before the financial crisis
of August 1998. Of course, most of the time this was normality at the lowest
point that prevented social upheaval and defused political protests, thus stabilizing the regime of involution. The third external condition that makes likely
the continuation of industrial involution are the international institutions of finance. Russia remains perceived as an enormous threat; therefore almost any
Russian government would be able to extort financial transfers from the core
states on the pain of unknown but invariably horrific consequences.

Undoubtedly, the post-Soviet system will deteriorate further, but it is difficult
to calculate for how long. Marginalization and dependency within the world-
economy are shameful and hurtful; however, they serve the immediate privatized
interests of many among the Russian elites. Organized crime and rampant corruption will be organic to such a scheme. The regime of normalized involution
would be highly resistant to domestic political change. Parliamentarism would
be too easily manipulated in this environment, while a limited sphere of market
exchanges, monopolized from the top by the post-Soviet conglomerates and left

at the bottom to the devices of the popular micro-strategies of survival, would actually reinforce involution.

FROM INVOLUTION TO SEMIPERIPHERAL METAMORPHOSIS?

A different regime can be introduced only by an extraordinary political upheaval amounting to another revolution. However theoretical this may appear at the moment, destruction of the existing regime will remain an ongoing possibility. Yeltsin's Russia resembled Brezhnev's Soviet Union, but it also differed in three crucial respects: the capacity of the elite to govern consistently, the existence of unquestionable ideology (hegemony in Gramsci's original meaning), and the ability of the populace to imagine alternatives and organize for collective action. All three add up to the questionable monopoly of social power. The eventual breakdown of the regime of steady involution opens two alternatives: the reversal of political and economic segmentation through dictatorship or, conversely, further segmentation that would create conditions for the popular takeovers in the chunks of post-Soviet segments that may (or may not) lead to democratic governance and wider access to markets.

Let me stress that it does not mean that such a revolution will inevitably establish a "better" society. The major goal and likely outcome will be a more efficient state that may turn out to be a militaristic nationalist dictatorship—and thus validate the dark prophecy of Andrei Amalrik regarding the end of the USSR. There is a historical parallel to such a trajectory. The strains of semiperipheral fascism and authoritarian populism of the 1920s and the 1930s, let us note, replaced the liberal progressivist regimes that had spread in the earlier wave of democratization through the semiperipheral zones of Latin America, southern Europe, and parts of Asia during the 1870 to 1910 period, in the tail phase of the British hegemonic cycle.[7]

Although fascism seems at the moment a rather dead bogey, an exclusionary form of globalization that leaves whole communities and countries superfluous to the cosmopolitan space of capital flows is bound to elicit radically nativist reactions including challenges through the use of state-organized violence. Even if violence remains directed against the fellow excluded zones and groups in the struggle to decide who is more superfluous (as in the wars of Yugoslav succession or the Algerian massacres), it would be difficult to contain such conflicts and prevent spillages. There are many voices in Russia who call for an alliance of the excluded states (which Washington calls "rogue") against the core. Some even use the terms of world-systems analysis to advocate such an alliance. Consider the following emotional passage drawn from the pages of a respected Moscow journal:

The core establishes monopolistic control over the advanced technologies and the upper floors in the hierarchy of commodity chains [sic]. . . . [W]e [Russia] are not being invited. We don't care for an invitation! We still have our high-tech weapons. . . . We shall lead the alliance of advanced semiperipheral outsiders. . . . Good behavior will not earn us a polite invitation into the core. Positions in the core are taken by working with elbows, by crushing the bones of competitors. (Starikov, 1995: 235–41)

This is rhetoric, so far. An opportunistic world alliance of "rogue" states and nonterritorial warlords ("criminal/terrorist") is a distinctly futuristic threat. The very fact that the possibility is on the horizon mitigates against its realization. Furthermore, within the neo-liberal variant of globalization Russia may evolve into the mercenary ally of global capitalists selling protection services at a world scale. This line of development certainly has age-old antecedents, but historical precedents also show that in the end mercenary barbarians could be no less dangerous.

A more encouraging possibility opens with the cumulative crisis of post-Soviet segments caused by the exhaustion of an involutionary pattern (which will arrive perhaps sooner than later). It would unleash popular pressures from within, causing the breakdown of the segmentary and intermediary powers established after the Soviet disintegration. Further consequences would be a rapid generation change in the ruling elites and advancement of new leaders and movements. If the "new prince" indeed emerges and seizes the central state apparatus in a combination of elections and extra-parliamentary actions, the new political bloc would have to challenge the trading monopolies and regional bailiwicks by invigorating the existing democratic institutions and reining in the crime and corruption. (In which case the recent experience of Italy may provide an inspiration.) In short, this would be the road of democratic revolution simultaneously pushed from below and from above which in many respects would continue and build up on Gorbachev's improvised attempt to rationalize and capitalize the territorialist mechanism of the USSR.

Ideas assume an autonomous role in the moments of chaotic transition. If the grand theoretician of anarchism, Prince Petr Kropotkin, was right when he observed over a century ago that revolutions were nurtured by hope while despair produced only destructive rebellions, then the scariest aspect of post-Soviet drift is the pervasive demoralization, pessimism, and anomie. An optimistic turn in the affairs of post-Soviet states (and many other areas currently on their way to becoming "black holes") has to be preceded by a reformulation of geoculture that would offer the hope of inclusion. Reversing the Russian involution depends not only on the radical political change from within, but also on the invitation to join the capital flows and commodity chains from without. This is not entirely impractical, given the potential enormity of Russia's markets, educated workforce, the resources, and other factors usually cited by the more upbeat forecasters.

This will not happen without a concerted application of political will. Which means, let us state it clearly, a politically motivated channeling of economic processes at supranational levels. Ideological elements of a more inclusive globalization project are mature enough to become discernible in the recent debates on new security thinking that is seeking to replace the old "realist" notions of national defense and the bloc-limited multilateralism with the agenda of human rights and prevention of most brutal forms of violence even at the cost of violating the sovereignty of peripheral states. Furthermore, the discourses of sustainable development and environmentalism may prove to be no less practical than the management of global debt. In theory, the commodification of global eco-management can replace the military Keynesianism of the twentieth century and offer realistic hope to the deindustrializing Rust Belts such as the former Soviet economies.

This possibility should not look exceptionally ironic given the adaptability of a capitalist world-system that has integrated many antisystemic movements before, including the Russian Marxist revolutionaries who ended up building a military-industrial empire adequate to its times. Specifically, the European Union might be best positioned to adopt the former Soviet territories into its special zone of economic and political interests, but at the moment this remains a distant hypothesis conditional on too many factors including the consequences of the likely further disruptions at the world-system's level, including the breakdown of the U. S. monopoly. In any event the trajectory of Russia will be critically conditioned by the emergent configuration of geopolitics and geoculture. In its turn, Russia remains in every respect a pivotal area whose trajectory will indicate whether the world-system is evolving along the lines of exclusion and violent challenges or as it shifts in the direction of global reformism.

NOTES

1. Valerie Bunce provided an astute analysis of the taming effects and the limits to the Brezhnev-era stability (Bunce, 1983). She was also one of the few social scientists who theoretically predicted the Soviet abdication from empire (Bunce, 1985).

2. The analysis of Soviet strategic thinking, once a major component of Western Sovietology, though suddenly a historical topic, remains a contested terrain. I am particularly indebted to Vitaly Vasilievich Shlykov, former head of the U. S. economic analysis unit at Soviet military intelligence (GRU), and his bristling articles (Shlykov, 1996).

3. The aluminum example was lent to me by the former GRU Col. Shlykov. Personal interviews, Moscow, June 1998.

4. I am grateful to Anatol Lieven for directing me to Lampedusa's great novel, *The Leopard*.

5. Vadim Volkov, *Organized violence, market building, and state formation in post-communist Russia*. Manuscript.

6. This argument was developed by the late Andrei Fadin. Personal communication, January 1997.

7. To my knowledge, the extraordinary British journalist Anatol Lieven was first to apply Gramsci's analysis of Italian *Transformismo* to Yeltsin's Russia in the excellent book that bears the utterly misleading title *Chechnya: The Tombstone of Russian Power*.

Bibliography

ABACC. *ABACC News*. Rio de Janeiro, Brazil, 1993–1997.

———. *Annual Report*. Rio de Janeiro, Brazil, 1993–1997.

———. Bilateral Agreement, ABACC and SCCC. Rio de Janeiro, Brazil, 1997.

Abu-Lughod, Janet. 1989. *Before European Hegemony: The World System A.D. 1250–1350*. Oxford: Oxford University Press.

Acheson, Dean. 1965. *Morning and Noon*. Boston: Little, Brown.

Adler, E. 1987. *The Power of Ideology*. Berkeley: University of California Press.

African Rights. 1995. *Rwanda: Death, Despair and Defiance*. London: African Rights.

Agnew, John, and Stuart Corbridge. 1995. *Mastering Space: Hegemony, Territory and International Political Economy*. London and New York: Routledge.

Alvim, C. F., O. Mafra, and A. C. Raffo. May 1997. Nuclear Verification in Argentina and Brazil. Presented at the workshop "Safeguards: Verification Techniques and Related Experience." IAEA, Vienna, Austria.

Amalrik, Andrei. 1970. *Will the Soviet Union Survive until 1984?* New York: Harper and Row.

Andereggen, A. 1994. *France's Relationship with Subsaharan Africa*. Westport, CT: Praeger.

Anderson, B. 1991. *Imagined Communities: Reflections on the Origins and Spread of Nationalism*. 2nd ed. London: Verso.

Ansell-Pearson, Keith. 1994. *An Introduction to Nietzsche as a Political Thinker: The Perfect Nihilist*. Cambridge: Cambridge University Press.

Anwar, Dewi Fortuna. 1994. Sijori: ASEAN's Southern Growth Triangle: Problems and Prospects. *The Indonesian Quarterly* 22 (1): 22–33.

Apicella, V. 1996. Southern Italy and the Underdeveloped Regions of Europe. *Review of Economic Conditions in Italy* 1 (January–June).

Arrighi, Giovanni. 1993. "The Three Hegemonies of Historical Capitalism." In *Gramsci,*

Historical Materialism and International Relations, ed. S. Gill, 148–165. Cambridge: Cambridge University Press.

———. 1994. *The Long Twentieth Century: Money, Power, and the Origins of Our Times*. London: Verso.

———. 1998a. Capitalism and the Modern World-System: Rethinking the Nondebates of the 1970s. *Review* 21 (1): 113–129.

———. 1998b. Globalization and the Rise of East Asia: Lessons from the Past, Prospects for the Future. *International Sociology* 13 (1): 59–77.

Arrighi, Giovanni, Beverly Silver, et al. 1999. *Chaos and Governance in the Modern World System*. Minneapolis: University of Minnesota Press.

Asiaweek. 1995. Prying Open Pyongyang: North Korea Experiments with a Free Trade Zone (12 May), p. 2.

Axline, W. Andrew. 1994. "Comparative Case Studies of Regional Cooperation Among Developing Countries." In *The Political Economy of Regional Cooperation*, ed. W. Andrew Axline. London: Pinter.

Bairoch, Paul. 1993. *Economics and World History: Myths and Paradoxes*. Chicago: University of Chicago Press.

Barber, B. R. 1988. Spirit's Phoenix and History's Owl, or The Incoherence of Dialectics in Hegel's Account of Women. *Political Theory* 16 (1 February): 5–28.

———. 1995. *Jihad vs. McWorld*. New York: Times Books.

Barnet, Richard J., and John Cavanagh. 1994. *Global Dreams: Imperial Corporations and the New World Order*. New York: Simon and Schuster.

Bayart, Jean-F. 1984. *La Politique Africaine de François Mitterrand*. Paris: Editions Karthala.

———. 1990. France-Afrique: La fin du pacte colonial. *Politique Africaine* (39).

———. 1996. "End Game South of the Sahara? France's Africa Policy." In *Paris, Pretoria, and the African Continent: The International Relations of States and Societies in Transition*, eds. C. Alden and Jean-P. Daloz, 26–41. New York: St. Martin's Press.

Bellah, Robert N., Richard Madsen, William Sullivan, Ann Swidler, and Steven M. Tipton. 1992. *The Good Society*. New York: Vintage.

Bergesen, Albert. 1980. *Studies of the Modern World System*. New York: Academic Press.

———. 1996. Praxis, Shmaxis: Commentary on Wagar. *Journal of World-Systems Research* (on-line), March.

———. 1999. "Beyond Cycles of Hegemony: Economic, Social, and Military Factors." In *The Future of Hegemonic Rivalry*, eds. V. Bornschier and C. Chase-Dunn. Beverly Hills CA: Sage.

Bianchi, A. 1985. *La Deuda Externa Latinoamericana*. Buenos Aires, Argentina: GEL.

Blumenthal, Henry. 1986. *Illusion and Reality in Franco-American Diplomacy, 1914–1945*. Baton Rouge: Louisiana State University Press.

Boone, C. 1992. *Merchant Capital and the Roots of State Power in Senegal, 1930–1985*. Cambridge: Cambridge University Press.

Boulding, Kenneth. 1962. *Conflict and Defense*. New York: Harper and Row.

Bourgi, R. 1980. *Le Générale de Gaulle et l'Afrique Noire*. Paris: Librarie Générale de Droit et de Jurisprudence.

Braeckman, C. 1994. *Rwanda: Histoire d'un génocide*. Paris: Fayard.

Braudel, Fernand. 1980. *On History*. Chicago: University of Chicago Press.

————. 1979. *Civilization and Capitalism, 15th–18th Century*. 3 vols. Translated by Sian Reynolds. New York: Harper and Row.

Bresser Pereira, L. C., J. M. Maravall, and A. Przeworski. 1993. *Economic Reforms in New Democracies: A Social Democratic Approach*. Cambridge: Cambridge University Press.

Bunce, Valerie. 1983. The Political Economy of the Brezhnev Era: The Rise and Fall of Corporatism. *British Journal of Political Science* 13 (January): 129–158.

————. 1985. The Empire Strikes Back: The Transformation of the Eastern Bloc from a Soviet Asset to a Soviet Liability. *International Organization* 39 (Winter): 1–46.

————. 1991. Domestic Reform and International Change: The Gorbachev Reforms in Historical Perspective. *International Organization* 47 (1, Winter): 107–138.

Bunker, Stephen G. 1989. Staples, Links, and Poles in the Construction of Regional Development Theories. *Sociological Forum* 4 (4): 589–610.

Burawoy, Michael. 1985. *Politics of Production: Factory Regimes under Capitalism and Socialism*. London: Verso.

————. 1996. The State and Economic Involution: Russia Through a China Lens. *World Development* 24 (6): 1105–1117.

Burt, Ronald. 1992. *Structural Holes: The Social Structure of Competition*. Cambridge, MA: Harvard University Press.

————. 1997. The Contingent Value of Social Capital. *Administrative Science Quarterly*, 42: 339–365.

Castells, Manuel. 1997. *The Information Age: Economy, Society, and Culture*. 3 vols. Oxford: Blackwell.

Cerny, Philip G. 1988. From Dirigisme to Deregulation? The Case of Financial Markets. Paper presented at the International Conference on Thirty Years of the French Republic, Paris.

Chang, Maria Hsia. 1995. Greater China and the Chinese "Global Tribe." *Asian Survey* 25 (10): 955–67.

Chase-Dunn, Christopher. 1989. *Global Formation*. Oxford: Blackwell.

Chase-Dunn, Christopher, and Thomas Hall. 1997. *Rise and Demise: Comparing World-Systems*. Boulder, CO: Westview Press.

Chase-Dunn, Christopher, and Bruce Podobnik. 1995. The Next World War. *Journal of World-System Research* (on-line).

Chase-Dunn, Christopher, Yukio Kwano, and Benjamin D. Brewer. 2000. "Trade Globalization Since 1795: Waves of Integration in the World-System." *American Sociological Review* 65(1): 77–95.

Chen, Xiangming. 1994. "The New Spatial Division of Labor and Commodity Chains in the Greater South China Economic Region." In *Commodity Chains and Global Capitalism*, eds. Gary Gereffi and Miguel Korzeniewicz. Westport, CT: Greenwood Press.

————. 1995. The Evolution of Free Economic Zones and the Recent Development of Cross-National Growth Zones. *International Journal of Urban and Regional Research* 19 (4): 593–621.

————. 1996. Taiwan Investments in China and Southeast Asia: "Go west but also go south." *Asian Survey* 36 (5): 447–67.

————. 1998. "China's Growing Integration with the Asia-Pacific Economy." In *What Is in a Rim? Critical Perspectives on the Pacific Region Idea*, ed. Arif Dirlik. 2nd ed. Boulder, CO: Rowman and Littlefield.

Chia, Siou Yue. 1993. Motivating Forces in Subregional Economic Zones. Pacific Forum/ CSIS Occasional Papers (December). Honolulu: Pacific Forum/ CSIS.

Child, J. 1985. *Geopolitics and Conflict in South America*. New York: Praeger.

Chipman, J. 1989. *French Power in Africa*. Oxford: Blackwell.

Chirot, Daniel. 1980. The Corporatist Model and Socialism. *Theory and Society* 9.

———. 1986. *Social Change in the Modern Era*. San Diego: Harcourt Brace Jovanovich.

———. 1989, ed. *The Origins of Backwardness in Eastern Europe*. Berkeley: University of California Press.

———. 1991. "What Happened in Eastern Europe in 1989." In *The Crisis of Leninism and the Decline of the Left: The Revolutions of 1989*, ed. Daniel Chirot. Seattle: University of Washington Press.

———. 1996. *Modern Tyrants: The Power and Prevalence of Evil in Our Age*. Princeton: Princeton University Press.

Chirot, Daniel, and Thomas Hall. 1982. World System Theory, *Annual Review of Sociology* 8: 81–106.

Chrétien, Jean-P., Jean-F. Dupaquier, M. Kabanda, J. Ngarambe, and Reporters sans frontières. 1995. *Rwanda: Les Médias du Génocide*. Paris: Karthala.

Christaller, Walter. 1972. "How I Discovered the Theory of Central Place: A Report about the Origin of Central Places." In *Man, Space, and Environment*, eds. Paul Ward English and Robert C. Mayfield. New York: Oxford University Press.

Clark, J. F., and D. E. Gardinier, eds. 1997. *Political Reform in Francophone Africa*. Boulder, CO: Westview.

Clough, Shepard. 1964. *The Economic History of Modern Italy*. New York: Columbia University Press.

CNEA. 1997. *Argentina Nuclear* 11 (63, July). Buenos Aires, Argentina: CNEA.

Coleman, James S. 1990. *Foundations of Social Theory*. Cambridge, MA: The Belknap Press of Harvard University Press.

Collins, Randall. 1978. "Long-term Social Change and the Territorial Power of States." In *Research in Social Movements, Conflicts, and Change* 1, ed. Louis Kriesberg, 1–34. Greenwich, CT: JAI.

———. 1986. *Weberian Sociological Theory*. New York: Cambridge University Press.

———. 1995. Prediction in Macro-sociology: The Case of the Soviet Collapse. *American Journal of Sociology* 100: 1552–93.

Collins, Randall, Robert Hanneman, and Gabriele Mordt. 1995. Discovering Theory Dynamics by Computer Simulation: Experiments on State Legitimacy and Imperialist Capitalism. *Sociological Methodology* (1–46).

Collins, Randall, and David V. Waller. 1994. "Geopolitics and Ethnic Mobilization: Some Theoretical Projections for the Old Soviet Union." In *Legacies of the Collapse of Marxism*, ed. John H. Moore. Arlington, VA: George Mason University Press.

Collins, R., and D. V. Waller. 1997. "What Theories Predicted State Breakdown and Revolution in the Old Soviet Bloc? In *Research in Social Movements, Conflict, and Change* 14: 31–47. Greenwich, CT: JAI.

Coquet, B., J.-M. Daniel, and E. Fourmann. 1993. L'Europe et l'Afrique: flux et reflux. *Politique Africaine* (49).

Corvers, Fabienne, Ben Dankbaar, and Robert Hassink. 1996. "Euregions: Springboard to Regional Development? Innovation Policy and Cross-border Cooperation in the Euregion Mass-Rhine." In *Local Economic Development in Europe and Americas*, eds. Christophe Demazière and Patricia A. Wilson. London: Mansell.

Cumings, Bruce. 1982–83. Corporatism in North Korea. *Journal of Korean Studies* 4.
———. 1991. The Seventy Years Crisis and the Logic of Trilateralism in the New World
    Order. *World Policy Journal* (Spring).
———. 2000. Liberal Order in Our Time: Toward "A Moratorium on the Slaying of
    Dilemmas." *Diplomatic History* 24 (1, Winter).
Cumming, G. 1995. French Development Assistance to Africa: Towards a new agenda?
    African Affairs 94: 383–98.
Delacroix, Jacques. 1977. The Export of Raw Materials and Economic Growth: A Cross
    National Study. *American Sociological Review* 42 (5): 795–808.
Development. 1998. Special Issue. "Globalism and the Politics of Place." *Development*
    41 (2, June).
Diamond, Larry. 1979. Power-Dependence Relations in the World System. *Research in
    Social Movements, Conflict, and Change* 2: 233–258. Greenwich, CT: JAI.
Dirlik, Arif. 1994. *After the Revolution: Waking to Global Capitalism.* Hanover, NH:
    Wesleyan University Press/University Press of New England.
———. 1997. "Three Worlds, or One, or Many? The Configuration of Global Relations
    under Contemporary Capitalism." In *The Postcolonial Aura: Third World Criti-
    cism in the Age of Global Capitalism*, ed. A. Dirlik, 146–62. Boulder, CO: West-
    view Press.
———. 1999. Place-Based Imagination: Globalism and the Politics of Place. *Review* 21
    (1, Spring).
DiTomaso, Nancy. 1982. "Sociological Reductionism" from Parsons to Althusser: Link-
    ing Action and Structure in Social Theory. *American Sociological Review* 47 (1):
    14–28.
Douglass, Mike. 1995. "Global Interdependence and Urbanization: Planning for the
    Bangkok Mega-Urban Region." In *The Mega-Urban Regions of Southeast Asia*,
    eds. T. G. McGee and Ira M. Robinson. Vancouver: University of British Colum-
    bia Press.
Eisenstadt, Shmuel N. 1966. *Modernization: Protest and Change.* Englewood Cliffs, NJ:
    Prentice-Hall.
Elgie, R., and H. Machin. 1991. France: The Limits to Prime-ministerial Government in
    a Semi-Presidential System. *West European Politics* 14 (2, April): 62–78.
Eribon, Didier. 1991. *Michel Foucault*, trans. Betsy Wing. Cambridge, MA: Harvard
    University Press.
Evans, Peter. 1995. *Embedded Autonomy.* Princeton: Princeton University Press.
Featherstone, Mike. 1996. "Localism, Globalism, and Cultural Identity." In *Global/Local:
    Cultural Production and the Transnational Imaginary*, eds. Rob Wilson and
    Wimal Dissanayake, 46–77. Durham, NC: Duke University Press.
Filtzer, Donald. 1992. *Soviet Workers and De-Stalinization: The Consolidation of the
    Modern System of Soviet Production Relations, 1953–1964.* Cambridge: Cam-
    bridge University Press.
Forte, Maximilian C. 1998. Globalization and World-Systems Analysis: Toward a New
    Paradigm of Geo-historical Anthropology (A Research View). *Review* 21 (1): 29–
    99.
Foucault, Michel. 1980. *Power/Knowledge.* Edited by Colin Gordon. New York: Pan-
    theon.
Frank, Andre Gunder. 1998. *ReORIENT: Global Economy in the Asian Age.* Berkeley:
    University of California Press.

Frieden, Jeffrey A. 1991. *Debt, Development, and Democracy*. Princeton: Princeton University Press.

Frieden, Jeffrey A., and David D. Lake, eds. 1991. *International Political Economy*. New York: St. Martin s Press.

Frobel, F., J. Heinrichs, and O. Kreye. 1980. *The New International Division of Labor*. Cambridge: Cambridge University Press.

Fukuyama, Francis N. 1992. *The End of History and the Last Man*. New York: The Free Press.

Gamble, A., and A. Payne, eds. 1996. *Regionalism and World Order*. New York: St. Martin's Press.

Garrett, G. 1998. *Partisan Politics in the Global Economy*. Cambridge: Cambridge University Press.

Gellner, Ernst. 1983. *Nations and Nationalism*. Ithaca, NY: Cornell University Press.

Gerami, Shahin. 1985. Export Alliances as a Device of Dependence Control: A Comparative Analysis. *Social Science Quarterly* 66 (1):105–19.

Gerbet, Pierre. 1994. *La Construction de l'Europe*. Paris: Imprimerie Nationale.

Gereffi, Gary. 1995. "Global Production Systems and Third World Development." In *Global Change, Regional Response: The New Context of International Development*, ed. Barbara Stallings. New York: Cambridge University Press.

———. 1996. Commodity Chains and Regional Divisions of Labor in East Asia. *Journal of Asian Business* 12 (1):75–112.

Gherardi, Sophie. 1996. Europe: l'Union comme Unique Horizon. *Bilan du Monde: Année économique et sociale 1995*. Paris: Le Monde.

Giddens, Anthony. 1991. *Modernity and Self-Identity: Self and Society in the Late Modern Age*. Stanford, CA: Stanford University Press.

Gill, Stephen. 1990. *American Hegemony and the Trilateral Commission*. Cambridge: Cambridge University Press.

———. 1995. Globalization, Market Civilization, and Disciplinary Neoliberalism. *Millennium* 24:399–423.

Gill, Stephen, and David Law. 1988. *The Global Political Economy*. Baltimore: Johns Hopkins University Press.

———. 1989. Global Hegemony and the Structural Power of Capital. *International Studies Quarterly* 36: 475–99.

Gilpin, Robert. 1987. *The Political Economy of International Relations*. Princeton: Princeton University Press.

Godeau, R. 1995. *Le franc CFA: Pourquoi la dévaluation de 1994 a tout changé*. Paris: SEPIA.

Golan, T. 1981. A Certain Mystery: How Can France Do Everything That It Does in Africa and Get Away with It? *African Affairs* 80 (318):3–11.

Goldfrank, Walter. 1987. "Socialism or Barbarism? The Long Run Fate of the Capitalist World-Economy." In *America's Changing Role in the World-System*. eds. T. Boswell and A. Bergesen, 85–92. New York: Praeger.

———. 1996. Praxis, Shmaxis: Commentary on Wagar. *Journal of World-System Research II* (online).

———. 1999. "Beyond Cycles of Hegemony: Economic, Social, and Military Factors." In Volker Bornscheirr and Christopher Chase-Dunn, eds., *The Future of Global Conflict*. London: SAGE, 66–76.

Goldstein, Joshua, ed. 1988. *Long Cycles: Prosperity and War in the Modern Age.* New Haven: Yale University Press.

Goldstone, Jack A. 1991. *Revolution and Rebellion in the Early Modern World.* Berkeley: University of California Press.

Gourevitch, Peter. 1978. The Second Image Reversed: The International Sources of Domestic Politics. *International Organization* (Autumn): 881–911.

Gourevitch, Philip. 1997. Continental Shift. *The New Yorker* 73 (4 August): 42–55.

Gramsci, Antonio. 1971. *Selections from the Prison Notebooks of Antonio Gramsci.* Translated and edited by Quentin Hoare and Geoffrey Nowell Smith. New York: International Publishers.

Granovetter, Mark. 1985. Economic Action and Social Structure: The Problem of Embeddedness. *American Journal of Sociology* 91:53–81.

Greenfeld, Liah. 1992. *Nationalism: Five Roads to Modernity.* Cambridge, MA: Harvard University Press.

Greer, S. 1999. *Chacun pour soi: African Elites and the French State 1958–1998.* Evanston, IL: Northwestern University Program of African Studies.

Greider, William. 1997. *One World, Ready or Not: The Manic Logic of Global Capitalism.* New York: Simon and Schuster.

Grey, R. D. 1990. A Balance Sheet on External Assistance: France in Africa. *Journal of Modern African Studies* 28 (1): 101–14.

Griffin, Keith. 1981. Economic Development in a Changing World. *World Development* 9 (3): 221–226.

Grosser, Alfred. 1989. *Affaires extérieures: la politique de la France, 1944–1989.* Paris: Flammarion.

Guichaoua, A., ed. 1995. *Les crises politiques au Burundi et au Rwanda (1993–1994). Analyses, faits et documents.* Lille: Université des Sciences et Technologies de Lille.

Guth, S. 1991. Africanisation, enseignement, et coopération bilatérale française. *Genève-Afrique* 29 (2): 77–85.

Haggard, S., and R. Kaufman. 1995. *The Political Economy of Democratic Transitions.* Princeton: Princeton University Press.

Hale, David. 1998. *Developing Country Financial Crises During the 1990s.* n.p.: Zurich Group.

Hamashita, Takeshi. 1997. "The Intra-Regional System in East Asia in Modern Times." In *Network Power: Japan and Asia*, eds. Peter J. Katzenstein and Takashi Shiraishi. Ithaca, NY: Cornell University Press.

Hamlin, Kevin. 1995. Greater China's Business Future. *International Business* (May): 32–36.

Harvey, David. 1989. *The Condition of Post-Modernity.* Oxford: Blackwell.

Hayward, J., ed. 1993. *De Gaulle to Mitterrand: Presidential Power in France.* London: Hurst.

———, ed. 1995. *Industrial Enterprise and European Integration: From National to International Champions in Western Europe.* New York: Oxford University Press.

Helleiner, Eric. 1994. *The Reemergence of Global Finance: States and the Globalization of Financial Markets.* Ithaca, NY: Cornell University Press.

Hennings, Klaus H. 1982. "West Germany." In *The European Economy*, ed. Andrea Boltho. Oxford: Oxford University Press.

Hibou, B. 1995. Politique économique de la France en zone franc. *Politique Africaine* (58).

Hill, Christopher. 1967. *Reformation to Industrial Revolution*. Harmondsworth: Penguin.

Hirschman, Albert O. 1945. *National Power and the Structure of Foreign Trade*. Berkeley: University of California Press.

———. 1977. *The Passions and the Interests*. Princeton: Princeton University Press.

Ho, K. C. 1994. Industrial Restructuring, the Singapore City-State, and the Regional Division of Labor. *Environment and Planning A* (26): 33–51.

Hobsbawm, Eric J. 1990. *Nations and Nationalism since 1870*. Cambridge: Cambridge University Press.

———. 1994. *The Age of Extremes: A History of the World, 1914–1991*. New York: Vintage.

Hobson, John M. 1997. *The Wealth of States. A Comparative Sociology of International Economic and Political Change*. Cambridge: Cambridge University Press.

Hodgson, Geoffrey M. 1994. "The Return of Institutional Economics." In *The Handbook of Economic Sociology*, eds. Neil J. Smelser and Richard Swedberg. Princeton: Princeton University Press.

———. 1996. *Economics and Evolution: Bringing Life Back into Economics*. Ann Arbor: University of Michigan Press.

Hoffman, S. 1995. "Thoughts on Sovereignty and French Politics." In *Remaking the Hexagon: The New France in the New Europe*, ed. G. Flynn, 251–58. Boulder, CO: Westview.

Holmes, Stephen. 1993. *The Anatomy of Antiliberalism*. Cambridge, MA: Harvard University Press.

Hong Kong Trade Development Council (HKTDC). 1995. *Hong Kong Trader* 105 (January): 1–8.

———. 1998. *Hong Kong Trader* 147 (July): 1–8.

Hroch, M. 1985. *Social Preconditions of National Revival in Europe: A Comparative Analysis of the Social Composition of Patriotic Groups among the Smaller European Nations*. Cambridge: Cambridge University Press.

Human Rights Watch. 1994. *Qui a armé le Rwanda?* Brussels: GRIP.

Hunter, W. 1996. *State and Soldier in Latin America*. Washington, DC: United States Institute of Peace.

Huntington, Samuel P. 1968. *Political Order in Changing Societies*. New Haven: Yale University Press.

———. 1993a. The Clash of Civilizations? *Foreign Affairs* (Summer): 22–49.

———. 1993b. *The Third Wave*. Norman: University of Oklahoma Press.

———. 1996a. *The Clash of Civilizations and the Remaking of World Order*. New York: Simon and Schuster.

———. 1996b. The West: Unique, Not Universal. *Foreign Affairs* (November/December): 28–46.

International Monetary Fund (IMF). 1997. *World Economic Survey: Globalization*. Washington, DC: IMF.

Izraelewicz, Erik. 1996. Le retour du "dèfi américain." *Bilan du Monde: Année économique et sociale 1995*. Paris: Le Monde.

Javis, Anthony P., and Albert J. Paolini. 1995. "Locating the State." In *The State in Transition: Reimagining Political Space*, eds. Joseph A. Camilleri, Anthony P. Javis, and Albert J. Paolini. Boulder, CO: Lynne Rienner.

Jobert, A. 1995. An Italian Paradox: Unemployment among Young Graduates. *Sociologie du Travail* 37 (4).

Johnson, K. 1982. "Argentina: Pride and Weakness." In *US Influence in Latin America in the 1980s*, ed. R. Wesson. New York: Praeger.

Katzenstein, Peter J. 1997. "Introduction: Asian Regionalism in Comparative Perspective." In *Network Power: Japan and Asia*, eds. Peter J. Katzenstein and Takashi Shiraishi. Ithaca, NY: Cornell University Press.

Kaufman, R. 1990a. "How Societies Change Developmental Models or Keep Them." In *Manufacturing Miracles*, ed. G. W. Gereffi. Princeton: Princeton University Press.

Keeler, J.T.S., and M. Schain. 1996. "Presidents, Premiers, and Models of Democracy in France." In *Chirac's Challenge: Liberalization, Europeanization, and Malasie in France*, eds. J.T.S. Keeler and M. A. Schain, 23–52. New York: St. Martin's Press.

Kennedy, Paul. 1987. *The Rise and Fall of the Great Powers: Economic Change and Military Conflict from 1500 to 2000*. New York: Random House.

Keohane, Robert. 1984. *After Hegemony: Cooperation and Discord in the World Political Economy*. Princeton: Princeton University Press.

Keohane, Robert O., and Joseph S. Nye. 1977. *Power and Interdependence: World Politics in Transition*. Boston: Little, Brown.

Kim, Won Bae. 1994. Sino-Russian Relations and Chinese Workers in the Russian Far East: A Porous Border. *Asian Survey* 34 (12): 1064–76.

Kim, Young Soo. 1996. The Expansion of Ministries in Modern Nation-States. Unpublished Doctoral Dissertation, Department of Sociology, Stanford University.

Kindleberger, Charles P. 1973. *The World in Depression 1929–1939*. Berkeley: University of California Press.

Konrad, Victor. 1991. "Common Edges: An Introduction to the Borderlands Anthropology." In *Borderlands: Essays in Canadian-American Relations*, ed. Robert Lecker. Toronto: ECW Press.

Korllos, Thomas. 1991. World System: Its Nature and Implications for Social Theory. *International Social Science Review* 66 (3): 128–138.

Kornai, Jànos. 1980. *The Economics of Shortage*. 2 vols. Amsterdam: North Holland.

Krasner, Stephen. 1982. Regimes and the Limits of Realism: Regimes as Autonomous Variables. *International Organization* 36.

———. 1985. *Structural Conflict: The Third World Against Global Liberalism*. Berkeley: University of California Press.

Krop, P. 1994. *Le Génocide Franco-Africain: Faut-il juger les Mitterrand?* Paris: J. C. Lattès.

Landes, David S. 1998. *The Wealth and Poverty of Nations: Why Some Are So Rich and Some Are So Poor*. New York: W. W. Norton.

Latham, Robert. 1997. *The Liberal Moment: Modernity, Security, and the Making of the Postwar International Order*. New York: Columbia University Press.

Lavroff, D. G., ed. 1980. *La Politique Africaine du Général de Gaulle*. Paris: A. Pedone.

Le Monde. 1996. *Bilan du Monde 1995*. Paris: Le Monde.

Leventhal, P., and S. Tanzer. 1992. *Averting a Latin American Nuclear Arms Race*. New York: St. Martin s Press.

Lever-Tracy, Constance, David Ip, and Noel Tracy. 1996. *The Chinese Diaspora and Mainland China: An Emerging Economic Synergy*. London: Macmillan.

Liberman, Sima. 1977. *The Growth of European Mixed Economies: 1945–1970*. New York: John Wiley.

Lieven, Anatol. 1998. *Chechnya: The Tombstone of Russian Power*. New Haven: Yale University Press.

Linnemann, H. 1966. *An Economic Study of World Trade Flows*. Amsterdam: North Holland.

Linz, J., and A. Stepan. 1996. *Problems of Democratic Transition and Consolidation*. Baltimore: Johns Hopkins University Press.

Liu, Baorong, and Jiasheng Liao. 1993. *Zhongguo Yianbian Kaifang yu Zhoubian Guojia Shichang* [China's Opening Borders and the Neighboring Countries Markets]. Beijing: Legal Press.

Loriaux, Michael. 1991. *France After Hegemony: International Change and Financial Reform*. Ithaca, NY: Cornell University Press.

———. 1992. "The Riddle of the Rhine: France, Germany, and the Geopolitics of European Integration." In *The Past as Prelude: History in the Making of the New World Order*, eds. Meredith Woo-Cumings and Michael Loriaux. Boulder, CO: Westview.

———. 1996. "Capital, the State, and Uneven Growth in the International Political Economy." In *Capital Ungoverned: Liberalizing Finance in Interventionist States*, eds. Michael Loriaux, Meredith Woo-Cumings, Kent Calder, Sylvia Maxfield, and Sofia Perez. Ithaca, NY: Cornell University Press.

———. 1999. "Realism and Reconciliation: France, Germany, and the European Union." In *Unipolar Politics: Realism and State Strategies after the Cold War*, eds. Ethan Kapstein and Michael Mastanduno. New York: Columbia University Press.

Love, Joseph J. 1996. *Crafting the Third World: Theorizing Underdevelopment in Rumania and Brazil*. Stanford, CA: Stanford University Press.

McGee, Terry G. 1995. "Metrofitting the Emerging Mega-Urban Regions of ASEAN: An Overview." In *The Mega-Urban Regions of Southeast Asia*, eds. T. G. McGee and Ira M. Robinson. Vancouver: University of British Columbia Press.

McMichael, Philip. 2000. *Development and Social Change: A Global Perspective*. London: Pine Forge Press.

McNeill, William H. 1963. *The Rise of the West. A History of the Human Community*. Chicago: University of Chicago Press.

Manent, Pierre. 1995. *An Intellectual History of Liberalism*. Princeton: Princeton University Press.

Mann, Michael. 1993. *The Sources of Social Power. Vol. 2: The Rise of Classes and Nation-States, 1760–1914*. Cambridge: Cambridge University Press.

Manning, P. 1998. *Francophone Sub-Saharan Africa 1880–1995*. 2nd ed. Cambridge: Cambridge University Press.

Marchesin, P. 1995. Mitterrand l'Africain. *Politique Africaine* (58).

Marcuse, H. 1964. *One-Dimensional Man: Studies in the Ideology of Advanced Industrial Society*. Boston: Beacon.

Marseille, J. 1984. *Empire colonial et capitalisme français. Histoire d'un divorce*. Paris: Seuil.

Martin, G. 1985. The Historical, Economic, and Political Bases of France's Africa Policy. *Journal of Modern African Studies* 23 (2): 189–208.

———. 1989. Uranium: A Case-Study in Franco-African Relations. *Journal of Modern African Studies* 27 (4): 625–40.

Martin, Hans-Peter, and Harald Schumann. 1997. *The Global Trap: Globalization and the Assault on Democracy and Prosperity*. Patrick Camiller, tr. London: Zed.

Martínez, Oscar J., ed. 1986. *Across Borders: Transborder Interaction in Comparative Perspective*. El Paso: Texas Western Press.

Marx, Karl, and Frederick Engels. 1888[1968]. *Manifesto of the Communist Party*, reproduction of the 1888 English edition. Peking: Foreign Languages Press.

Mearsheimer, John. 1992. Back to the Future: Instability in Europe After the Cold War. *International Security* 15 (1, Summer).

Mény, Y. 1992. *La corruption de la République*. Paris: Fayard.

Meyer, John, and Michael Hannan. 1979. *National Development and the World System*. Chicago: University of Chicago Press.

Meyer, John, J. Boli, G. M. Thomas, and F. O. Ramirez. 1997. World Society and the Nation State. *American Journal of Sociology* 103.

Meyer, John, F. Ramirez, and Y. Soysal. 1992. World Expansion of Mass Education: 1870–1980. Sociology of Education 65: 128–149.

Miller, Jon. 1980. Access to Interorganizational Networks as a Professional Resource. *American Sociological Review* 45 (3): 479–96.

Milward, Alan. 1984. *The Reconstruction of Western Europe*. Berkeley: University of California Press.

Modelski, George, and William R. Thompson. 1988. *Seapower in Global Politics, 1494–1993*. London: Macmillan.

———. 1996. *Leading Sectors and World Powers: The Coevolution of Global Politics and Economics*. Columbia: University of South Carolina Press.

Moody, Kim. 1997. *Workers in a Lean World*. London: Verso.

Morgenthau, Hans J. 1948. *Politics among Nations*. New York: Knopf.

Mountjoy, Alan B. 1973. *The Mezzogiorno*. Oxford: Oxford University Press.

Munford, Clarence. 1978. Africa and the Political Economy of Underdevelopment. *Black Scholar* 10 (1): 22–30.

Myrdal, Gunnar. 1957. *Rich Lands and Poor: The Road to Prosperity*. New York: Harper and Brothers Publishers.

Nemeth, Roger, and David Smith. 1985. International Trade and World System Structure: A Multiple Network Analysis. *Review* 8 (4): 517–60.

Nietzsche, Friedrich. 1997. "On the Uses and Disadvantages of History for Life." In *Untimely Meditations*, ed. David Breazeale. Cambridge: Cambridge University Press.

Nitzan, Jonathan. 1998. Differential Accumulation: Towards a New Political Economy of Capital. *Review of International Political Economy* 5 (2): 169–216.

Niveau, Maurice. 1970. *Histoire des faits économiques contemporains*. Paris: Presses Universitaires de France.

North, Douglass C. 1981. *Structure and Change in Economic History*. Cambridge: Cambridge University Press.

———. 1990. *Institutions, Institutional Change, and Economic Performance*. Cambridge: Cambridge University Press.

North, Douglass C., and Robert Paul Thomas. 1973. *The Rise of the Western World: A New Economic History*. Cambridge: Cambridge University Press.

Northcraft, Gregory B., Margaret A. Neale, Ann Tenbrunsel, and Melissa C. Thomas-Hunt. 1995. The Allocation of Benefits and Burdens: Does It Really Matter What We Allocate? *Social Justice Research* 9:27–46.

O'Donnell, Guillermo. 1973. *Modernization and Bureaucratic Authoritarianism.* Berkeley: Institute of International Studies.

Ohmae, Kenichi. 1995. *The End of the Nation State; The Rise of Regional Economies: How Capital, Corporations, Consumers and Communications Are Shaping Global Markets.* New York: The Free Press.

Palat, Ravi Arvand. 1993. *Pacific Asia and the Future of the World System.* Westport, CT: Greenwood.

Parsonage, James. 1992. Southeast Asia's "Growth Triangle": A Subregional Response to Global Transformation. *International Journal of Urban and Regional Research* 16 (2): 307–17.

Péan, P. 1983. *Affaires Africaines.* Paris: Fayard.

———. 1988. *L'Argent Noir: Corruption et sous-développement.* Paris: Fayard.

Perroux, François. 1950. Economic Space: Theory and Applications. *Quarterly Journal of Economics* 64: 89–104.

Petrella, Ricardo. 1991. World City-States of the Future. *NPQ (New Perspectives Quarterly)* (Fall): 59–64.

Poidevin, Raymond, and Jacques Bariéty. 1977. *Les Relations Franco-allemandes, 1815–1975.* Paris: Armand Colin.

Porter, Michael. 1990. *The Competitive Advantage of Nations.* New York: The Free Press.

Prunier, G. 1995. *The Rwanda Crisis: History of a Genocide.* New York: Columbia University Press.

Przeworski, A., and F. Limongi. 1997. Modernization: Theories and Facts. *World Politics* 49 (January): 155–83.

Raffo, A. C., and E. Palacios. 1997. A Importancia de um Organismo Regional (ABACC) na Aplicação das Salvaguardas Modernas, ABACC Internal Document, Rio de Janeiro, Brazil.

Ragin, Charles C. 1980. "Celtic Nationalism in Britain: Political and Structural Bases." In *Processes of the World-System,* eds. T. K. Hopkins and I. Wallerstein, 249–65. Beverly Hills, CA: Sage.

———. 1986. "The Impact of Celtic Nationalism on Class Politics in Scotland and Wales." In *Competitive Ethnic Relations,* eds. S. Olzak and J. Nagel, 199–220. Orlando, FL: Academic Press.

———. 1994. *Constructing Social Research: The Unity and Diversity of Method.* Thousand Oaks, CA: Pine Forge Press.

Ragin, Charles, and York Bradshaw. 1992. International Economic Dependence and Human Misery, 1938–1980. *Sociological Perspectives* 35 (2): 217–47.

Rau, William, and Dennis Roncek. 1987. Industrialization and World Inequality: The Transformation of the Division of Labor in 59 Nations, 1960–1981. *American Sociological Review* 52 (3): 359–369.

Rawski, Thomas, ed. 1996. *Economics and the Historian.* Berkeley: University of California Press.

Redick, J., J. Carasales, and P. Wrobel. 1995. Nuclear Rapprochement: Argentina, Brazil, and the Nonproliferation Regime. *The Washington Quarterly* (January).

Reid, Peter, and Andrew Church. 1996. "New Forms of Local Economic Development in the Global Economy: Transfrontier Cooperation and Internationalization." In *Local Economic Development in Europe and Americas,* eds. Christophe Demazière and Patricia A. Wilson. London: Mansell.

Reilly, John E, ed. 1995. *American Public Opinion and U. S. Foreign Policy 1995.* Chicago: Chicago Council on Foreign Relations.

Reyntjens, F. 1994. *L'Afrique des Grands Lacs en Crise: Rwanda-Burundi 1988–1994*. Paris: Karthala.

Riesman, D. 1950. *The Lonely Crowd: A Study of the Changing American Character*. New Haven: Yale University Press.

Rigby, T. H., and Ferenc Fehér, eds. 1982. *Political Legitimation in Communist States*. New York: St. Martin's Press.

Robertson, Roland. 1994. "Mapping the Global Condition: Globalization as the Central Concept." In *Global Culture: Nationalism, Globalization and Modernity*, ed. Mike Featherstone, 15–29. London: Sage.

Robinson, William. 1996. *Promoting Polyarchy: Globalization, US Intervention and Hegemony*. Cambridge: Cambridge University Press.

Rokkan, Stein. 1975. "Dimensions of State Formation and Nation-Building: A Possible Paradigm for Research on Variations within Europe." In *The Formation of National States in Western Europe*, ed. Charles Tilly, chapter 8. Princeton: Princeton University Press.

Rosenau, James N. 1997. *Along the Domestic-Foreign Frontier: Exploring Governance in a Turbulent World*. Cambridge and New York: Cambridge University Press.

Rostow, Walt. 1960a. *The Stages of Economic Growth: A Non-Communist Manifesto*. Cambridge University Press, New York.

———. 1960b. *The U. S. in the World Arena: An Essay in Recent History*. New York: Harper.

———. 1980. *The World Economy: History and Prospect*. Austin: University of Texas Press.

Rouvez, A. 1994. *Disconsolate Empires: French, British, and Belgian Military Involvement in Post-colonial Sub-Saharan Africa*. Lanham, MD: University Press of America.

Roxborough, Ian. 1976. Dependency Theory in the Sociology of Development: Some Theoretical Problems. *West African Journal of Sociology and Political Science* 1 (2): 116–133.

Rubinson, Richard, and Deborah Holtzman. 1981. Comparative Dependence and Economic Development. *International Journal of Comparative Sociology* 22 (2): 86–101.

Rueschemeyer, D., E. H. Stephens, and J. D. Stephens. 1992. *Capitalist Development and Democracy*. Chicago: University of Chicago Press.

Russett, Bruce M., et al. 1993. *Grasping the Democratic Peace: Principles for a Post-Cold War World*. Princeton: Princeton University Press.

Sacks, Michael Alan, Brian Uzzi, and Marc Ventresca. Forthcoming. Global Institutions and Networks: The Structure of World Trade Advantage, 1965–1980. *American Behavioral Scientist*.

Sassen, Saskia. 1991. *The Global City: New York, London, Tokyo*. Princeton: Princeton University Press.

———. 1996. *Losing Control? Sovereignty in an Age of Globalization*. New York: Columbia University Press.

Scalapino, Robert A. 1995. "Natural Economic Territories in East Asia—Present Trends and Future Prospects." In *Economic Cooperation and Challenges in the Pacific*, ed. Korea Economic Institute of America. Washington, DC.: Korea Institute of America.

Schraeder, P. J., S. W. Hook, and B. Taylor. 1998. Clarifying the Foreign Aid Puzzle:

A Comparison of American, Japanese, French, and Swedish Aid Flows. *World Politics* 50: 294–323.

Schumpeter, Joseph A. 1942. *Capitalism, Socialism, and Democracy.* New York: Harper.

Scott, Allan J. 1995. The Geographic Foundations of Industrial Performance. *Competition and Change* 1 (1): 51–66.

Selden, Mark. 1997. "China, Japan, and the Regional Political Economy of East Asia, 1945–1995." In *Network Power: Japan and Asia,* eds. Peter J. Katzenstein and Takashi Shiraishi. Ithaca, NY: Cornell University Press.

Shapin, Steve. 1996. *The Scientific Revolution.* Chicago: University of Chicago Press.

Shlykov V. V. 1996. Rokovye proschioty amerikanskoi i sovetskoi razvedok. Gonka vooruzhenii i ekonomika. [The fatal miscalculations of American and Soviet intelligence services. The arms race and economy]. Mezhdunarodnaia zhizn', no. 9 (September): 47–55.

Shuman, Michael. 1998. *Going Local: Creating Self-Reliant Communities in a Global Age.* New York: The Free Press.

Sikkink, Kathryn. 1991. *Ideas and Institutions: Developmentalism in Brazil and Argentina.* Ithaca, NY: Cornell University Press.

Simon, Julian L. 1996. *The Ultimate Resource 2.* Princeton: Princeton University Press.

Singapore Economic Development Board. 1995. Singapore's World-Class Infrastructure. *Singapore Investment News* (August): 1–12.

Skocpol, Theda. 1979. *States and Social Revolutions.* New York: Cambridge University Press.

Smith, David, and Roger Nemeth. 1988. An Empirical Analysis of Commodity Exchange in the International Economy: 1965–1980. *International Studies Quarterly* 31: 227–240.

Smith, David, and Douglas White. 1992. Structure and Dynamics of the Global Economy: A Network Analysis of International Trade 1965–1980. *Social Forces* 70 (4): 857–93.

Smith, S. 1995. "France-Rwanda: lévirat colonial et abandon dans la région des Grands Lacs." In *Les crises politiques au Burundi et au Rwanda (1993–1994). Analyses, faits et documents,* ed. A. Guichaoua, 447–54. Lille: Université des Sciences et Technologies de Lille.

Snyder, David, and Edward Kick. 1979. Structural Position in the World System and Economic Growth, 1955–1970: A Multiple Network Analysis of Transnational Interactions. *American Journal of Sociology* 84 (5): 1096–1126.

Solingen, E. 1996. *Industrial Policy, Technology and International Bargaining.* Stanford CA: Stanford University Press.

Starikov, Evgeny. 1995. Derzheteli hartlenda ili obitateli ostrova? *Novy Mir,* No. 3 (March).

Steiber, Steven. 1979. The World System and World Trade: An Empirical Exploration of Conceptual Conflicts. *Sociological Quarterly* 20 (1): 23–36.

Steinmetz, George. 1994. Regulation Theory, Post-Marxism, and the New Social Movements. *Comparative Studies in Society and History* 36 (4): 176–212.

Sternhell, Zeev. 1995. *Neither Right Nor Left: Fascist Ideology in France.* Princeton: Princeton University Press.

Stinchcombe, Arthur L. 1968. *Constructing Social Theories.* New York: Harcourt.

———. 1982. On Softheadedness on the Future, *Ethics* 93 (October): 114–128.

Storper, Michael, and Bennett Harrison. 1991. Flexibility, Hierarchy and Regional Development: The Changing Structure of Industrial Production Systems and Their Forms of Governance in the 1990s. *Research Policy* 20: 407–22.

Su, Tieting. 1995. "Changes in World Trade Networks, 1938, 1960, 1990." *Review* 18(3): 431–59.

Tang, Min, and Myo Thant. 1994. "Growth Triangles: Conceptual and Operational Considerations." In *Growth Triangles in Asia: A New Approach to Regional Economic Cooperation*, eds. Myo Thant, Min Tang, and Hiroshi Kakazu. Hong Kong: Oxford University Press.

Tarrow, Sidney. 1994. *Power in Movement: Social Movements, Collective Action, and Politics*. Cambridge: Cambridge University Press.

Thompson, E. P. 1980. *The Making of an English Working Class*. Harmondsworth: Penguin.

Ticktin, Hillel. 1992. *Origins of the Crisis in the USSR. Essays on the Political Economy of a Disintegrating System*. Armonk, NY: M. E. Sharpe.

Tilly, Charles. 1984. *Big Structures, Large Processes, Huge Comparisons*. New York: Russell Sage Foundation.

———. 1990. *Coercion, Capital, and European States. AD 990–1990*. Oxford: Blackwell.

———. 1993. *Coercion, Capital, and European States, AD 990–1992*. Oxford: Blackwell.

———. 1995. Globalization Threatens Labor's Rights. Responses by Immanuel Wallerstein, Aristide Zolberg, Eric Hobsbawm, and Lourdes Beneria. *International Labor and Working-Class History* 47 (Spring): 3–55.

UNDP. *Human Development Report 1996*. New York: Oxford University Press, 1997.

Urban, Michael, with Vyacheslav Igrunov, and Sergei Mitrokhin. 1997. *The Rebirth of Politics in Russia*. New York: Cambridge University Press.

Valette, Jacques. 1976. *Vie économique et sociale des grands pays de l'Europe occidentale et des États-Unis: Début du XXe Siècle—1939*. Paris: S.E.D.E.S.

Verschave, François-X. 1994. *Complicité de Génocide? La politique de la France au Rwanda*. Paris: La Découverte.

Vogel, Ezra. 1992. *The Four Little Dragons: The Spread of Industrialization in East Asia*. Cambridge, MA: Harvard University Press.

Wagar, W. Warren. 1989. *A Short History of the Future*. Chicago: University of Chicago Press.

Waller, David V. 1992. Ethnic Mobilization and Geopolitics in the Soviet Union: Towards a Theoretical Understanding. *Journal of Political and Military Sociology* 20 (1): 37–62.

Wallerstein, Immanuel. 1974a. The Rise and Future Demise of the World Capitalist System: Concepts for Comparative Analysis. *Comparative Studies in Society and History* 16 (September).

———. 1974b. *The Modern World-System I. Capitalist Agriculture and the Origins of the European World-Economy in the Sixteenth Century*. San Diego: Academic Press.

———. 1979. *The Capitalist World-Economy*. Cambridge: Cambridge University Press.

———. 1980. *The Modern World System II. Mercantilism and the Consolidation of the European World-Economy*. San Diego: Academic Press.

———. 1983. The Three Instances of Hegemony in the History of the Capitalist World Economy. *International Journal of Comparative Sociology* 24 (1–2, April): 100–8.

————. 1989. *The Modern World System III. The Second Era of Great Expansion of the Capitalist World Economy, 1730–1840s*. San Diego: Academic Press.

————. 1991. *Unthinking Social Science: The Limits of Nineteenth-Century Paradigms*. Cambridge: Polity Press.

————. 1995. Social Science and the Communist Interlude, or Interpretations of Contemporary History. *Polish Sociological Review* 1: 117.

————. 1996a. "The Global Possibilities, 1990–2025." In *The Age of Transition*, eds. Terence K. Hopkins, Immanuel Wallerstein, et al., 226–243. London: Zed Books.

————. 1996b. "The Inter-state Structure of the Modern World-System." In *International Theory: Positivism and Beyond*, eds. Steve Smith, Ken Booth, and Marysia Zalewski, 87–107. Cambridge: Cambridge University Press.

————. 1998. The Rise and Future Demise of World-System Analysis. *Review* 21 (1): 103–12.

Wauthier, C. 1995. *Quatre Presidents et l'Afrique: De Gaulle, Pompidou, Giscard d'Estaing, Mitterrand*. Paris: Seuil.

Whiteman, K. 1983. President Mitterrand and Africa. *African Affairs* 82 (328): 329–43.

Williamson, Oliver. 1994. "Transaction Cost, Economics, and Organizational Theory." In *Handbook of Organizational Sociology*, eds. Neil J. Smelser and Richard Swedberg. Princeton: Princeton University Press.

World Bank. 1997. *World Development Report 1997: The State in a Changing World*. New York: Oxford University Press.

Young, Crawford, and Thomas Turner. 1985. *The Rise and Decline of the Zairian State*. Madison: University of Wisconsin Press.

Yu, Guozheng. 1994. Guanyu jianli tumenjiang sanjaozhou kuaguo jingji tequ de zhonghe yanjiu baogao [An integrated research report on the establishment of a cross-national special economic zone in the Tumen River delta]. *Dongbeiya Yanjiu* [Northeast Asian Studies] 14 (Supplemental Issue): 12–29.

Zakaria, Fareed. 1998. Will Asia Turn Against the West? *New York Times* (July 10).

Zaslavsky, Victor. 1994. *The Neo-Stalinist State: Class, Ethnicity, and Consensus in Soviet Society* (rev. ed.). Armonk, NY: M. E Sharpe.

Zysman, John. 1983. *Governments, Markets, and Growth: Financial Systems and the Politics of Industrial Change*. Ithaca, N.Y.: Cornell University Press.

Index

About the Editors and Contributors

ISABELLA ALCAÑIZ is a Ph.D. candidate in the Political Science Department, Northwestern University. A National Science Foundation graduate fellow since 1997, she is currently working toward completion of her doctoral thesis on nuclear integration between Argentina and Brazil.

BERNARD BECK is Associate Professor of Sociology at Northwestern and Associate Chair of the Department of Sociology. He has studied comparative institutions, social problems, and ideology, and he has written on welfare, poverty, popular culture, and the performing arts. He has served as president of the Society for the Study of Social Problems. His current work concerns the social organization of the performing arts, and he reviews films in the journal *Multicultural Perspectives*.

XIANGMING CHEN is Associate Professor of Sociology at the University of Illinois at Chicago. He has published extensively on China's integration with the global economy and China's urban and regional development. He is completing a book manuscript tentatively entitled *The Borderless Pacific Asia*.

DANIEL CHIROT is Professor of Sociology at the Jackson School of International Studies at the University of Washington. His most recent books are *Modern Tyrants* (1996) and a book he edited with Anthony Reid, *Essential Outsiders: Chinese and Jews in the Modern Transformation of Southeast Asia and Central Europe* (1997). He is the editor, with Martin Seligman, of the forthcoming *Ethnopolitical Warfare: Causes, Consequences, and Possible Solutions* (2000).

RANDALL COLLINS is Professor of Sociology at the University of Pennsylvania. His books include *Conflict Sociology* (1975), *The Credential Society* (1979), *Weberian Sociological Theory* (1986), *The Sociology of Philosophies: A Global Theory of Intellectual Change* (1998), and *Macro-History: Essays in Sociology of the Long Run* (1999).

BRUCE CUMINGS is Norman and Edna Freehling Professor of History at the University of Chicago. His publications include *The Origins of the Korean War* (2 vols., 1981, 1990), *Korea's Place in the Sun: A Modern History* (1997), and *Parallax Visions: American-East Asian Relations at the End of the Century* (1999). He is presently completing a book on the industrialization of Japan, both Koreas, Taiwan, and parts of China, and the ways that scholars and political leaders have thought about that development.

GEORGI M. DERLUGUIAN holds doctoral degrees in African history from the Soviet Academy of Sciences and in sociology from the State University of New York at Binghamton. He is currently an assistant professor at the Department of Sociology, Northwestern University. The title of his forthcoming book is *Chechnya: A Field Study of the End of History and the Clash of Civilizations*.

ARIF DIRLIK is Professor of History at Duke University. His most recent publications include *Hougeming fenwei* (The Post-Revolutionary Aura; in Chinese, 1999), *The Postcolonial Aura: Third World Criticism in the Age of Global Capitalism* (1997), *Postmodernity's Histories* (2000), *Postmodernism and China* (ed., with Zhang Xudong, 2000), and *Places and Politics in the Age of Global Capital* (ed., with Roxann Prazniak, 2000).

STEPHEN GILL is Professor of Political Science at York University, Toronto, Canada, specializing in International Political Economy and International Relations. His published work includes about 50 articles and chapters in edited collections and numerous books, including *The Global Political Economy* (co-authored with David Law, 1988); *American Hegemony and the Trilateral Commission* (1991); *Gramsci, Historical Materialism and International Relations* (1993); *Globalization, Democratization and Multilateralism* (1997), and *Innovation and Transformation in International Studies* (co-edited with James Mittelman, 1997).

WALTER L. GOLDFRANK is Professor of Sociology and of Latin American and Latino Studies at the University of California, Santa Cruz. He was most recently the lead editor of *Ecology and the World System* (1999).

SCOTT L. GREER is a doctoral candidate in political science and international studies at Northwestern University and most recently a Fellow in Law and Social Science at the American Bar Foundation. He is currently researching a dissertation on regional politics in Scotland, Catalonia, and Northern England. He has researched and published work on French regional government, American health care policy, and the development of war crimes law.

MICHAEL LORIAUX is Associate Professor of Political Science at Northwestern University. His books include *France after Hegemony: International Change and Financial Reform* (1992) and *Capital Ungoverned: Liberalizing Finance in Interventionist States* (co-authored, 1997). He has written or co-written articles on the political thought of Augustine and Thucydides and is currently researching the political economy of Franco-German reconciliation.

CHARLES C. RAGIN is Professor of Sociology and Political Science at Northwestern University. His publications include *The Comparative Method: Moving Beyond Quantitative and Qualitative Strategies* (1987), *What Is a Case: Exploring the Foundations of Social Research* (with Howard S. Becker, 1992), and *Constructing Social Research* (1994). His newest book is *Fuzzy-Set Social Science*, published by University of Chicago Press in 2000.

MICHAEL ALAN SACKS is Visiting Assistant Professor of Organization and Management at the Goizueta School of Business, Emory University.

BRIAN UZZI is Associate Professor of Management and Organizations at the Kellogg Graduate School of Management at Northwestern University. In addition to articles on organizations and social networks, he is co-author of *Athena Unbound: Social Capital and Women's Career Advancement in the Hard Sciences* (2000).

MARC VENTRESCA is Assistant Professor of Management and Organizations at the Kellogg Graduate School of Management at Northwestern University and holds a courtesy appointment in the Department of Sociology. His current projects include work on the structuring of the world economy, the succession of college presidents, organizatonal environments, and social movements.

DAVID V. WALLER is Assistant Professor of Sociology at the University of Texas at Arlington. He is author of several articles and book chapters on macrosociology and science studies.